FRIENDS *of the*
Livingston Public Library

**Gratefully Acknowledges
the Contribution of**

Richard Kosson

For the 2020-2021 Membership Year

Inventory

Inventory

A

Memoir

Darran Anderson

FARRAR, STRAUS AND GIROUX

New York

Farrar, Straus and Giroux
120 Broadway, New York 10271

Library of Congress Control Number: 2020012288
ISBN: 978-0-374-27758-1

Designed by Abby Kagan

Our books may be purchased in bulk for promotional, educational, or business
use. Please contact your local bookseller or the Macmillan Corporate and
Premium Sales Department at 1-800-221-7945, extension 5442, or by e-mail at
MacmillanSpecialMarkets@macmillan.com.

www.fsgbooks.com
www.twitter.com/fsgbooks • www.facebook.com/fsgbooks

1 3 5 7 9 10 8 6 4 2

This is a memoir and a work of nonfiction. The names and identifying
characteristics of some individuals have been changed or
combined to protect their privacy.

To Caspian

Describe your street. Describe another street. Compare. Make an inventory of your pockets, of your bag. Ask yourself about the provenance, the use, what will become of each of the objects you take out.

—GEORGES PEREC, *L'infra-ordinaire*

"No, don't! Don't dig up the past! Dwell on the past and you'll lose an eye."

But the proverb goes on to say: "Forget the past and you'll lose both eyes."

—ALEKSANDR SOLZHENITSYN, *The Gulag Archipelago*

Inventory

Prologue

It took months before the full symptoms made themselves known. In the distant frozen north, having abandoned his ship in the ice, Sir John Ross discovered that a scar, from a bayonet thrust through his body in a sea battle off the coast of Bilbao thirty years before, was transforming back into an open wound. Eighty years later, in the distant frozen south, Captain Lawrence "Titus" Oates, thirty-one and already dying, found that a long-healed gunshot wound to the leg, which he'd received a decade earlier in the Boer War, had never truly gone away.

Two million sailors died slowly and terribly of scurvy during the Age of Discovery, without knowing that vitamin C is needed to bind tissue, including scars. Scurvy killed more men on the seas than drowning. Gums rot; the skin ulcers; bones turn black. The circulatory system begins to rupture. Feelings accentuate, including melancholy and a desperate yearning for land.

The sickness was even thought to be tied to nostalgia, dreams, ecstasy, terror, and fatigue, as well as diet. Sailors knew when one of them was touched by it and shunned him, lest they, too, fall under its spell. It had its own memory, resurrecting those long-forgotten injuries. It seemed to rise up from each man's past. Sailors died nursing bloody lacerations they had received in their youth, mystified that being healed was somehow just a temporary condition.

How might it be possible to reconstruct a lost person? To thread bone onto soul and muscle onto bone and skin onto muscle without creating a monster or a marionette. To rebuild a human being from photographs, documents, contradictory fragments of memories. The objects and impressions they left behind perhaps form a silhouette of negative space resembling a figure. A presence in the shape of an absence. Perhaps it is also worth establishing what first took people apart. To follow the unwinding thread.

PART ONE

Derry, 1984

Longwave Radio

God knows how long the radio had sat in the rain or where it had come from. My father, a man of few words, admitted it might not work, but we would never know unless we tried. He hauled it into his huge Popeye arms and carried it up the banking from the sodden ditch. I followed, clumsily, behind. We moved through the trees and along the rough trail at the backs of the houses. A dog barked furiously at the bottom of a gate as we passed.

The Glen was a dumping ground, a wilderness that had once marked the edge of town but that the city had grown around, never quite absorbing, it being too steep and marshy to build on. Its wildness never defused.

We turned onto our street, went up the concrete steps and past the railings. I thought my father, sleeves rolled up, veins bulging on his tattooed arms, might stop and place the radio into the discarded shopping trolley. I had watched the older boys swing each other around the car park inside the trolley, in great whooping arcs, but my father just walked on past. The glass glistened on the tarmac as I ran to catch up.

For several days the radio just sat there on the living room floor, in the space where a television might be. I eyed it fearfully, suspecting it might explode or burst into flames when turned on. I knew what a radio was. It was a box with voices inside. A puzzle box. How did the voices get in there? Who did they belong to? How had they become detached from their owners? What if they escaped?

My mother wiped down the wooden cabinet with a towel— "Your father's always bringing bloody junk into this house"— then dried out the speaker with a hair dryer, filling the room with a hot, artificial smell. Then it sat there. Mute. Goading me into flicking the switch. I closed my eyes and braced myself.

It started to life with a hum.

The lid lifted slowly, almost hydraulically, and a series of colored lights blinked on, as if part of a control panel from a science-fiction film. It felt delicate, like a prized artifact and not a piece of junk that had been discarded. Somehow simultaneously futuristic and ancient, as if belonging to some advanced alien civilization that had long since died out.

The dial creaked and then gave, gliding a red line along mysterious numbers and hieroglyphs. A horizontal bandwidth of places with unearthly sounds between each channel. I would tell my little sister, half-believing it myself, that they were transmissions from other galaxies, ones that I would later try to point out to her in my books—the spiral Andromeda, the starburst M82, the Magellanic Clouds—while she ignored me, busy rehearsing dance routines and reenacting musicals to invisible audiences.

I had to steady my hand to tune in. There was always the

garbled, disintegrating echo of a voice or music just before I could lock onto the signal precisely. Then, just as quickly, I would lose it. The slightest movement, a tremble, could knock it off.

The marker moved along, through Paris, Cairo, Leningrad, Bombay, Peking. Some cities were out of reach, but occasionally I would catch a glimpse of the other side of the planet: the night side of the world, or the day side when we were enveloped in darkness. The slightest fragments of voices and melodies would conjure up images I'd seen in books—stave churches, karst forests, Hong Kong junks, torii gates, the shimmer of neon lights on rain-drenched streets—all appeared holographically in front of me, until my mother's call from another room broke my hypnosis.

I'd always return to the radio. First thing in the morning before school, last thing before bed. If I could unlock its secrets, everything in the world would surely make sense. Below the names of the cities were the transmitter stations, which sounded even more fascinatingly unreal: Petropavlovsk, Béchar, Motala, Dalanzadgad. It made me wonder which places were real and which were not—Gotham, Timbuktu, Transylvania, Atlantis—and what distinguished one from the other.

There was something illicit about listening in. I felt like a secret agent prying into distant lands, where language sounded like verse, incantations, ciphers. Even the Eastern European football teams, some behind the Iron Curtain (which I imagined as a literal mountainous wall of rusting metal), had names that sounded impossibly enigmatic: Red Star Belgrade, Rapid Bucureşti, Dynamo Kyiv. By contrast, there was little mystery to be found on the BBC channels. It was always gardening, mirthless comedy, interest rates, the ruminations of vicars full of dust and spiders. Except, that is, for the shipping forecast.

There the mystery seeped in, almost despite itself. It was too late to listen most nights, but one evening while lying ill with a blazing fever on the sofa, a damp cloth on my brow, I had been allowed to stay up and had heard it. I would, from then on, at opportune moments, sneak downstairs when everyone else in the house was sleeping and listen with my ear pressed against a whispering speaker. And the radio would conjure up before me in the half-light night ships in Viking, Hebrides, Finisterre, setting course for Venice, Valparaíso, Yokohama.

In the daytime I would lie there listening, staring up at the swirls and swishes of the Artex on the ceiling, sprawled on a mock-Persian carpet, threadbare but as detailed as any medieval manuscript. It was placed on the solid stone floor that I'd once split my head on, hyperactively flipping out of a baby-bouncer that had hung in the doorway. I had no memory of that incident and would not even know of it until, much later as a teenager, I shaved my head and found the scar, underneath all that time.

The music I found on the strange, exotic channels fascinated me more than anything on *Top of the Pops*. I would listen to the songs in foreign languages, without ever knowing what they were called or who sang them or what they were about, aware that I would never hear them again. The transience and mystery made them seem precious, as if they ceased to exist upon finishing, or were lost forever and I'd have to walk the entire earth to chance upon them again.

Before radar, the authorities in Britain would build huge structures out of concrete on headlands facing the sea. Acoustic mirrors. Sound waves would hit them and swirl around, and those standing within them could hear the hum of planes advancing, long before they appeared visually on the horizon. I lay there next to another kind of acoustic mirror in that little room in our rickety Victorian terraced house. Tuning in the radio, I would occasionally pick up police and army exchanges, quite by accident at first and then intentionally. There were invisible voices in the air. I would listen in to foot patrols, to the armored Land Rovers, perhaps even to the omnipresent helicopters droning high above our rooftops. At times their conversations, in accents familiar from soap operas, were discernible. At other times there were too many codes and numbers to make sense; the empire, with its lion and unicorn, moved in mysterious ways. Often the voices were calm, but sometimes they were frenzied. Gradually I became frightened of what I might be listening in to, for fear perhaps that it could listen back.

At the beginning, though, it felt empowering. I felt that I was party to secretive riddles, like the characters in my picture books—Ali Baba spying on the forty thieves, the miller's daughter who watched Rumpelstiltskin dance around a midnight fire, Jim Hawkins overhearing Long John Silver's dastardly plots. I was listening in on the world of adults and slowly trying, slowly learning, to translate. At times it felt dangerous, especially when, as I knelt there hearing the patrols of soldiers speak among one another, I'd see their silhouettes walking, ghostly through the net curtain. I would exhale only after they'd passed.

My mother noticed me once listening in—"Look at you, eavesdropping"—and, embarrassed, I immediately turned the radio off, wondering what an eaves was and how I'd dropped it. No sooner had her head turned than I sidled back, tuning in again, trying to catch the transmission, but it was once again lost. I did not yet know that glimpses were not complete access or revelation, that sometimes you uncover what they want you to uncover or things that are best left unheard.

I was not the only person listening. My father listened in too. My mother would tell me so, years later.

"It was a Sunday," she began. "Your grandmother Needles used to come down for company. I'd keep her a bite to eat. She'd sit you on her knee. She was a sharp woman, no doubt about it, but affectionate, especially to you. I was waiting for her . . . *we* were waiting for her, and she didn't come. I don't know why, but I had this sinking feeling, like something was wrong—badly, badly wrong. She had no phone we could call, and neither did we, come to think of it, so . . . I don't know, I just had this physical feeling. Not telepathy or anything like that, more a horrible rush. Like the start of a panic attack.

"We'd no TV at the time. It's stupid really, looking back. We probably could've afforded one, just about, on hire purchase. But we'd no real money to spare, and we definitely couldn't afford the TV license. I was scared of those vans that went around with the radar dish on top and could tell if you had a TV. So we didn't get one. They still sent threatening letters. They wouldn't believe we didn't have one. It was inconceivable to them. The silly thing is the inspectors were too afraid to come into Catholic areas back then, so we'd have been grand, but that's hindsight. Instead, we listened to the radio a lot. And someone realized you could tune in to the army's frequencies."

Until this point I had been listening absentmindedly, but at those words I turned to look at her directly.

She continued, "You could get the gist of what they were saying if they were close enough by, and there was that watchtower, of course, up the street. That's how your father found out. Secretly listening to the radio. That's how he heard they were searching for someone in the river. That's how we found out she'd gone in. His mother. Your grandmother. And that she was gone forever."

House Key

An electric fire. Food in the pantry. A clothes horse. A sewing kit. A St. Brigid's cross. A wireless. A doll's house. All were burning. The lino floor was bubbling. A Bakelite phone was melting and dripping off the table. The beds were ablaze. The owners had already fled, to cries of "Fenian bastards." They did not know the word *pogrom* before that night, but that's what it was. Maybe they never knew the meaning of that word, because this was just something that happened. Undeserving of a name. The house, the houses—the entire street they would never return to— burned right through the night until the next day. Until all the things they'd owned, what little they had, were just smoldering ash and debris, charred imitations of what they had once been, in rooms with no roof, under a sky innocent in its ignorance.

Map

ontrary to popular opinion, you can read too many
books. It did something to my brain at an impressionable age. It left me not quite adjusted to real
life, always one step removed. An observer, always
seeking out dramas, consciously or otherwise, but in a dislo-
cated way. I would look out the windows of cars, buses, trains,
and see the projections of cinema on the panes, rather than a
solid world go by. It instilled in me a dangerous curiosity and
an even more dangerous hesitancy.

The world of books seeped into my life until the borders
of reality seemed permeable. I would climb up the banisters of
the stairs, hoisting myself onto the floor above like it was the
rigging of a pirate ship. The stairs split in two directions. To
the left were the other bedrooms, one of which housed the hot
press and boiler, which would growl and splutter demonically
at night. To the right were the bathroom and my bedroom at

the back, colder than the rest of the house, as it was in an extension and there was no attic or insulation. The dry season does
not last long here, and the flat tarpaulin roof turned the rain
into music, lullabies. I lay for countless nights listening, as if in
a cabin in a storm, a guest to the night's own secret soundtrack.
At the top of the landing was the huge, cavernous hulk of a
wardrobe. It had dark, thick stained wood, and though it was
massive on the outside, it was even larger inside. My mother
had inherited it from a deceased great-aunt. It was filled with
endless rows of moth-eaten, unworn fur coats. I would wander between them as if they created corridors, and eventually I
would make it to the back. And then I would crouch down and
tap the wood, as if a door might suddenly open if I tapped the
right number of times, in the right pattern, to reveal a snowy
landscape and a single Victorian gas lamp.

I dreamt too much as a kid. Waking dreams. Eyes semi-
glazed and mouth hanging open. "You'll catch flies," my mother
would say, or "If the wind blows, your face will stay like that." I
was always floating off elsewhere, especially at the first sign of
trouble or raised voices. Once, my mother came into the living
room and saw me gazing up, spellbound, framed in a beam of
light, and she thought for a second that her son was seeing some
apparition of the Virgin Mary. I was watching a mouse very
carefully climbing up the net curtain.

Sometimes I would go out into the dank Dickensian backyard, where my mother used to place me as an infant in the
basin, and pull out the spout from the kitchen to bathe and play
in the running soapy water as she did the dishes. The yard had
no exit door and was closed in by a high, decaying wall covered with cracks and moss. Shimmying up the rusted pole of the
clothesline and then balancing dangerously on top, I could leap,
grab hold, and pull myself up. There was a little alcove there,

below the roof, where I could sit in all weathers, looking down on the gardens of the mansions behind, almost a gated community tucked away in an otherwise working-class area. I climbed up there often—my dog and trusty sidekick, Patch, far below, making tiny jumps to try to join me. It was like looking into another world, unreachably distant in time and space, except now and then, in the spring or summer, one of the visiting girls picking berries would wave tentatively, before her grandparents would chase her back into the house and glare at me until I left.

I inhabited a place between fiction and reality, whether I wanted to or not, and so I tried to chart it. Like many children, I had long been obsessed with flags. Flags and maps. The hammers and sickles. The crescent moons. The suns. What could the symbols possibly mean? And yet there was order to it all. A fixity. This was the way things were and always would be. The German Democratic Republic. The Soviet Union. Yugoslavia. Only later would I learn of other flags. The flags of imaginary countries, like the starry plough and the sunburst flags I'd seen hoisted on neighborhood lampposts; and when I asked my mother what countries they were, she said, "None." The flags of countries that once existed but no longer did. The Republic of Biak-na-Bato. Ryukyu Kingdom. The Most Serene Republic of Venice. All flags were temporary, in the long scheme of things, and depended so much on whether people believed in them or not.

Inspired, I began to make maps myself. I copied the features without really knowing what they meant. Wind rose. Compass. Scale. Cherubs and bearded gods blowing prevailing winds. I drew maps of the tumbledown terraced streets of our neighborhood, like it was the center of the world, which for us it was. Everywhere is, for someone. I sketched the main routes first, then I added the tiny lanes that my friends and I hung around in, exclusively and jealously guarded. Largely unseen, behind the lives of the adults. The alleyways with their garbage sentinels, marked "No Hot Ashes," which we'd pretend were shrieking Daleks or Darth Vader with his Stormtroopers. The backyard walls crowned with broken bottles lodged in concrete. Rusting tin cans of Scottish lager with crumpled models on them, like cubist paintings. The acrid smell as we poured the rainwater out of them. Clues left of nights before by now-vanished apparitions. I mapped the gates that we were able to bypass, being small and agile enough to squeeze through the gaps and shimmy up the drainpipes. You couldn't take bicycles or even skateboards down such routes, as they were strewn with debris, so we'd venture in on foot, dragging sticks along the moss-dripping walls. I marked those areas on my charts: "Here be dragons."

All discovered space becomes territorial. And we boys, without thought or instruction, colonized our immediate surroundings and its promontories. We'd give one another "heevies" up walls, joining our hands in downward prayer to hold each other's heel and hoist upward. And we'd scramble, hands gripping tiny footholds, knees scratched against ragged red brick, to sit triumphant eventually, perched on high, graffitied walls, shimmying over to give each other room, the soles of our feet stinging when we finally tired of surveying our small council-house kingdom and leapt down onto the pavement slabs.

There were dodgy places that boys and girls did well not to hang around, especially alone, and especially after sunset. Areas that drinkers would frequent. Certain houses where the front doors were hanging off and the occupants seemed to regularly shape-shift. The darkened concrete staircases of the flats at the end of our street. I drew quicksand, tiger traps, pitfalls, trolls at these points on my map. I would find—in incidents I dared not think about, let alone speak of—that it paid to keep your wits about you in such places. I grew to have a healthy suspicion of intriguing characters, and not just old creeps: those wearing camouflage gear, for instance, especially young men who were too old to be hanging around with kids. My friends did too, responding with excuses and insults when the atmosphere changed. Sometimes the strangers would become distinctly unpleasant, inexplicably enraged, as if arguing with someone who wasn't there, but we found safety in numbers. There were no other adult intrusions into our map world, bar once a week when the garbagemen would barge in, whistling, and we would run after them, alongside their trucks, jumping up onto the running boards as they cursed us. No one else bothered us really. Except, of course, for the army.

I sketched in pencil the front gardens, opposite the pub and the bakery, where we would do our "donkey derby" dash. The more hazardous challenge of the backyard run, bursting through clothes dangling on washing lines and clambering onto coal bunkers. I drew the maze of housing that led down into the valley. I drew cubes within cubes, until it resembled the brutalist tower block a stone's throw from our street; and I drew us as stick figures climbing to the top, above the perilous drop, where we would sit on the glowing concrete and watch the cinema of the skies, half-believing it was a performance by God every night. And we would watch the sun go down behind the bread factory, behind the mountains of Donegal, out there beyond the border. Perched as we were on the very edge of Europe, an outland, we would watch the sun boil into the wild Atlantic. And we would make sure we got home before the moon, covered with barnacles and shaking off kelp in my sketches, started to rise out of the sea.

The real wilderness was the Glen. I had written "X marks

the spot" on that expanse on my map, and rubbed it out and moved it so many times that it gave the space an impression as opaque and chaotic as the place actually was.

There was something about the wastelands of the Glen, and the deep, dark woods on its periphery, that I needed in order to feel the snug safety of my room in contrast. I found myself drawn there, both with my friends and alone. All sorts of stories clung to the place. Tales of murder, long enough ago to be in ballads or close enough to be word-of-mouth. Famine roads cut through the wasteland, where the British establishment and the landowners had made the starving Catholic Irish build roads to nowhere, to justify the charity of a bowl of soup. They made the people, all of them close to starving to death, construct architectural follies too—huge structures it was willfully impossible to live in, built by many who effectively had no homes. Some of the roads they laid down ended in the middle of fields, in the middle of nowhere, because all those working on them simply died where they stood.

If there were any treasures in the city, surely they would be found in the Glen, the most foreboding of places. That's where *I* would hide something if I had to. A place where it was always raining or lashed with sleet, or choking in a thick fog. So I ventured there, trudging among the heather, wrenching my boots out of rabbit holes, climbing over ivy-covered, half-collapsed walls. I had a pair of shoes with compasses in their soles. Once I found a catacomb amid the greenery. It formed a perfect room around me when I crawled into it, insulated from the world outside, but I was unable, on subsequent expeditions, to find it again and wondered if I'd dreamt it. Throughout the wasteland were cracked warning signs, missing letters and falling to pieces. Each one documenting a tragedy perhaps, as warnings do, but also acting as an invitation, like the curses of pharaohs to stay away, do not venture in, there is nothing but death here—all to keep the grave robbers from the precious grave goods of kings.

Most of the time I would set off with our gang, at least partly reluctantly, on some harebrained scheme of their devising. I was neither the quietest nor the most vocal, and I lagged behind, surveying the scene, always primed to take to my heels at the first sign of trouble. Our leader, a charismatic boy named Jamesy, could handle himself and had a natural flair, and it was not unusual for him to lead us while somehow smoking a cigar, its origin never adequately explained. There was Carl, who was crafty; and Danny, who was jolly; and Gareth, who was timid; and there was me, who had no idea what I was or how I appeared. I could write the characters of others in my head, in a silent commentary, but I struggled with seeing myself, even in mirrors. Face-blind to my own face.

The Glen was forbidden, but only to the degree that trespassing there gave us delight. To venture out of our neighborhood, which we patrolled as sentries, really was forbidden. We'd end up in the territory, and at the tender mercies, of other gangs of street urchins. Behind enemy lines. Streets and alleyways and crossover points were defended with sticks and stones, and kids would return home wailing, with throbbing eggs on heads and fat lips, if they intruded too deeply. I had not yet realized, having not worked out the meaning of the painted curbstones of my town, that humans did not grow out of this impulse. It only darkened as they aged.

Cardboard Box (Marked "This Way Up")

I'll see you when I see you," my father would tell my mother when they first met as teenagers, and he would disappear accordingly, off gallivanting and hitchhiking across the thirty-two counties; the elusiveness irritated and attracted her. "I'd be damned if I let him get the better of me," she thought. I had seen photos of my father out at Inch Island, where he'd gone to "live off the land." He and his brother and their friend look like a stranded prog rock band. My mother thought he looked like Bob Marley from behind, with his long hair and denim jacket; and thought, with some delight, and accurately, that he'd outrage her parents. It was a time when having long hair was an invitation to get your head kicked in, and so they learned to scrap early on. The lads would drink Mundies fortified wine, listen to British blues-boom records like Peter Green's *Fleetwood Mac*, wear pirate earrings, and smoke Woodbines and Park Drive. They'd put metal tips on the heels of their brogues to make an authoritative click when they walked through the dance and punk clubs. Girls would go to the riots in gangs, linking arms, to "check out the talent." The guys would wear their Sunday best while throwing bricks and petrol bombs. Hair done. Boots polished. Aftershave dabbed. Preparing for battle. The key was to get noticed, but not too noticed.

Briefly my parents-to-be had escaped together from the Troubles-strewn North, hitchhiking the entire length of the country to Cork—a kind of twin town that suggested what Derry might have been without the conflict. My father had worked there for a while on the docks, unloading cargo, recalling later a huge African spider scuttling off into the rainy streets from a crate of bananas. While they were there, my mother, only eighteen and unmarried, learned she was pregnant with me, and so they decided to return north, to the imaginary comfort of their families. I was almost a Cork man, they'd say, but they returned north, over the border and into the conflict, as if disaster had a strange kind of magnetism or gravity.

They had gone to Cork for no other reason than to escape, but their path had been pointed out by my father's record collection. Growing up, Da had become a fan of the blues singer Rory Gallagher, from listening to his older brother's LPs. He'd grown his hair, bought lumberjack shirts in imitation, learned guitar and harmonica. Da and his friends would roadie for bands that came to town. Gallagher never stopped coming, even in the darkest days of the Troubles, when musicians like the Miami Showband were being butchered. Punks appeared in *NME* posing next to barricades in Belfast, but bottled out of actually playing, while Gallagher just turned up quietly and played loudly. He was born in Donegal but moved to Cork, and so, seeing a path, my parents followed suit. They also resolved, if their firstborn was a boy, to name him Rory as a tribute. In the end they were three weeks too late, and my cousin received the name instead.

We chimed as toddlers. Rory was boisterous, while I was cautious, but we were both curious little fellows. We lived three streets apart and were inseparable. We would climb on bunk beds, and peel the colors off Rubik's Cubes and stick them on each other, and make forts with cushions and blankets that would transform into the Wild West or carry on forever like the sea.

One day, a stranger was driving down the street past the corner shop, with its boxes of fruit and veg spilling out onto the pavement. The cars would take shortcuts through the terraces to bypass a series of traffic lights on the main road—a safety decision made by a well-meaning civil servant. The driver was making up time and was idly about to drive over a cardboard box near the faded white line when something stopped him. It moved—perhaps there was a dog inside?—and so he stepped out of his car and went to kick it out of the way, when a child suddenly crawled out from inside it. It was an uncomfortably close call for everyone, and the kids were told emphatically not to hang around on the road, but bar a sliver of pavement outside their front doors, there was nowhere else to play.

One day, Rory was kidding around, trying to pinch turnips from the shop a few doors away from his house, and he bolted, not pausing for a second to look, and was struck by a passing car. The driver was distraught. Perhaps never the same again. There was nothing that could be done, and so Rory stayed a little boy forever.

The first night that it rained after he was buried, Rory's mother became terribly upset, wanting to bring a blanket to the cemetery so that her child could be warm. They stopped her from leaving the house. They stopped her from going to him because he wasn't really there anymore.

As a small boy myself, I was shielded from the grief, but something entered the world right then, just as my little cousin exited it. Something fathomless. Rory wasn't coming back, I was told in gentle terms by my mother, her mascara streaked from tears. "Back from where?" I wondered but did not ask. It was the first sense—one that would never go away—that there was a shadow world, a world largely ignored but ever present, within this one.

Chalk

Opposite the house was a blank gable wall that rarely remained blank for long. Messages would appear on it continually, and yet, for all the time I spent looking through my window, I'd never seen anyone write any of the words on it. I had seen people painting blocks of white over the slogans, but never once had I seen the messages being delivered. It was as if they just appeared, like the scene we'd been told about in Bible studies at school, the words of doom appearing at Belshazzar's feast, written by an invisible hand.

The owners of the house took great displeasure in noise, and would come out frothing at the gob, but when their pristinely polished Lada car was not parked up on the pavement, I was free to cross the street and draw goalposts on the wall. There were other games we'd play—Curby, where we'd throw the ball to bounce back off the curb from the white line; and the

hide-the-ball game Alla Balla, which we didn't realize was centuries old—but those games required at least two people. When
I was solitary, which was often, I would thud the ball against
a two-dimensional goal, commentating in my head as if I were
Maradona, George Best, Paul McGrath, or Totò Schillaci.

Sometimes I'd have to draw the lines of my chalk goalposts across the graffiti, and I'd thud the ball against the letters. What they meant seemed cryptic to me. "IRA." "INLA."
"IRSP." "SS RUC." "Fuck the UDR." I thought of the painting
of the crucifixion in my classroom and of the letters above Jesus's
head. "INRI": "Jesus the Nazarene, king of the Jews." Perhaps
these were the kings of these streets. I found out only later that
they were the acronyms of the combatants—rebels versus the
state, state versus citizen, people versus people—in our little
war. Depending on where they were from, often an accident
of birth, they were terrorists or freedom fighters. Forces of law
and order or brutal tyrants hiding behind the law. Rebels fighting injustice or each other or themselves. Them against them.
You against you. I against I.

Sentences would appear. "Up the Provos." "Brits out." "*Tioc-
faidh ár lá.*" "Mickey D is a tout." "Death to hoods." Sometimes
there'd be something I'd recognize. "Fuck the Queen." "Celtic
FC." Mostly they were puzzles, and I'd go inside and summon
up the courage to ask my mother, "What is a sex pest?" or "Who
are snitches?" After reading "Free all POWs now," I asked her,
"What is a pow?" thinking it was the noise Batman made when
he fought the Joker or the Riddler in my comic books.

"It's just people writing nonsense. You don't need to worry.
I remember all sorts of messages being written when I was a
girl. There used to be one that went around called 'Kilroy was
here.' And another called 'Big Aggie's Man.'"

"Who were they?"

"No one really. Just make-believe people. You know, like Jack Frost. And San—oh, you know, made-up people."

"Like imaginary friends?" I asked.

"Sort of."

"But who writes them?"

"They're just messages. Sometimes you get funny ones. Like the one in Belfast that said, 'Is there life before death?'"

"I don't get it."

"Someday you will. You think too much, Professor Anderson." She ruffled my hair.

I sat on the floor, legs crossed, for an hour, wondering about life before death.

I knew nothing of how the messages worked. The graffiti. That they were threats and warnings, made specifically with an audience in mind. The court of public opinion. I didn't know that they were ordering people to go into exile voluntarily or go into the afterlife permanently. At best, those singled out might have a beating with spiked bats, or have their kneecaps blown out. Sex offenders, drug dealers, informants, pariahs. The messages were to them but also to the community, like Martin Luther posting his theses on the doors of the Schlosskirche. Back then, I knew nothing of the schisms between the groups, personal or ideological—men in Ford Escorts punched full of holes while dropping their kids off at school, or blasted standing in phone boxes in the midst of calls to their wives that gave birth to new acronyms. I did not know the meaning of the other acronyms, of the terrorists from the other side, UVF, UDA, UFF; but I knew enough, even at a tiny age, to fear them and avoid any area where those letters appeared. Death was brought to you today by the letter "U."

There were deeper clues to some other reality everywhere, it seemed to me. Shoes hung mysteriously over telephone wires.

Cracks in the pavement would have diabolical consequences if stepped upon. Coal holes were hatches to other dimensions. Messages sprayed by council workers and electricians on the pavements were runes. If you came from my background, you dared not set foot anywhere with red-white-and-blue-painted curbstones, or Union Jack flags (the "butcher's apron," republicans called them), or bunting or murals with William of Orange on horseback, or celebrations of being massacred at the Somme, or our province's self-mutilated symbol, the blood-soaked severed red hand, thrown onto the land when two princes raced each other to be the first to touch and claim its soil. The adults would stir up the fear in you, like joking about the bogeyman. "You go there, they'll put you in the sack. Or you'll end up in the bonfire." And the other side—*they*—told their children likewise.

It was the same on maps. I'd read the tantalizing poetry of the names of villages and towns all across the province in which we lived—Blackskull, Desertmartin, Mazetown, Moneyglass, the Birches—and I knew, deep down, that these were places surely I could never go.

The graffiti appeared all through those years, warnings or gloatings over atrocities and deaths, which read like supernatural curses from dark storybooks.

"Fenians, remember Hyster."

"Mull of Kintyre . . . bodies rolling in from the sea."

My memory of the text was always in black and white. Life was in newsprint. The only colors I remember were those of flags. Or of accidents, like the spilled rainbows of oil along the gutters slick with rain.

The most famous graffiti in the city was "You Are Now Entering Free Derry," painted on the gable wall of a demolished terrace of houses. It marked the autonomous territory that the citizens had claimed against the empire—a word I'd always associated with the villains of *Star Wars.* Really it was a couple of housing estates that were unruly enough to keep the army and the cops at bay. They did so from 1969 until 1972. War photographers had come there when Derry was part of the nexus of rebellion from Paris to Vietnam to the civil rights movement in the United States. The graffiti itself had been adapted from a student protest message at the University of California, Berkeley. Eventually the existence of a people's republic of Derry within the United Kingdom could no longer stand, and the army was sent in to seize back the Bogside and Creggan in Operation Motorman, a massive invasion involving over twenty thousand military personnel and tanks transported by HMS *Fearless*, launched from the river. A young witness to the operation was shot dead alongside his friend. A single teenage terrorist was shot in a tree and was left alone to bleed out in the back of a meat wagon. My father, only a kid then, had stood on the shore at Moville, a fishing village over the border, and watched the vessels moving up the river, knowing what was coming before the defenders in Derry did. The "Free Derry" sign remained. The idea still existed in people's heads. After the Bloody Sunday massacre of protesters took place, British soldiers painted their own graffiti: "Paratroopers 13, Bogside 0." The "Free Derry" sign was attacked and vandalized many times. Once, the army even drove an armored vehicle into it, but it stood firm. Time and again the locals would paint it afresh.

Floppy Disk

In *The Wizard of Oz*, when Dorothy's house crash-lands on the witch, she opens the door from her sepia world into one of vivid Technicolor. I watched the scene on the mounted television in the video store, with the clerk perpetually irritated in the background. "Are you going to rent anything?"

"I'm waiting for my friends."

On our street we had our own secret arcade. It consisted of a single machine. It was clandestine, in the back of the video shop. We usually went in, nodded at the store clerk, who was usually busy watching some hideous B-movie, arguing with one of those guys you thought worked there but who just hung around, unpaid, all day. We would pester the irritated clerk for posters from the window, hoping to get *RoboCop* or *Predator* for our bedroom walls, to hang next to the Mr. T poster, though you never knew what you had been given until you got outside and unrolled it, and then we would mock each other incessantly if it was a rom-com. We walked past the rows of VHS tapes, getting more obscure the farther we went in— sci-fi, then horror, taking a right at European art house. The soft porn, the stuff of hell and damnation in the eyes of the Church, was kept under the counter and had to be asked for in hushed tones, and sniggering boys would shout things as the blushing couples grabbed the tapes and exited swiftly. The arcade game was technically outside, in a chilly half-finished concrete annex. It was kept there, it was said, because the proprietor didn't have a license, which made it seem underground and illicit.

The game was *Street Fighter II*. Blessed were the rare days when I would walk into the back of the store, with a pocketful of change, and find the room empty. Sometimes, most times, I'd go in there totally skint and just watch the demo play. What intrigued me wasn't really the characters or the monkish learning of elaborate special moves. Rather it was the backdrops. Other worlds were suggested in pixels. I found myself staring at the Hong Kong streets, the prone Buddhas, and Indian shrines, wanting to leave the fights and explore the scenes in the background, knowing these places existed somewhere out there. Sometimes I walked into the lion's den: all the older kids hogging the machine, but all short of funds and resentful, trying in vain to break into it. Naive as I was, I could already spot who the neighborhood psychopaths were: they usually got your character into the corner and repeated the same move over and over until your energy depleted. Or tested out the assaults of the game in real life if you promised to beat them. Mostly I hung back, sitting on crates, hoping not to be noticed, and watched the bloodbaths, both in pixels and in reality. Nevertheless, the time came when you had to step up, be tested. It was an initiation ceremony. A crucible. The way you won mattered, but maybe what mattered most was the way you lost.

My cousin DD was the first person I knew who had a computer at home. There was a myth that he'd constructed it himself. I was always enamored with my cousins. Older, wiser, cooler, they had posters of bands that kids my age weren't allowed to listen to—the bands we were thus obsessed with—on their walls. They had satellite television with surreal Japanese game shows. In their sheds they kept terrapins and their BMX bikes. DD heard that I liked computer games and invited me up to his room: "Come and see." He took out the disk, blowing any dust off, and slid it into the slot, and it took a while to load, with patterns of different colors sequencing on the screen. Then suddenly we were in an infinite blue landscape, with vector tanks moving around with impossible deftness. It was another world. I stood there, openmouthed.

"How . . . how did you do this?"

He showed me the reams of code he'd written. It seemed like some arcane magic, the kind of riddles and diagrams on gnostic medieval manuscripts. How typing certain numbers and letters in a certain order could create a different universe. It was like knowing the secret name of God and creating golems with it.

"This is the future," DD claimed, and he was right, though he would not live to see much of it.

I admired DD a great deal from a distance, but the age gap was slightly too much. I knew that time spent with him took the form of kindness on his part, rather than friendship. In childhood, a span of just a few years appears a chasm, before it narrows to insignificance in adult life, but we never made it that far. An older, future friend of mine eventually worked with DD at a technology firm out in an industrial estate at the edge of town. They used to get lifts to work together, and my mate said that DD was one smart cookie and that he'd mentioned me, and I thought that I must get in touch with him soon. I had this image in my head, given that several years had passed, that he must have been working on mind-blowing things on his computers. What worlds could he have conjured up since, now that the technology is so much more advanced? Where had that blue landscape of vectors led?

Early one morning, not long thereafter, DD came back from a night out and bumped into his brother, who was on the way out for a morning jog. In hindsight, DD seemed fine, with no visible signs of distress, in fact no warning signs at all, no need even for anyone to look particularly hard. And so there was much conjecture later on, given what happened and the unexpectedness, especially given that he was quiet and "getting on with things." DD said nothing to anybody. That was the last anyone saw of him, in the land of the living. He walked up to the farms beyond his housing estate and entered one of the barns. There he found some discarded baler twine and tied it to a rafter and then around his neck, and he climbed up and then dropped. The coroner was able to determine that his first attempt had failed. The rope had snapped. DD had not taken this as a message or a second chance. He tried again and made sure this time.

They say drowning in real life is different from how it looks in the movies. There are rarely any screams. People drown silently, grasping and panicking for sure, but soundlessly, because they are too busy trying to breathe to speak. It takes a trained eye even to notice it, especially when someone is drowning on dry land.

Periscope

erry means "oak grove," but the trees were largely quarantined in the parks. Where did all the other oaks go? Perhaps into smoke, burning through ten thousand winter nights. Perhaps into the sea. It took over two thousand oak trees to build a single battleship, before the iron ships came. Whole forests sailed on the oceans, were splintered in battle, and ended up in their depths or floating in their vast gyroscopic currents.

At Christmas I had received a gift. It was a periscope, which, through some alchemy of mirrors, could enable me to see around corners through a spyglass. I had wished for a long time for a telescope, but it was pointless, given the yellow glare of the street-lights and the smog, which extinguished the stars overhead and even gave the moon a blurry nicotine glow. But the periscope had its uses: to see and not be seen. At the beginning, I made myself a nuisance to my parents, watching them talking, eating, or simply minding their own business without their knowledge, until they felt my prying eyes and voiced their displeasure. So I took the periscope away upstairs. From my bedroom, I could see rooftops to the horizon, mostly slate, chimneys, and aerials. The bay window let in an arctic breeze in winter but trapped the heat like a microclimate in summer. I remember gazing at the river from this vantage point, which seems impossible now, and perhaps a false memory implanted somewhere along the way; or perhaps I was remembering a dream or a photograph of somewhere else. A memory of someone else's memory. Memory has its complications, contradictions, collages, and it has times when it aspires to fiction. I would turn the light off in my parents' room when they were downstairs, and pulling the curtain closed but just wide enough to allow in a sliver of light, I'd survey the activity at night: staggering drunks, nestling couples, scuffles, and barbarisms. When the streets were empty, I'd watch rubbish blowing along, thrown from cars, and would move upward and along the windows, gazing at bedroom ceilings, and the impossible mystery of a candle in a window, and someone coming and going in rooms I'd never visit, and the car lights in the street that would momentarily startle me back to my senses.

In the distance, lit up from below, was St. Patrick's Church, Pennyburn. I would notice how its mock-Russian onion dome turned a darker hue during storms and glistened like dragon scales in the sunshine. It was a glorious, exotic note on the skyline, and in my mind it merged with Edmund Dulac's illustrations for *One Thousand and One Nights*, which I would pore over, as if the book were leaking into reality. It reinforced—this innocuous spire in a landscape of rooftops—that the border between the worlds of fact and fiction might be navigable and there might be roles for smugglers.

"You've been stuck indoors too much. You'll get cabin fever. Go on—go out and play with the traffic," my mother commanded, shooing me onto the street. As I left with my periscope under my arm, she saw the glint in my eye and thought twice, one eyebrow raised. "Where do you think you're going?"

"Just along the street."

At first, my reply had not been a lie. I'd used the periscope to see over walls and through the knotted holes in wooden fences. I'd peer into letter boxes, my eye huge and magnified like an octopus at a porthole. Gradually, though, as always, I drifted toward the Glen, the wildwood.

It was not long before I lost track of where I was and found myself surrounded by thickets. As I leaned down by the bough of a fallen tree, there was a skirmish of wings high overhead. It was then that I heard the radio chatter, ten or twenty seconds before I saw the trees become figures, secreting past in formation, a patrol of British soldiers in camouflage, shades that were as slow as ships with broken masts. I watched them through the periscope. They had not seen me and were too close for me to casually reveal myself without startling them. I felt the fear rising, knowing I was trapped. They could not see me, and they must not. I lowered myself farther onto the earth, sodden with leaves, and delicately weighed each breath. My heart was beating in my throat. They grew so close, I could hear their treads. The light splintered through the trees and onto the ground, but I could not even look up. Slowly they passed, like a herd in some distant future long after humankind has disappeared, and eventually my heartbeat subsided. As I watched them, their backs turned, head into the trees again, I thought to myself, giddy with relief, "One nil." It would be years before I realized how close I'd come to being shot.

Torch

In the living room, under the stairs, was an impossibly dark space that my parents called the "spider cupboard." It contained a perpetual fragment of night when the door was closed. It enveloped anyone who entered, and even when your eyes accustomed to it, there was minimal vision. You could feel the darkness. You could not see your hand in front of your face. The air tasted faintly of coal. Everything became still in there. It was as if the walls of the house had fallen away and you were standing in an infinite, starless cosmic black and it would take all your nerve to remain there for long. One day, someone locked me in there. Everyone has their breaking point, and as I finally snapped and pounded on the door to be let out, I could hear laughter through the door, and the panic rose in my chest. I was frantic before they relented and I spilled out onto the carpet, reaching for my inhaler. Even when the door was open and the light was shining in, it did not penetrate far. And yet the darkness still lured me in.

Always a hoarder ("Steptoe," my mother joked), Da kept a lot of his junk in there, hanging on little hooks and piled up in boxes. Rarely would he throw anything away. The hoarding seemed to be the echo of a deep, lingering habit, a kind of need that went beyond need.

I would take my father's torch into the spider cupboard and search through the items: concert posters, sheet music, strange photographs of groups of young men with their arms around one another standing in front of rows of lights and wire fences, and photos of family members now deceased, which seemed taboo to even look at but utterly compelling. Turning the torch around, close enough to create a halo of light, I could see writing of indeterminate age faintly scrawled in different colors on the stone wall. It was always cold to the touch, like a castle wall. I shone my flickering light along the wooden panels descending: the inverse side of the staircase above. I always dreaded shining the light down into the farthest reaches for fear I'd see something. The darkness there swallowed even the battery's power. I could never see where it ended or if it ended at all, convincing myself that perhaps it went down into the darkness of a hollow earth, to hell or limbo, and if you did terrible things, or even just questionable things (and who was to know what they were?), you'd go there and never be let out. I kept one foot in the doorway at all times, never entirely crossing the threshold.

Football

I lost all track of time, trying to curl the ball into the corner of the two-dimensional chalk-drawn net. My concentration was interrupted by a familiar voice. My older cousin Robert. An edgy guy with the gift of the gab. Handsome and cocky, but boyish with it, so you couldn't be angry with him. He was a magnet. He'd say things like, "I can't wait until tomorrow . . . 'cause I get better-looking by the day," knowing how ridiculous he sounded but kind of believing it, and people would laugh rather than cringe. One of the untouchable few. Charismatic. Indestructible. Always joking around with my mother and any other woman in sight: "You know me—I'm a lover not a fighter." One of those relatives who gave you kudos with the other kids. I liked Robert a lot, but I always felt myself getting shy with extroverts, and awkward with people I wanted to like me back.

"What's the craic, kid? Keeping her lit, I hope."

I nodded silently, without the remotest idea what he was talking about.

"Good stuff. Is your auld boy in?"

I shook my head.

"Well, tell him I've left in that thing he was after." Robert winked and nipped into the house.

I nodded to no one and went back to pounding the ball against the wall. Every time it hit, it left a damp circular print. I carried on for a while, until many circles were overlapping, and then sat down on the curb. Chimney smoke was drifting down the street. It had a blue tinge to it. The smell of turf. Slowly drifting along, gradually disappearing—the moment it vanished imperceptible in the drizzle. I sat and watched it, so hypnotized that I didn't realize I was soaked right through.

The ball was suddenly kicked out from between my legs with a spray of water. "You snooze, you lose, kiddo." Robert started dribbling the ball along the pavement, then flicked it up onto his knee. "Still got the magic." He started keeping it up then, attempting some ridiculously ambitious bicycle kick–style move, and walloped the ball onto a nearby roof. "Could've played for Liverpool."

He was laughing to himself as he walked away and out of my memory. I stood there in the rain, staring up at the ball.

Aerial

Time was of the essence. My mother had just nipped down to the corner shop. The devil makes work for idle hands, and I treated the house, secretly, as a laboratory. I realized I had only a few moments for the experiment. The electricity, the very substance of lightning, lived inside the walls. Wires like snakes. I'd seen it strike the church tower once, and somehow scientists had bottled it and contained it, and I could let the genie out of the bottle, just a peep. Out of curiosity, I lifted the aerial from the top of the television and very delicately slotted it into the socket.

I woke up sometime later, lying on the floor. My head was ringing as if it were inside a colossal bell. The dimensions of the room were all wrong. I thought I remembered a flash and a *whoomph* sound, but it felt like it had happened in a dream a week earlier. My mother was standing over me, screaming, but I couldn't hear her. Everything sounded like it did at the swimming baths. There was a sickening smell of burning, and as she wrenched me up onto my dangling feet, her hands trembling, I noticed the wallpaper was very lightly on fire: a scorch mark rising to the ceiling, following the path of the electric wire. I felt ill, dizzy, but as my voice and hearing returned, I realized I was not injured enough to tell the truth. "It just . . . fell into the socket."

There was no hiding this incident, but next time would be different. Concealment was the key.

"Results inconclusive," I wrote in my notebook, when my double vision had finally subsided.

Television

There was something nightmarish about that television. Perhaps it was the wait to get one that built up the expectations and trepidation. When it arrived, I was appalled. It was amazing, and yet it was like a window into bedlam. A Punch and Judy cavalcade of grotesques. 'Roid-rage wrestlers, dart-throwing stand-up comedians, drunken snooker players, deranged adverts of leering serial-killer clowns and dancing golliwogs—all the nonsense figures that filled people's heads the way medieval saints once did—tap-dancing light-entertainment lounge lizards, crazed hand puppets, Gary Glitter chants, and Jimmy Savile tracksuits. Plywood sets and sequined costumes. A nightmare from which the times struggled to awake. It was the 1980s, and the apocalypse was beamed in on our handful of channels. I was mesmerized.

My mother warned me that I'd go blind, sitting so close to

the television, the screen enveloping my panorama of vision almost entirely. I had to, or so I justified it, so that I could painfully move the tiny dials to change the channels. There was static in between. My father gazed up from his book. "You know what the Swedish call that? *Myrornas krig.* 'The war of the ants.'" My father didn't talk much, but when he did, it was full of things that no one else ever said. "Deep and meaningless," my mother would joke. My father would laugh and return to his reading. He always had his head in a book.

My friends would boast of having barely believable things like remote controls, Ceefax, even satellite dishes; and after they told you, they'd read your face for envy. I didn't mind, or at least I didn't flinch. I really liked only two or three shows, the ones I'd rush home from school once a week to see, which transported me somewhere else, the future perhaps, or another world, like *Knightmare* and *Ulysses 31*. I used to stare at the little girl playing tic-tac-toe on a blackboard while a deranged toy clown sat next to her. I was fascinated by the television because it seemed like a portal. Where to didn't matter. Perhaps it was a fragment from some other world, intruding on ours. Watching it was like gazing into the fire, hypnotized, uncomprehending. My face illuminated by the light.

The news was, however, a cursed interloper. Famine in Biafra, children with their bones breaking through their skin. The space age seeming to die, live on television, as I watched the astronauts plummet to earth in the *Challenger* disaster. The main television stations were in London and Dublin. No one spoke like me, or anyone around me. I watched *The Angelus* on RTÉ and *EastEnders* on the BBC, and they felt . . . disconnected, like I was on the wrong side of the aquarium glass.

The local news was much worse, though. It began every day with a litany. Three people shot one day, two people the next.

A bomb in a dumpster in a crowded high street. The tide of the
bloodbath ebbed and flowed between Catholic and Protestant
("Other" was a novelty). The newsreader would make the an-
nouncements like they were the football scores. I watched as
people in the room with me would respond, and I clocked the
differences in reaction. If people on the "other side" were killed,
they'd shake their heads and say, "That's a sin. No one deserves
that." If it were one of their own, the reaction would be rage
and curses. Every report was filled with the minor incidents. An
Orange Order hall attacked. Shots fired at a house. A Gaelic
Athletic Association club targeted. Scorch marks. Charred tim-
bers. A spiderweb of cracks on glass. A "viable" explosive device found on the bottom of a car. *Viable* meant "could have."
Viable meant how close you'd come to the end. How thin the
ice was, upon which, unwittingly, you walked.

Sinn Féin representatives were not allowed to speak in their
own voices. They had an actor speak over them, like a badly
dubbed kung fu movie. I wondered how actors got these jobs?
Out-of-work Shakespearean thespians, perhaps, phoned by
their agents to attend a recording studio, to repeat a political
denunciation. In the absence of their mysterious real voices, I
always imagined bizarre ones, deep and operatic perhaps, or
squeaky and cartoonish. I asked my mother and she laughed,
saying they sounded like us.

The news repeated every day, like a loop. Stuck in limbo.
Always something nice at the end to lift the spirits, finish on a
high note. A cat rescued from a tree. A fundraising initiative.
Mirthless comedy. Our wee nation. God's own acre.

People were shot in their own homes. That was the lesson
that sank in. It was a simple one. I began, every night without
fail, to place the latch on the front door before bed. My mother
caught me once and, embarrassed, I mumbled some excuse that

only waded me further into the lie the more I talked. Yet I still sneaked back to put the latch on regardless.

When the sun set, I discovered I had a fear of darkened windows, a fear that faces would suddenly appear at them. I would scurry past the one on the landing on my way to bed, without ever looking out of it, afraid I'd see something, even though rationally it made no sense, as it was on the first floor. The fear came into my mind—a fear both rational and irrational—from outside, and the television was the conduit for it. It let the monsters in.

My sister and I would sit all Saturday morning watching cartoons and adverts for things that weren't on sale here; competitions, stores, fairgrounds that existed only across the sea or south of the border. And when the news came on, the politicians, the salespeople, I would hold a magnet, pocketed from the fridge door, up to the television screen, and the figures would gently warp and a rainbow halo would encircle them. I was simultaneously dissuaded and encouraged by my parents telling me that the television would explode if I kept doing it.

Totem

The boys were playing cowboys and Indians. None of us had wanted to be the latter. My father overheard and arrived back home a few days later with a book on Crazy Horse, Geronimo, and Sitting Bull. He set it on the living room table and didn't say a word. He would do that. Leave things out for me to find myself. I was soon transfixed, and I would gaze over the other maps of America, before the states, and chart the routes and lands of the different tribes. My father even made me a totem pole for my room, which reached the ceiling, painting birds and faces on it.

Underdogs were almost sacred in Derry. I grew up thinking that Pancho Villa, Rosa Luxemburg, Biko, Allende, Mandela, Guevara were somehow saints. When a priest at school, after an hour of lecturing on Catholic martyrs, asked the class if they knew of anyone who had died for their beliefs, I even, foolishly, put up my hand.

Bird's Egg (Smashed)

A peregrine falcon used to soar above the school. It nested somewhere on the cathedral spire, up by the stone crucifix. I would watch it—noisily at first, trying to get other pupils to look, and then silently, sullenly—high above the playground and the hopscotch squares. I was intrigued by the spire, and the idea fostered in my mind by the teachers that it was somehow a celestial transmitter and receiver. It was a holy space, and yet a mason had been killed in its construction, as often happened in those days. Was it cursed then? Haunted? Our teacher claimed it was all the more holy because there'd been a martyrdom. The mason's name went unremembered, though.

The spire seemed impossibly high, surely one of the tallest buildings in the world, given that there were days when it was above the clouds, though I could find no mention of it in my books. I watched the bird orbit. It would dive astonishingly fast, its wings pointed, sharp as blades. All the noise around me—the chants and handclaps and haggling over silver football stickers, the talk of Bruce Lee's one-inch punch, whether sharks ever slept, and whether astronauts explode in the vacuum of space—would fade away into a bubble of silence. Occasionally small dead birds would be found, spattered across the playground. The children would circle around them, nudging each other to prod them with a stick.

The girls were chanting and clapping some elaborate memory feat. The boys were kicking a crushed tin can around, in lieu of a football. The cool kids boasted patches on their jackets, pinched from older brothers, of bands they'd never actually heard, like Iron Maiden, Slayer, and Anthrax. I was smart or dumb enough to hang around with the kids who were "bad news." It allowed me to be bookish but protected. You might be nearly the last to be picked for football, but they weren't even allowed to take part. They'd be given their own ball and you'd look over at their pitch and they'd be lighting fires or hurling rocks at one another. It seemed more interesting than teams competing for silver jugs. Their activities were ludicrous. They would raid the nature table for frog spawn, firing tadpoles through straws at each other. They would bring in actual ninja stars to embed in the wood of cubicle doors to freak out those inside. One of the kids, an expert shot, had become a legend by launching an orange over the height of the school, after a seemingly impossible dare, and while he was being carried around the playground on the pupils' shoulders in triumph, the orange kept going on its trajectory. It fell out of a clear blue sky and into the face of an elderly crossing guard, who retired and declined terminally shortly thereafter. They were innocent japes until they weren't.

I had proved my mettle to the gang by getting into fights on knee-scraping gravel pitches, straddling the chests of other boys before being hauled off by the scruff of the neck by teachers on their route home. The pièce de résistance, though, was kicking through a reputedly haunted window in a school basement cloakroom, in a misjudged attempt at "ghostbusting." I ended up alone in the empty school with the stern headmistress-nun, while the rest of the children went to the circus, but I knew it would earn me kudos. The nuns were particularly merciless, however, with my ma, as they assumed that she was a single mother, given that my father—through shyness or distraction, or working every hour God sent—never came to any parents' meetings, and thus that I'd hailed from a broken home, or my parents were "living in sin" or some lifestyle that did not fit the endlessly narrowing worldview of the puritan. The walk home was heavy and fraught with silence, and I felt hollow when I realized my mother was on the point of tears. I thought, suddenly and for the first time, how young she looked.

Back in the playground, one of our group was holding court in the midst of a circle of pupils, carving with a key what he claimed was a Ouija board on the wooden steps to the Portakabin classroom. A girl leaned over their shoulders and told them that they were idiots and how she had recited the Hail Mary backward at midnight facing the mirror, and Satan had appeared and offered her three wishes; and having gained the other girls' attention, she recounted her wishes in great detail. Meanwhile I silently watched the falcon orbit the spire.

In other parts of Ulster, right then, children our age were walking unbeknownst into crime scenes, led in by the sickly-sweet smell of cadaverine. A game of hide-and-seek uncovered the brutalized corpse of a young man, gagged and hooded. Kids playing near a cricket ground found two men shot dead. Other bodies were discarded directly into playgrounds. What do the children dream of after these discoveries?

The falcon kept orbiting the spire.

Gargoyle

We would dare each other further and further into danger, drunk not just on our own bravery, or the imitation of it, but on the possibility of one another having an accident. We'd climb higher and higher, onto more death-defying ledges, creaking drainpipes, scurrying across moss-covered rooftops. Fatalities were somehow averted. One unintended side effect was that we found ourselves in blind spots above the town. We would find an entire forgotten world on that rooftop layer, unseen by the street dwellers or even by those within the buildings, full of alcoves and huts and ramparts where we hung out for years. There was an unmapped world up there and it was ours for the taking.

We were tempting fate, of course. Walking along tin rooftops or placing bending planks between buildings and over sheer drops, or leaping between them, running in an instinctual form of parkour long before a name for it existed. Health and safety was a rarity then, but the dangers were still obvious. In Brooke Park, Gwyn's Institute had been an orphanage for the children of typhoid victims and had been taken over by the army before a fire incinerated it, causing its roof to fall in. Its shell was too tempting, however, and a kid scaling it fell amid collapsing masonry and was seriously injured. As we got older, injuries mounted among us too, most often inflicted during moments of complacency. One of my friends gouged his back open, like it was meat, on the metal hook of a clothesline after falling backward as we sat together. Another sliced his foot to ribbons while splashing around in the fountain in Brooke Park, where drunks threw their bottles. He was carried back in a mock pietà by our friends. I remember laughing with nerves, not for the last time, at the sight of trauma.

When I tired of the dares, the relentless nicknames, the jibes, the prepubescent talk of each other's mothers, I'd go off on my own. I would walk down to the Gander's Neck, a curiously named stretch of road with Georgian housing, past the huddle of garages and furtively past the house of a voyeur who photographed and filmed (with a Super 8 video camera) any trespassing youngster, and whom we'd nicknamed "Candy Camera." Then I'd slide in the back of a hedge, disappearing into the foliage, and wrest myself up into a tree and shimmy onto the low shoulder of the church. It seemed abandoned, but it was only dormant. They still had special services there once in a blue moon, but otherwise it had been left behind in the flight of Protestants from the west bank of the city. I would climb up there often and sit silently in the folds of the neo-Gothic architecture. Watch the sky change under every kind of weather. A place that was uniquely mine. Sometimes I would test myself and my vertigo by climbing upward, hanging off the edge. Mostly

I would sit watching the world go by, hidden from view, impassive as the gargoyles nestled next to me. A line from *The Hunchback of Notre-Dame* would circle in my mind, like a fluttering bird: "Oh, why am I not of stone, like you?" and then it would fly off into the sky.

Shovel

Kids were merciless with each other at school. Any point of difference was seized upon, especially about each other's parents. For years I'd been plagued by taunts of "Your parents are hippies," especially given that Da had a beard and long hair, which were anathema to the other children and their militantly respectable parents. These were decent God-fearing Catholics, and the last thing a Catholic would respect is someone with a beard and long hair. For too long I listened to them and longed to grow up quickly so that I could rebel and have cropped hair and wear a big suit, like the one the singer from Talking Heads wore on *The Chart Show*. I'd eventually learn to shrug off the accusations that my parents were hippies, which there was no point contesting, as they were (Da had nailed a Green Man sculpture where the holy-water fonts would be in other people's houses, next to the front door), but another recurring taunt was that my da was a gravedigger. I never understood why such a job was viewed so badly. It was something that almost every person would one day need, but the taunts still came. My father was a gardener-groundsman in the local cemetery that overlooked the town, high on the hill. He tended the graves and the trees, arranging the flowers for the grieving, keeping the lawns trimmed, and stopping the place from being swallowed up by nature.

Occasionally Da would bring back objects he'd dug up, relics of earlier times. Occasionally he'd tell horror stories of having to euthanize rabbits that had myxomatosis, bleeding from their eyes, with his shovel—feeling the terrible weight of mercy. Occasionally he'd tell stories of paupers who lived so long that everyone they'd known had already died and the only people at their funeral were a priest and my father, leaning on a rake. He'd stood and watched lavish, well-attended funerals of people who'd been feared and hated in life. Another time he told the story of how, at the burial of a young IRA volunteer, the army and the police had turned up and fired on the mourners, and they'd had to run while carrying the coffin. The authorities often turned up at memorials, not just to intimidate but to film and photograph people in the crowd, and attempt to arrest the masked figures who would play the "Last Post" at the graveside and fire volleys of bullets over the coffin, draped in a tricolor.

The cemetery suited my father's stoicism. Da treated death as a great leveler. No castle or fortress could keep it out indefinitely. "The real tragedy is an unlived life," he would say, half to himself. My father tended the plots of young and old alike. A moment's contemplation and then back to digging, back to planting. I asked him once, "Was it ever scary working there, especially when it got so dark so early in the winter?"

"There's nothing to fear from the dead. It's the living you have to worry about."

Once or twice I visited him at the cemetery, following him around as he worked, a tiny sidekick of greater hindrance than help. I would pick up single leaves, looking at the lines on them as if they were highways or tributaries, as my father slung huge sacks of compost over his shoulder. Sometimes curiosity got the better of me.

"Don't touch that, son. That's giant hogweed. It'll give you a nasty rash."

I pulled my hand back quickly.

"Is that the difference between weeds and flowers?"

"Sometimes. Most of the time they're the same. One just gets bad press."

Being built on a steep hill overlooking the city and the river, the cemetery could be seen from various points in the streets, a memento mori on the horizon. It was also possible, however, to watch games of football in the Brandywell Stadium below, from the vantage point of the tombs. My friends and I went there as young men on sweltering early-summer days. My father would notice us and saunter over, cool as a cowboy. He'd stick around, have a chat with the bolshie boys. I would always get an acknowledgment as he left—"Your da's sound"—and I'd nod. I didn't disagree, but even then I'd given up trying to impress my father, with thoughts or things I'd found, like a cat bringing dead birds to the door. We used to sit on those tombs and watch the football, and when it was done, I used to turn round and, under my breath, thank whoever it was who rested beneath us, reading their names on the headstones—something he had taught me.

LP

When we were small, my father would perform tricks for my sister and me, suddenly accelerating into flips on the beach or walking on his hands through the house, humming circus music. He was built like a Victorian strongman. He would do push-ups with us sitting on his back, laughing as we pounded on him with tiny fists. Once, he did pull-ups from a bridge in the woods, dangling over a waterfall, as we yelped and bounced in ecstatic terror on the planks above. As we got older and grew out of childhood, he became more withdrawn. My friends would always be impressed in his presence, but when they left, he and I would just drift to other rooms. It was no big thing. My friends did that with their fathers too. And besides, heavy things seemed to be worn lightly with my father, if at all. He never raised his voice or needed to. His disdain was shown with a laugh and rolled eyes. The silences were rarely uncomfortable, but they nevertheless grew the older I got. I never knew precisely why.

His sanctuary, and mine in turn, was music. Da was obsessed with the blues, from the Mississippi Delta to Chicago. He played a mean guitar and harmonica (the blues harp, he called it) and had a fine voice. I would ask him if he'd been in any bands as a teenager, but he'd always change the subject. In a strange way, I felt like I got to know my father more from playing his records than from talking. What he listened to was one method of trying to understand him, just as I learned something about my mother from her Leonard Cohen and Sandy Denny records. Da had a treasure trove of LPs in the attic that gradually made it down the stairs as the years went on, mainly through my impish climbing and dangling from the attic hatch. Dusty, scratched, warped at times, but with mesmerizing interstellar covers of other planets or ancient-sounding folk singers standing on misty headlands. Discovering artists was like discovering entire planets to explore. It began early. As soon as I learned to toddle around, I would sidle over to the record player, knowing exactly where to drop the stylus to play particular songs. It really kicked in, though, as it does with everyone, in the second age of discovery that is the teenage years.

Other houses had photos of the pope, JFK, maybe a china plate of the Queen Mother. My father had shrines to Muddy Waters and Howlin' Wolf, and an almost life-size portrait of Robert Johnson looking impossibly dapper in a pinstripe suit, trilby on, guitar in hand. For years I thought they were saints. Perhaps they were. The self-harming martyrs and ascetic neurotics offered up by the Church paled next to Skip James, Mississippi John Hurt, and Reverend Gary Davis. The tricks of holy men seemed far too austere and too absurd compared with the crackling clairvoyance of vinyl.

My father always sang. He sang more than he talked. It took me an awful long time before I realized it wasn't just a form of communication, but could also be a way of avoiding it.

Clock

The future was elsewhere. We were all stuck in the present. You could feel it coming—the need for it, the tug of a vacuum for air. It was close, we were on its scent, but really it was on ours.

My pals and I would walk around our neighborhood theatrically, as if on a tightrope, on the small walls that ran parallel to the roads. We'd heave ourselves up lampposts like sailors toward crow's nests, searching for land. When someone got a possession—a BMX, say—there was a clamber of grabbing hands until someone prevailed, and then they were off, not only with little respect for the bike or the owner or their own safety, but actively trying to deliver it back to them in a diminished, disintegrating state. We broke into derelict housing, jabbing holes in stained-glass windows older than our grandparents and leaping onto furniture that hadn't been touched since the 1950s. We lay on warm, porous tarmac and frosted concrete to kick footballs free from underneath parked cars, dislodging the occasional exhaust pipe. We played football between the battered gates of two facing lanes, stopping regularly for passing traffic, and on marshland with a sodden ball, painful to head; it went on for hours, until the tally reached way into double figures. We cultivated wounds on our way, little scars ranging from scraped knees to stitched scalps as medals, the amount of stitches defining each rank. That was before we got real injuries, the ones that stayed with you, the ones you didn't want, inside and out. Those were still to come.

Occasionally we'd overstep the mark. One monumentally stupid way was getting "hangies." We'd stand around roadsides, using discarded hubcaps as Frisbees, waiting for the opportunity, then we'd run up behind trucks and cling to the back as long as we could. Usually the driver would notice at the next traffic light or even straight away, given the extra weight on the suspension, and we'd leap off and scatter. We were as dedicated as trainspotters for rare vehicles to attach ourselves to: horseboxes, car haulers, boats on trailers.

Our favorite was an ice-cream van that had a huge Uncle Sam Perspex face on the back. We'd dangle from the Stars and Stripes hat, trying to get a foothold on the slippery beard as it drove down the road, playing a shrieking robot version of "Dixie's Land." From time to time we'd get a driver who was in a daze and didn't notice the change in the vehicle's weight or failed to spot us in the rearview mirror. Or, worse still, a psychopath with road rage, who'd deliberately speed up or try to physically shake us off. They'd drive for miles until some of us, clinging on, white-knuckled, were weeping and threatening to jump in front of other horrified drivers. We'd be left miles into unknown territory and we'd return exhausted, to the laughter of the younger kids of the neighborhood, saying,

"Ha-ha, you're dead. Your folks have been shouting for you for hours. You're dead." They'd follow me like I was the Pied Piper, right to my front door.

We were nine years old, Gareth and I. The other boys were ten, and thus a lifetime our senior. We all filed into line as they led the expedition. The bravado was almost believable. When there was any risk, the elders were not stupid and sent the younger ones in first, to take point, like they were expendable grunts. Gareth and I held our breath, treading lightly through the alcos' house with no front door, stepping over the barely breathing mannequins scattered in swastika shapes over the floor. We dangled and dropped into a torched, abandoned squat whose occupants had signed off their tenancy by setting fire to a gas bottle, blowing holes full of sky in the roof. In a third house it was always the 1950s, since its owner had died or simply left. Everything had lain in place, undisturbed, since. A sudden departure, frozen for forty years—it was like time travel. Everything remained still in situ, impeccably ordered but covered in a shroud of moths and dust. A sliding glass cabinet, a light switch and shaving sockets in the bathroom, a clothesline spanning the kitchen: we were afraid to touch anything for fear it would all crumble or stir into life; afraid of the ladder that led to the attic, afraid of the dial phone that might suddenly break its long silence.

Once the area was secure, we were dispatched outside as lookouts. We were almost glad to be posted outside while the others plundered. We huddled together in the yard, out of reach of the rain and out of sight of the neighbors, under a wall crowned with broken bottles, not caring if the others got caught; and we'd talk about what we wanted to be when we grew up, where we wanted to go, occasionally interrupted by the sound of shattering glass or a muffled whoop of delight or an insult thrown from one of our gang mates at some high window ("Are you two homos snogging?"). When the conversations were interrupted, we forgot to return to them.

Fate was not kind to our group of street urchins. One of the boys began to suffer from liver failure at an early age, before we'd even begun drinking. Though he survived, it appeared touch and go as he bloated and turned yellow. Another was exiled from the city for drug dealing. Gareth died in the Swiss Alps, of all places, falling into a ravine. He wasn't found for some time.

He was always called in from the street earlier than the rest. I was always second, having time to watch him walk away under the yellow glare of the streetlights. Sometimes he would whistle.

Fence

Legal territories were mapped out by aristocrats in drawing rooms, but everyone drew their own borders in some way, from the earliest age: the division of a shared bedroom into zones, like occupied Berlin. Chalk on a playground. Beyond the singular house, the terraces were defined according to risk. There were safe areas, where we knew every passageway and escape route and could mount defenses against roving gangs of ne'er-do-wells from elsewhere. Then there were absolute no-go areas, where trespass risked life and limb. There weren't many transitional places. The demarcation lines were well established. One exception was the fairs that drew in gangs from all over town, so that the excitement of the swirling rides and pounding dance music and flashing lights always had a distinct and delicious element of peril.

Later, we'd escape over the border to camp in Donegal, a beloved place full of mysteries and wonders (from the Poisoned

Glen to the Bloody Foreland), but where we found territories guarded by the local young men of the villages. Though the inhabitants of Derry and Donegal were essentially the same people, there was acrimony due to the narcissism of small differences. Some of the villages were deceptively crazy, for all their picturesque qualities. In one, a mass brawl between drug gangs had been broken up, not by the Irish police, the Guards, who sat it out on the sidelines, but by a spooked horse. We learned to keep to ourselves, to camp in hollows and woods or inside Napoleonic forts, burning bonfires by the sea as comets blazed in the skies. We drank and sang to the stars through those nights. But we were always called back over the border.

In the city, on the periphery of my neighborhood, I could venture up to Rosemount far enough to visit relatives and pick up a subscription to the comic *2000 AD*, which led me to assume that the adjacent Brooke Park was a safe zone, or a DMZ at worst. It faced dead-end terraces that I never dared intrude upon, but the park itself was a pastoral sanctuary I'd loved when much younger, being taken up there regularly by my mother. It didn't even matter that I'd contracted blood poisoning after falling off the roundabout and busting my knee on the glass-flecked gravel. I had, after all, earned a scar and, melodramatically, "nearly died" in stories to follow, including this one. And so it was still a sanctuary and a place of boundless imagination: climbing on a metal frame designed to look like a Soviet satellite with a wooden seat facing skyward, dreaming that I was Gagarin.

A statue was at the bottom of the park, of a banker, baron, and MP known to locals as the Black Man, due to the darkened bronze, which had once stood between traffic in the central square ("the Diamond") of town. At night, my classmates would whisper, the statue would descend and hunt trespassers to their doom. Aside from spectral effigies, the park seemed safe. It had a feeling of serenity, with its fountain and oaks and weeping willow trees. I did not know that the violence had reached even there. Once, for example, at the bowling green pavilion, two soldiers were blown up when someone nonchalantly handed them a package wrapped up like a present. A relative, then a passing schoolgirl, had looked into the aftermath and seen bodies through the smoke and the barrel of a rifle zigzagged by the force of the blast. She recalled a female soldier, one of the Wrens, screaming. "Blood pumping out of a head wound." There was no counseling for anyone in those days. You were told not to talk about it. This is how quickly the abnormal becomes normal. Time carried on without mercy. Weeks later, another soldier was killed by a sniper, leading to gun battles throughout the city. Unforgettable things were "forgotten."

Trespassing there was a folly that was rewarded with a busted head when I was set upon by a gang of older kids, who caught me and a friend kicking a football around, without sufficient papers. Gazelles away from the pack. I'd almost gotten away, until felled by a slide tackle, and had tried to roll into a ball as boots flew and stomps came down. It was only halted by a passing jogger, by which stage I was bashed around, trying to catch my breath through sobs. The worst part was then being driven by a friend's father, who was above the etiquette of the street, to confront those who'd done it—"Look at him, you ghastly wee brutes. Look at his face"—and having them beam in at me in the back seat, like I was being held up as a trophy from a safari hunt.

I had broken not only the silent code of territory but also that of omertà. You took your beatings, I told myself, and you retaliated, biding your time, for years even, until the gang had forgotten who you were; and then you saw one of them strutting along, absentminded, and the odds were in your favor. You didn't snitch. It was the worst of crimes where we lived. The absolute worst. Worse than murder. From then on, when we ventured into other areas, we went in numbers and we answered attacks by responding in kind. I had thought of it as something we could shake off as we got older, like the shell of a chrysalis, but it only intensified.

And yet I cherished where we lived with a sense, even then, that it was impermanent. I knew I would leave one day, unwillingly, and so, curling back the carpet in my bedroom, I would hide objects beneath the floorboards and scratch messages on the stone walls underneath the wallpaper. Transmissions to the future.

Most of the time we evaded the gaze of adults and explored the boundaries. We unweaved holes in wire fences. On waste ground we set up Evel Knievel jumps for bicycles with dodgy brakes, putting a flattened drinks carton under the mudguard to make an approximation of a motorbike *vroom*. We climbed the precarious heights of trees to attach ropes to make death-swings, achieving increased g-force and then blackout by winding them up and spinning on them, or breaking bones when the swinging rope snapped, sending the swinger careering through the air at an unnatural angle, still optimistically holding a portion of rope flapping in the breeze as they headed toward plumes of nettles.

The names of the streets puzzled me as I wrote them carefully onto my maps. I had been told that the courts and terraces had Scottish names (Glasgow, Argyle, and so on) because the houses had been built for shipbuilders a hundred years before. They were long gone now or assimilated. The docks were still there, decaying behind locked gates, but the ships were no longer being constructed. Nor were there any on the river. What puzzled me were the other names—the names of trees. We lived at the corner of Cedar Street and Hawthorn Terrace, but there were no trees in sight. My forest was one of lampposts, chimneys, and drainpipes. One morning my father took me cycling up to the Grianán of Aileach fort, a stone refuge for ancient sun-worshipping Celts high on a Donegal ridge—my father's old boyhood haunt, where he would flee for temporary respite from the madness of those years. Delicately wheeling our bikes out onto the street at five in the morning, I was struck instantly by how the mundane, familiar streets seemed to have transformed. Everything was unearthly silent, I could feel the silence on my skin, and the air was filled with the unmistakable smell of pine trees, as if we were in the middle of an invisible wood, separated from it only by time.

Salt

Across from our house was the chip shop. It had a mosaic of tiny colored windows on one side, which drunks kept falling through. On the other side were portholes and pipes emanating steam, as if the building were a machine. Above, there was a flat where the electric neon-blue of a sunbed glowed radioactively at night. My mother worked in the chip shop in the evenings, while she studied to be a nursery nurse in the daytime. My pals always wanted to go in and hang out, cadge free chips, but I knew even then to keep them away, that trouble followed in their wake and they'd push things. Ma would work late, serving those staggering back from the local pubs. I would always lie awake until she returned, recognizing the sound of her step on the stair, and she would always check in on me and I'd let on to be asleep.

My parents were smart but had no qualifications, so it didn't count to the kids at school or in society at large; my father had an endless pile of books, while my mother was always crafting things. Once, looking through photos, I found a picture of someone kneeling with a welding mask on and a flare so incandescent it dazzled, even from a photograph. "Who's that?" "That's me," Ma said, laughing, "when I was a teenager." I took my parents to be, as everyone does, vaguely biblical, when in hindsight they were just kids. My mother was only eighteen when she got pregnant. She had a tentativeness that bordered on the fearful, a fear that, when you knew her, seemed not to belong to her but be imposed from outside or from experience rather than personality. The quiet kind of introversion she wore was always mistaken or misrepresented as snobbery. She reacted with bolshiness, by saying loudly that she didn't care, as those who do care often do. In the photograph, she is welding with a cigarette in one hand. She is wearing some kind of poncho. To this day, I have never seen a superhero more impressive or nonchalant. She'd watch endless soaps, but was happiest sitting in front of paranormal programs or films where huge robots bludgeoned each other through disintegrating cities. I wondered if my fascination with seeing the mechanics inside things came from her.

Poverty is continual low-level anxiety. It is ambient. The step of children without poverty is perceptibly lighter. Most families didn't have much in Derry, and still don't, but there was nevertheless a pronounced sense of shame at living in a small house, or in getting free meals at school, or not wearing certain brands of clothing. The teachers encouraged it, by getting the children to stand up and tell the class where they'd been on holiday, or bring their Christmas toys into school, or count how many rooms were in their houses and describe them. They could even tell from the wallpaper that covered their notebooks. I used to hate no-uniform days. Once, my mother had bought me a counterfeit football top, because we could not afford a real one. The lads at school were scathing, and I went home and took it off, and my mother found it hidden and was hurt, and I felt guilty for my petulance and spent the rest of the day trying to make her laugh, like a shamed jester. The Traveller kids got it especially hard. Even the poorest among us gave them a desperate time, seeking perhaps someone to stand between us and the bottom.

Our house had no central heating, but it did have a Japanese room. This seemed normal to me, until I began to stay over at friends' houses for sleepovers and found out that Japanese rooms were conspicuous by their absence in working-class Derry, and ours was part bohemian affectation and part genuine fascination on my parents' behalf. They were hippies who'd gone off track, and I guess there was some kind of yearning for Zen, in the midst of the chaos and mundanity of then-and-there. Inside the room were lacquered boxes decorated with bamboo forests, fans with cherry-blossom harvests, a statuesque monk with a begging bowl with frozen mist rising and transforming into a dragon around him, eggshells in tiny glass cabinets, figures twisting like gnarled polished driftwood. They were cheap counterfeits, but I took them for precious relics that had made it from one edge of the world to another. There were woodblock prints of *The Great Wave off Kanagawa*, immaculate tearooms, samurai battles on bridges, and, above all, the rain falling on nocturnal Japanese streets in another century. I wondered if there was a word for feeling intensely nostalgic for a time and place in which you had never actually lived.

There was a Japanese mask that I knew to take very delicately off its hook (an earlier bone or ivory incense-holding Confucius had been knocked off the mantel and smashed when my sister and I had been playing, and we'd had to construct a house of cards of lies that soon collapsed). I'd wear it, facing the mirror. Looking upward, it seemed to smile. Downward, it seemed to frown. Comedy and tragedy depended on the angle. A perspective trick, a trick of light. It all depended where I was standing.

One day the teacher told us to bring in an object from our house to talk about. I made the mistake of bringing the mask. The other boys snatched it away and wrestled over it. Wrenching aside the tussling children, the teacher confiscated it, saying it was pagan and most likely satanic. Terrified all day that my parents would notice it missing, I went at the end of the school day, when the bells had rung and the other kids were jostling through the cloakroom and onto their buses, and tentatively approached the teacher to ask for it back. She handed it back, broken.

Mostly the children aped their elders, sometimes literally, posing as if smoking invisible cigarettes or adopting swaggers, claiming their fathers had had trials for Spurs or could lay waste to every other kid's father. It was rare that my da picked me up at school, but I was always secretly proud when I burst out and he was standing at the gates. Usually it was Ma who picked me up, until I was old enough to walk home on my own.

I knew to keep the delinquent world of my friends away from my home and my school. Some worlds were best kept separate. They always seemed to be hatching plots: raids, cheevies, knick knack, the casual terrorizing of anyone different. You targeted others for fear of being targeted yourself. That was the logic. A reverse golden rule. Some of these targets were formidable, and you toyed with them at your peril. One such character seemed to have survived from a lost world. Wabbits was a scrapyard tinker, a rag-and-bone man, a poacher, a thief of copper and lead from church roofs (a not-unusual undertaking;

my father remembered people prying lead from church rooftops to melt down and make tiny crosses for themselves). It was said that Wabbits kept no furniture in his house and slept on the floor. He always left his keys in the lock of his front door, yet no one would have dared to enter. One kid, seeking a chance to put himself at the top of the pecking order, stole the keys one day and dropped them down a drain. It was a costly decision.

We usually goaded Wabbits from a safe distance. He had a deceptively impish look, like a bedraggled gnome or a leprechaun. He would zip around at high speed on his bicycle, which had no brakes, never sitting but always standing on one pedal, and would freewheel to ludicrous speeds. We would laugh and mock, but the way he rode made it possible for him to suddenly accelerate off the bike at a full sprint, the bicycle carrying on beside him, as we would soon find out. All it took was a single call of his name and the chase was on. We didn't fully realize what we were unleashing until one of us was caught. The beating was savage. The kid was thrown around like a rag doll as if in the jaws of a wild animal, and all the while Wabbits was smiling a deranged but unequivocally happy smile. We still couldn't resist shouting his name after that. Sometimes he would chase us for what seemed like hours, until some of the weaker members of the group would start to cry and beg the others, "Why won't he stop?" and some of the more conspiratorial of the group would try to trip up their friends as a sacrifice.

There were other people in our neighborhood who attracted unwanted attention. One was the Karate Woman, an American lady who wore a bandanna and would do martial-arts moves on unsuspecting passersby. What brought her to this part of the world was unknown, but someone claimed they saw her daughter visiting her once, which suddenly made her seem real to me and not a caricature. Then there was "Mad Elizabeth," who wore jam-jar glasses and would throw her possessions out her window in great heaps, and we would sift through them, tentatively, like creeping into the lion's den. We'd see her early in the morning, walking up the street, clenching a crowbar in one hand and a shopping bag in the other, as if it were perfectly normal. The Tories had shut down a lot of the psychiatric care and turned those with severe mental illness out onto the street, under the guise of "empowerment" and care in the community. We might have thought of these people as dangerous predators, but they were the prey. And although we were children, we were innocent only up to a point. To our victims, we were harpies.

Take the case of Danny Bird. The kids would stand outside his home, with his overgrown garden and plastic sun-bleached Virgin Mary on the windowsill, and we'd shout abuse and accusations, one of which was the unfounded rumor that he'd killed his own brother. We could never be sure when he'd come. The timing was always unexpected. We would taunt for hours and then, in an instant, as we walked away, he'd appear; at other times he'd burst out at our initial approach. He'd propel himself, arms and legs akimbo and flailing after us. Once, as we ran away from him, he caught up with us and, running parallel at the same speed, started looking backward, as if we were all running away collectively from someone or something else. I didn't take part in the tormentings anymore after that. I felt a deep sense of shame and would feign boredom, trying to get the others to relent without losing face. It rarely worked.

The dares had become gradually more extreme, along with the peer pressure. It was no longer enough to bolt through box gardens. The mischief had turned to malevolence. I could see their hearts harden with time and experience. A couple of humiliating and threatening incidents with British soldiers, and all lightheartedness was gone from their interactions. We exchanged not only insults but also stones, no longer playing games but instead taking to our heels for dear life, pursued through the routes that only we knew—sometimes bursting at high speed through strangers' homes, in the back door and out the front, as they sat openmouthed with their dinner on their laps. Coming up to Halloween, we'd get our hands on brightly colored boxes of Chinese fireworks and would construct spectacular explosive devices, tying them to aerosol cans, even firing them at each other or daring one another to hold on to Roman candles as long as we could (once I almost lost an eye when an aerosol sliced across my eyelid; my friend's doting grandmother dabbed it with the heady sting of TCP). We'd make prank calls to random numbers from the phone book and then blow up the telephone booth, with Catherine wheels or air bombs ricocheting inside, trying to lock each other in the booth, gripping the door, laughing and screaming. Hanging out now, almost entirely on waste ground, behind fences, on rooftops, in derelict buildings, disused factories, and never-finished building sites, we would launch our firework-missiles at passing army patrols, then use flares and smoke bombs to disguise our escape, not quite realizing how close we came to getting killed. Given that the state had colluded in the murder of lawyers and the bombing of cities in the Republic, the death of an errant Fenian youth wouldn't carry much weight or earn many headlines, especially on the "mainland."

Kids younger and more innocent than us had their brains blown out, often for nothing except being in the wrong place at the wrong time—their heads fractured by the direct point-blank impact of a rubber bullet. The soldiers who did so were rarely punished. If it even went to trial, the judge would commend their unblemished character and speak of regrettable tragic accidents that should not blight an impeccable, promising career. In one case, the coroner declared that one such dead child had an abnormally thin skull, which the soldier could not have known, of course. In another case, a schoolboy in uniform was said to clearly be a terrorist. The newspapers concurred, and the unfortunate cases were quickly forgotten by anyone who mattered in the scheme of things.

There used to be a remarkable object that initially had no real name. It had been due to be part of the third nuclear bomb on Japan that was scheduled to be dropped, had the imperial administration not surrendered. It was a split orb of plutonium. The two halves were kept apart to prevent a nuclear reaction from taking place. A physicist called Harry Daghlian was experimenting with it one day when it slipped out of his hand, and in the brief instant when the pieces touched, it began to go critical; he received enough of a radiation dose to kill him within a few weeks. A year later another scientist, Louis Slotin, was playing around with the same object, holding the two halves apart with a pencil, when again there was a slip and the air briefly turned blue and he could taste the radiation before he started vomiting. After the two deaths, the object earned the name "the demon core." Handling it was called "tickling the dragon's tail." I read about it in my books. We did not realize it then, but we, too, were tickling the dragon's tail with something even more unpredictable than a chemical element: scared and psyched-up young men on patrol in a hostile environment. All it would take was a slip.

It was a time of watching. There were so few CCTV cameras that we would dance in front of them, amazed to see our own images moving in real time. I still watched the patrols from my parents' window. They seemed black and white with a dash of dark jungle-green, smudged as newsprint, mixing in with the smog that hung over the city, smoke from the chimneys indistinguishable from the sky. Now, however, they slowly began to have electronic eyes looking back.

At the top of the hill on my map, looming over the Glen and the houses, was the watchtower. Built by the army, such towers were alien structures. Some of them looked industrial, almost like water towers or smokestacks, except they were located in the middle of residential areas, where people washed their cars, and kids went from door to door with sponsor sheets. The watchtowers dominated desolate mountaintops near the border, surrounded by a web of scaffolding. Tolkienesque. Others were squat and bunkerlike, nestling in protectively between houses. Some loomed, dark green and gray, over the streets like sentinels, like invaders that might suddenly start to walk, insectlike, across the city.

The Troubles were blazing then. There was always talk about how much the army could listen in on the locals and how much they could see. Women complained about voyeurs gazing into their bedrooms. Reaching above the houses as a kind of anti-lighthouse, the watchtower extended a reach over the streets and drew in emotion, speculation, ire. It also drew fire. Always a light sleeper, my mother would leap out of bed at the sound of nearby shots as gun battles at Rosemount Barracks echoed through the streets, followed by the sound of speeding cars and the inevitable helicopter response. When the bullets sounded especially close, she would throw the duvet on the floor, so the bed was in front of the window, and lay us down with her body between us and the window until the cacophony finally petered out. Even when they were distant, she'd take no chances. She'd read somewhere that a bullet could travel over a mile, and they could, and did, ricochet. Kids were shot in the cross fire when the IRA opened up on the army. A nine-year-old boy was shot in the back of his skull in his bedroom when the police, the Royal Ulster Constabulary, opened up indiscriminately on Divis Flats with a machine gun. People forgot about that incident; it was in the interest of many for people to forget, but she remembered.

My grandmother Needles, as she was nicknamed, had to walk in the shadow of the watchtower of Rosemount Barracks to come see us. I traced the route on my map, past the derelict shirt factory and the derelict little church, down the hill that served as our Cub Scout hall.

The army had its own maps. I saw the officers consulting them, even asking kids for directions or to show them where specific places were. Their patrols—and every day they'd make their presence felt—were well rehearsed. They would highlight safe areas, populated by unionists friendly to their presence, and antagonistic Catholic areas in different colors. They would pinpoint intersections like Bishop Street, flashpoints like "Aggro Corner" at the bottom of William Street, and ghettos like the Fountain, where my mother had worked in a nursery but had been forced out by loyalist paramilitaries, stepping over toys and waving goodbye to the infants as she left. Potential sniper positions would be pinpointed. Death zones for ambushes. Attacks could take place anywhere, though, with combatants blending back into the crowd from whence they came. Numerous soldiers were shot dead on the low-lying stretch along the waterfront at the Foyle Road by snipers up on the heights of the town. "One shot, one kill" was the rule, so the soldiers' screaming colleagues could not get a bead on them. Watchtowers would have to climb higher then, as snipers looked for snipers above the heads of people coming and going to work, to shops, to school.

There was safety in numbers around the Brits. On my own, I learned to keep my head down and skirt past the soldiers, for fear of getting a thump or being seen as too friendly. When I first became aware of their presence, I'd approach them as if we were in a zoo, unclear on who was observer and who observed. My friends would follow them, in a continual to and fro. The bolshie Artful Dodger types among the group would throw banter back and forth with the soldiers, strutting with their hands in their pockets. "Give us a look through your sights." And sometimes the soldiers would let them.

Once, Jamesy, always mouthing off, persuaded the soldiers to let him inside the armored Land Rover. A clatter of noise came from inside and he suddenly appeared out the top with a helmet on, laughing his head off. The soldiers were laughing too. "Stick the nee-naw on. Come on, drive, for fuck's sake," Jamesy was shouting, thumping the metal armor plates at the top. The laughter died down, but Jamesy kept going, pushing it. His head suddenly vanished. It reminded me of the opening scene of *Jaws*. Then the latch door reopened and he was bundled out, kicked onto the street and onto his face by a standard-issue boot. The Land Rover lurched abruptly and then took off and soon vanished into the streets. My friend, ordinarily the cock of the walk, suddenly appeared like the little boy he was, squealing for his mother and blinded with tears as he ran toward his house. Our group, minus our leader, nervously stood frozen in the porch of his house, unsure of what to do and somehow implicated, as muffled shouts came from inside. The porch had a mosaic floor. One of my friends asked, "What should we do?" I couldn't look at him and began counting the tiles, stopping and beginning again repeatedly.

Later, when the moment had passed and Jamesy had regained

his resolve, wiping his eyes with his sleeves, he and I found ourselves walking together. I thought it best not to say anything,
but remembering my friend's vulnerability, I turned and said,
"I'm sorry about what happened to you earlier. How upset you
g—" And I found myself immediately pinned up against the
pebbledash wall, gripped hard at the throat. Jamesy's face had
changed completely. There was rage and pain in his eyes. "You
mention that again, to *anyone*, and you're fucked. Do you hear
me?" I nodded and Jamesy let me go. We continued walking
silently. I was out of step with him and gradually fell away to a
halt as he kept walking, huffing and puffing to himself. Memory is a sketchy thing, especially chronology, but I can't recall if
I ever visited his house again, or vice versa.

The soldiers emitted authority, a clunking swagger, but they
seemed skittish, too, when I looked closer. They weren't much
older than I was, but half a decade was a lifetime at that age.
They would make their way cautiously, almost geometrically,
through the streets, winding at angles like a single creature, an
arthropod. I joined the dots between them in my imagination.
There was a tension between the wish to be seen, to assert their
presence, and the urge to take cover. I watched them intently.
They would cradle their rifles and adjust their posture, barrel-
chested and baby-faced beneath the war paint. Some would
shelter in porches, while others knelt at corners. They wore
camouflage in the midst of brick, concrete, and tarmac. One
would take point, a stalking horse, surveying windows and corners while the others followed. A signal would be exchanged
from time to time in sign language, and I could see it filter
through the unit and their tension ease, and they would adopt
a slightly more informal march through the territory, between
the corner shop and the bakery. "Tail-End Charlie"—that was

the last guy on patrol. I heard them say it. I listened in, close enough to hear such phrases. It was dangerous to be first in the patrol, but even worst to be last, waiting to be picked off.

I heard other words too. Slang. It changed with each regiment. You could tell they were different by the color of their berets and badges, even before you heard their accents. They'd use words like *numpty* and *scunner,* and I'd try to place them as Geordie or Welsh or whatever. The first black people I ever saw in real life wore those uniforms. The soldiers walked through housing estates like the ones where they grew up in Manchester or Glasgow, but this place was different. Same dimensions, but somehow warped in their minds. The heavy firepower they brought said it all. To me, it was home, but to them it was hell. There were moments of stilted connection. A local girl would walk past and they'd wolf-whistle and make gestures I didn't understand, and she'd say, "You wish!" and they'd shout, "Slapper!" And then a moment or two later, after the laughter, you'd see the concentration coming back, the fear rising again. They'd momentarily let their guard down and they knew it.

My ma, barely a teenager on her way to school, had been one of those girls. She had bolshily passed one such patrol. She overtook a young soldier crouched down at one of the telephone exchange boxes, a sight so common it no longer warranted more than a second glance. Suddenly she was thumped forward onto the pavement, and a fraction of a moment later she was enveloped by a sound so loud it shook the ground beneath her and she couldn't tell which way was up. Then silence. She covered her face instinctively and turned, her hands and knees cut, to see dust everywhere, slowly dissipating. There was a crackling charred stump where the box had been. Debris was scattered outward, and in its midst, the soldier was scattered across the road. Ma could not remember if it was him who was screaming, if that was even possible anymore, or one of his mates, before she was shepherded into school. Other girls were trembling and blessing themselves. She sat there in shock at her desk. Her friend motioned to her face, and as my mother touched her cheek, she looked at her fingertips and saw they were covered in soot.

When the army passed through, most adults shied away, by force of habit as much as intention. A few left their homes, though, and went out and put on a show of defiance just by going about their business. It was a process of mutual demoralization. You'd get occasional exchanges of insults between the teenagers and soldiers, but from a safe distance, given that the teenagers were old enough to be fair game and risked getting nabbed into one of the Land Rovers by a snatch squad and carted off for a battering, a sleepless night, and a court summons, to be read through a throbbing, seeping welt of a black eye. The matriarchs of the area, who had ruled the roost in Derry since the shirt-factory days, would stand on their doorsteps with their arms brazenly crossed, their children or grandchildren pulling at their hems, occasionally snarling a caustic observation— "They say bullies are cowards, you know"—before turning to their kids and telling them to button their lips or she'd get the Brits, the bogeymen, to snatch them away.

Mostly the kids would be playing kick-about, and they'd pause their game as the patrol passed. Holding the ball. Staring in slow motion. Now and then one of the squaddies would try to show off his skills: "On the 'ead, mate." You could hold the ball and refuse to pass it, if your nerve held. They *hated* that. Most of the time they passed by grudgingly, full of suspicions. I realized only later, with genuine surprise, that I and my kind were supposed to be the villains in this story.

The strange thing was that none of it seemed strange.

Everywhere people think their life is the norm, the default. A childhood, however abnormal to others, is always normal to those living it. Knowing nothing different, you grow so used to bomb scares, armed checkpoints, turnstiles into town centers, eyes at metal slots when ordering taxis, cages and cameras at the entrances to pubs, that you no longer even really see them. Old ladies cursed paramilitaries for emptying their bus at gunpoint so that they could take it away and use it as a burning barricade: "I have an appointment, you know. You should be ashamed of yourselves. That mask doesn't fool anyone—I know your grandmother."

I would sit with my cousins on the low walls of their housing estate, a place nicknamed Bally-Bosnia, listening to them talking, deferential to them, as wise elder teenagers.

"You'd never catch me going to London. Or Dublin, for that matter. I heard muggers come up and threaten you with infected needles."

"That's nothing; I heard they throw rats in your car window at traffic lights, and when you jump out, they jump in and drive off."

We all agreed that the big cities were mad, round about the time that a tank passed us in the background, driving through the housing estate.

Sweets

Time is relative. There are places, rooms even, where time moves slower or faster than elsewhere. Forced to go to Mass at school, I found that time stretched, while my hours with my friends accelerated. Halfway down our street was a sweetshop where time had not passed for fifty, maybe one hundred years. When you stepped into Auld Mick's tiny but cavernous shop, a bell, attached by a string to the door, rang. He would shuffle out, impossibly ancient to us but probably barely sixty or seventy, an amiable old chap with bad hearing and a stoop, who'd take a lifetime, using a stepladder, to reach up to glass jars filled with flying saucers, bonbons, foam shrimps, and vats of sherbet. There were chocolate cigarettes on the counter and chewing gum with little comic-book cards inside. Two old gentlemen, with flat caps and pipes blazing, chatted to Auld Mick in a steady flow of unanswered observations and maxims. I heard them many times, but their philosophies go unrecorded. There was a shutter into the family's house that would regularly open, and a head, usually one of Auld Mick's legion of grandchildren, would pop through from their living room to demand "messages" from their grandfather.

We began to push our luck, even though Auld Mick had been nothing but courteous. We started ribbing each other to steal, asking the shopkeeper to get the farthest-away sweets and, when his back was turned, leaning over to ransack under the counter. I didn't want to take part and said I would keep lookout outside, to no avail. I was dragged in as an accessory. My friend was reaching over one day when the shutter opened and one of the family saw what my friends were up to, and all of the gang were barred. I kept this a secret until my mother sent me down to the shop one day, to get a pint of milk, and I made up a list of unconvincing excuses—increasingly elaborate lies that I was soon entangled in—as to why I couldn't, and she read my face like an open book.

I did not like keeping secrets. Shame had a weight that only grew when concealed. One day I had walked over to my friend's house and was introduced to another boy our age. I had seen him before, on the periphery of our area. He had a different accent and his clothes were always grubby and he looked older than he should. Unkempt. Slightly feral. He had strange ways of doing things. Odd quirks to his language, the way he carried himself. I was intrigued, threatened, and attracted, I suppose, but I kept a distance. The other boys admired the new kid, as he had no bedtime and could freely roam the streets. He seemed afraid of nothing, but in a dazed kind of way.

One day I went to his house with a mutual friend to play on the new kid's computer. It was in an old building down near the Glen, and the stairwell was full of rubbish and smelled musty.

We played for a while, fighting over the joystick, but something seemed off and I wanted to leave almost the minute I arrived, counting time until I could make an adequate excuse. There was no mother around. It soon became apparent he didn't have one. When the kid's father arrived, he announced his presence with a bellow that jolted everyone in the room, bar the new kid. He was steaming drunk, and the son got into a row with him. I felt alarm bells going off in my head and said to my friend that we should leave, but he was wrapped up in the game and oblivious to any danger. The pressure in the room felt unbearable, so I asked to go to the toilet. I thought about fleeing, but the exit was in the other direction, back through the living room. As I came back along the landing, the father cornered me, crazed, violent. I was a deer in the headlights. I made it out, babbling excuses that seemed to potentially implicate me in something fearful that I did not understand.

The baleful encounters with strangers in childhood, the experiences of being cornered, and the shame that came from others finding out about this vulnerability only grew, until the places we hid shameful things we didn't understand strained to the bursting point and endlessly ingenious methods would have had to be employed to keep them hidden. The lies would have to deepen. This was the slightest experience of shame in my youth but, in a sense, the most evocative, because it was so near the surface and thus more perilous and imperative to keep secret. Going through such experiences in childhood and learning the gravity of secrets was like discovering a tear in the very fabric of being, finding it there underneath my little bed and seeing it grow, horrifyingly, to become a black hole, sucking in matter, destroying things around it. I'd attempted to hide it, but it only grew, exponentially, the more I tried. It fed off its concealment and the complexities of the subterfuge, damaging the reality around it, but always remaining unacknowledged until it was too big, too destructive, too imposing ever to reveal and explain to anyone else, even the adults who loved me. These are the weights that children bear that are not theirs to carry.

Doll's Eyes

Every night in autumn and winter my father would have to listen to the weather reports on the news to find out if the temperature would sink below, or even approach, zero. If it threatened to, Da would have to get up at five in the morning to go salt the roads as part of his job for the council. He never complained, but it was harsh work, all the seasons showing on his skin ("weathered like an old oak table," he would claim), and dangerous too: braving the treacherous black ice ("The worst ice is the ice you cannot see, and the worst mistake you can do is to steer against it," he'd say) so that sleeping commuters, who'd earn more in an hour than he did in a day, could make it to work. I would go to school and listen to the posh kids tell me, "All poor people are just lazy," mimicking the talk of their parents, whose fortunes rested, for example, on the impeccably moral entrepreneurship of simultaneously owning holy shops and gambling establishments.

That was part of my father's job for decades—still is—out in the razor-cold pitch-black of winter mornings, when all the rest of us are still tucked in our beds. Just as there are people fixing pylons in storms or in the sewers beneath us. The unseen. "Working indoors would've killed a man like your father," my mother would say. I wasn't so sure, but who was I to know?

Salting one of the roads that ran along the borderlands, Da saw something spectral-white flit across the road like a sudden apparition. He swerved his Land Rover and braked sharply. He found the owl illuminated by the red taillights. It had been struck sometime earlier. It was already too late. He gathered it up into his arms and placed it in the back of the car. It died somewhere along the way, with the stars moving unnaturally above it. Ma went ballistic when he returned days later from the embalmers with the bird inside a heavy glass case. He put it up in the living room, perched over us, standing guard. My sister asked, "What if it escapes?" Da was fascinated by birds of prey. He knew their calls and the various ways they flew and hunted. I grew up thinking they were tender, noble creatures and not simply killers at the top of the avian food chain. Da paid no attention to talk of bad luck or superstition about the creatures: that they were emissaries of the underworld that survived from Celtic times and the Gaelic side of the country, where *the owl* translates as "the night hag" and "the screeching entity of the cemetery." Da didn't mind. He seemed more at home with the owl than with most human visitors.

At nighttime I would stare at it through the glare of my reflection, hoping and fearing it would crank its head. It *did* seem otherworldly, even though its marble eyes never moved. My mother's issue was not so much with the owl as the place where it had been found. Bad luck in the past (rather than future) tense. Years earlier a British armored car—they called them Ferrets—had been driving there, with a soldier on look-out through a turret at the top. The roads were in a desperate condition (before the EU fixed them up), with potholes, flooding, bumps, dips, and blind spots. Pedestrians couldn't walk the roads safely. They were essentially driftways for cattle, ineptly repurposed for the automobile age; too narrow for two vehicles to pass at the same time, so that one would always be forced toward the verge. The army vehicle was driving quickly, believing the coming car, driven by a local Orangeman, would defer, but he stood firm in what he saw as his right to drive unencumbered on the Queen's highway. The armored vehicle swerved and slipped into the ditch and flipped over, instantly decapitating the soldier on the roof.

The road had irrevocably changed for my mother since then, as if the impact of what happened had warped the landscape permanently. That's what ghosts were—memories of terrible things that had happened in a given location, and the disbelief that the landscape could carry on as if nothing had happened. Walking along that road always unnerved me, as I imagined I'd meet a ghost figure in fatigues and helmet, still in shock, asking in an English accent where he was, why he was still there.

I'd gaze at that owl, trapped in its glass case, its consciousness gone completely, or gone somewhere else. At night, the birds that crossed the skies in the daytime vanished into the trees, and these other creatures emerged, invisible in the daylight and profoundly unusual to the human eye, which rarely chances upon them. It was not difficult to understand why they seemed to be more than simply animals. Why they became harbingers, witnesses, emissaries of some other place. And that other place is all around us. The most silent, innocuous stretches of land contain memories of what once happened there, and we are sheltered from tragedy and brutality only by the thin ice that we call time.

Telephone

or a long time there was no telephone in our house, and it was blissfully quiet. It became even quieter on days when bill collectors came to the door (I learned to recognize the difference between the knocks of the milkman, the lemonade man, the coal man, the parish draw, and the bailiffs). Eventually my parents relented, and they came to install a line for incoming calls only, initially. The quiet was broken. Modernity seeping into a house unchanged in decades.

At first I did not appreciate the phone. It shrieked like a demanding child and continued even when ignored. I would regularly pull the cord out of the wall, to my mother's frustration. "What's the point of having a phone if no one can reach us?" When my parents had enough regular income to open the line to outgoing calls, I could ring my friends. You had to remember long lists of numbers in your head, especially for those who were not in the phone book. Their parents would answer, always with a degree of irritation, as if expecting someone else.

For a long time the line was plagued by odd clicks and phantom sounds, not voices necessarily, but glitches and malfunctions that sounded like a voice trying to be born. Perhaps a plane was passing high overhead, or a telegraph line was felled in some distant field, or wires were crossed in the babel of a telephone exchange. My mother noticed and cautioned me to watch what I said. Be careful. Someone might be listening in. "Who?" I wondered. "And why?"

Perhaps they listened in to everyone, but who were *they*? What was the right and wrong thing to say? It occurred to me that you could say something and mean an entirely different thing. Sometimes the right words did not come out. Sometimes people heard what they wanted to hear.

I would walk past the telephone and then pause and return, and I would lift up the receiver and listen, to detect if someone was listening. I would talk nonsense, babble, speak in tongues, mimic the languages I heard on the radio. I dropped the words like stones down into a bottomless well and listened for a sound to echo back.

I had no idea, at that age, of the role that telephones would play in the Troubles, which were unfolding right there and then. Knowing that the emergency services recorded their calls, paramilitaries would call up television stations, newspapers, and the Samaritans, authenticating themselves with their official passwords, and would warn of imminent bombs—fictional or otherwise—giving people in public places only minutes or seconds to get out, before they "initiated." They would also claim ownership of attacks and murders, and give ideological justification for why a child might no longer have a parent or a parent might no longer have a child. There was one man who received the message, from someone he likely knew, saying, "Keep your head low," not long before he was shot dead. There was the garbled message that led police to direct shoppers toward, rather than away from, the Omagh bomb, and the conspiracy theories around it. There were the bombers who couldn't warn of the devices they'd planted that would blow little girls through windows and into ribbons in Claudy, or turn the members of the Irish Collie Club into blazing human candles in the La Mon Hotel, all because the phone boxes they'd gone to had been vandalized. The informer was discovered, tortured, and executed when one of his comrades pressed redial and rang a police inspector. There were the "legitimate targets," selected via their names and addresses in the phone book. And there was the guy who'd bested an IRA volunteer in a bar brawl, who was then shot in the legs in front of his girlfriend and child, and she ran in a blind panic from door to door in her tower block after they'd ripped out her phone line, but no one opened the door, and he bled out, dying because of silence on the receiver.

Newspaper

I lay on my bed, on my side, watching the shadows shift on the floor, almost imperceptibly, as the sun moved across the sky. They began to grow and join and climb up the walls, and the room became enveloped in darkness.

I had a bad chest. One of my lungs had been damaged when I'd had whooping cough as a baby, and because the hospital had been overcrowded, I was kept at home and barely made it. It flared up now and then. I would listen to my own lungs, half amused, wheezing like a waterlogged accordion; feeling oddly detached, as if they were disconnected from me, just inanimate objects like the creaking springs of the army-surplus bed I lay upon. The damage left me prone to illnesses, bronchitis, asthma, but because of my childhood obsession with reading arcane books, most of which I couldn't remotely understand, and my overactive imagination, I believed myself to be suffering from baroque fevers, the "rising of the lights," inflictions from bad airs and the kind of medieval maladies one could get rid of only by touching the king's garments. My main ailment, it seems, was hypochondria. I thought I could see illness in my face in the mirror, the perpetual bags beneath my eyes. It had made my mother even more protective.

The cold got in and grew, like the darkness but different. It had its own methods. It came in under the door and through the keyhole. It rattled the window. There was no heating in our house. On school mornings I'd dread crawling out from underneath the blankets. I would lie there as long as I could, watching my breath as mist in the air in front of me, imagining shapes forming from the plumes—ships with intricate rigging of vapor, which would then swirl and dissipate. I knew I could wait until my mother's third call before hastily moving, skin bonewhite, goose-bumped, and shivering as I pulled on my uniform and dashed down the stairs.

There were no radiators in the house. Each bedroom had a fireplace, but they were unused and boarded up. Birds' nests were in the chimneys and my mother was afraid of smoking them out. My parents had painted scenes from children's picture books onto the wooden panels in my own and my sister's rooms, alongside a life-size Morph turning off the light. Children waving outward from a window and into my room.

When winter struck, it reminded us all abruptly how far north we were. It could have been much worse. I drew a line from Derry along the latitude on my atlas. It was adjacent to Moscow, the lands of the Siberian Cossacks and the Trans-Siberian Railway, Lake Baikal, the "land of fire and ice" Kamchatka Peninsula, the lands of the Aleut and the lands of the Inuit. The world outside my window should be barren and frozen. The rooftop I could see from my bed should have been covered in frost and snow, but we were saved, for the moment, by the Gulf Stream. It was not always so. Once, all this lay under a miles-deep glacier. And the land remembered, even when people forgot.

The only sources of heat were hot-water bottles and, if there'd been a win on the parish draw, a gas heater in the kitchen. My mother would spark the gas alight and it would flow across the squared grid, igniting each cube, and I would stare into it as if it were the photosphere of an electronic sun. Otherwise there was the living room fire. I would rush down on Sunday evenings— bath night—having washed myself in my sister's tepid water, and stand in front of the flames to dry, covering myself, embarrassed, when my mum's friends were there, but needing to stay inside that glowing golden bubble of heat. The other rooms were blue with cold.

The wind often howled down the chimney, so each time my father prepared the fire, it was like a military operation or, rather, a ritual. Lifting the brass fireguard out of the way, Da would remove the old ash from the night before, all the incinerated fossils and compressed forests that made up the coal, in great shovelfuls, filling the air with a strange taste. Through the gray, I could see the glint of gold from the grate, shaped like the portcullis of a castle. Then my father would send me out with a scuttle to the coal bunker in the backyard, and I'd fill it, blackening my hands. I took childish pride in the job, beaming at the responsibility, but would overload the bucket and have to shimmy back holding the handle tightly with both hands, my skinny arms trembling with the strain. My father had huge hands, skin like leather and tattooed, and would grasp the handle and swing the coal with almighty force into the hearth. Then he'd place kindling, crackling sticks, and firelighters strategically and tell me to bring the matches over. There was a ship on the box. He'd light a taper and a series of tiny fires would ignite. Da would reach for yesterday's paper and construct an updraft, manipulating the winds. Invisible currents, as if the air were an ocean. "Drawing the air," it was called. Soon it would provide a bellows for the fire, and once it caught, my father would scrunch up the paper and lob it into the flames.

Something about the fire was hypnotic. The colors, the way it moved. The memory it had, or that people had of it, fire dancing in the eyes of all our ancestors, whose names we will never know. It seemed mysterious to me. If everything was solid, liquid, or gas, as I was told in school, what was this? An element? A process? A creature? Magic? The newspaper made it even more intriguing. The way the paper would shift, crinkle, and change color as the fire took hold, and only then erupt. The flames would nestle at first, then curl outward, traveling as if it were topography.

The newspaper retained the type until the very last moment, and I would try to read the stories as the paper buckled and fizzled into glowing ash. Stories of unarmed Iranian boys walking to paradise through minefields, of students in Latin America being thrown from helicopters into the sea, of the ex-president of Afghanistan hanging from a lamppost. Football hooligans were on the loose. Mandela was condemned by the Tories. The Soviet Union had shot down a Korean airliner, killing everyone. Sarajevo was hosting the Winter Olympics. Off the coast of Ireland, an Indian flight had suddenly vanished off the radar. Over a small Scottish village, a bomb in a cassette player had rained down people still strapped in their seats, burning fuselage and Christmas presents. In Somalia the Isaaq people were being blown to pieces in their homes in Hargeisa: a "genocide that would surely never be forgotten." Fiction began to lose its hold on me then. Outside, the drunks in the street shouted themselves hoarse like they were roaring to the summer to return.

I never got used to the cold. It seeped into my bones. I would sit by the hearth as often as I could, drunk on the heat at times. They called such kids "ashy pets" in Derry—kids who were more inclined to stay indoors with their parents than to go out with their own kind ("Tell them I'm not in," I'd often shout out to the hall). We should never have come here, I thought. Our ancestors, tracing them back in my mind to the Great Rift Valley of Africa. I wondered why they had bypassed the Silk Route, forsaking sunbathed islands and opal seas. Why they stayed here was easier to work out; they simply ran out of land. Some, like St. Brendan, went beyond and became myth, landing on a whale that he mistook for an island. My lineage had never fully acclimatized. Our genes remembered the kiss of the sun.

I lay there on an archipelago at the hinterland of Europe, where the tides of rain from the ocean first make landfall. Hibernia, the land of winter, the Romans had called it; and they, at least, had left it alone. Perched at the edge of the flat earth. Not far over those rooftops, framed in my window and out to sea, ships were sailing off the rim into the abyss. And the cold that entered my room had blown through their sails to reach me.

Blindfold

In Victorian times, they used to think the murdered retained the memory of their killer on their retinas, photographed, and it could somehow be extracted. An optogram, they called it. They tried to create an optogram from the dead gaze of at least one of Jack the Ripper's victims, twenty-five-year-old Mary Jane Kelly, formerly of Limerick, who was quiet and sang Irish songs and started fights when drunk, and called herself, touchingly, Marie Jeanette after the briefest spell in Paris. No image was ever found. What she had seen was gone forever.

Those taken away by paramilitaries were often tied up, gagged, and hooded. The perpetrators didn't want to be identified if the victim survived, but perhaps there was a lingering superstition there too. Perhaps they didn't want to be cursed in this life or the next by the accusing gaze of their victims. Perhaps the eyes, as windows to the soul, would remind them of their victim's humanity and of their own humanity, or lack thereof, and make it difficult for them to carry out the butchering. When the army executed people—deserters, for instance—they tied them to a post and blindfolded them, not so they wouldn't have to see the firing squad, but so that the firing squad wouldn't have to make eye contact with their target. It was an act of kindness for the perpetrators.

In many cultures there are spells and remedies for the evil eye. Amulets can be worn to deflect it. Symbols are painted above doorways to keep it away from homes. I wondered if there were spells that could keep away the power of the innocent eye. Or all the shades of gray in between. It happened within organizations, when there were ideological splits or schisms, according to personal, financial, or territorial rivalries. Two young loyalists said the wrong thing at a house party and were led off, on the guise of continuing the party elsewhere, taking it up a notch, and were savagely beaten and then had their throats hacked open by fellow loyalists of a marginally different stripe. One of the victims stared up at his assailant, who responded by slotting a knife deep into his eye. When the mother of a young exiled informer went to the IRA to beg forgiveness for him, they assured her that he would be free to come back to Derry, provided they could question and debrief him. He'd been naive, they suggested, but he was only a kid, and he was one of them and deserved a second chance. They questioned him all right. He was found blindfolded not long afterward, shot in the back of his head, with his eyes blown out.

Those who were found in the blue light of morning by dog walkers or joggers received little sympathy. Their deeds, like those of drug dealers or sex offenders or informants, had led them there, many concluded. Yet they had been boys once, eyes opening for the first time, gazing on a new world, adjusting or failing to adjust to the light and shadow.

Belt

George Orwell once had a fascist in his sights, during the Spanish Civil War, and didn't pull the trigger because the soldier was running along, trying to hold his trousers up. There was something innately human about the gesture that saved the man's life, without him ever knowing. Again and again during the Troubles, in the midst of everyday life, intruders arrived and defiled what was human. A teenage Catholic girl is shot four times in the head, sleeping next to her Protestant boyfriend. A father of ten is shot five times in his kitchen while making bottles for his twin babies. People are shot watching soap operas or *Top of the Pops*, while having a drink or chewing food. Two brothers are shot dead at their sister's eleventh birthday party. A man lifting his one-year-old nephew in the air is shot three times. A pregnant girl begs them not to shoot her boyfriend as they lie in bed, then begs him not to die. Wrapping Christmas presents. Babysitting four grandchildren. Fixing a washing machine. Reading the paper. Having an argument. A father comes home at 4:00 a.m. to find his seven-month-pregnant wife lying dead, surrounded by her four children. A wife thinks fireworks are going off outside as her husband is killed next to her; another that her husband is hammering in the next room. The television show continues as bloodstains spread on the carpet, sofa, wallpaper. A man lies dead in the back of a shop that he named after his wife. The sign on the door is still turned to "Open."

Cassette

What were the noises at night across the land? The screech of the fox across fields, the splicing of the owl through the trees, the breathing of something unidentified in the undergrowth. I had heard tales of the *púca*, shapeshifters inhabiting the gray area between good and evil. The land we inhabited was the same. It was beautiful, enticing, but could turn at any moment. Rivers, slurry pits, traps, even the weather could change drastically in exposed places; even seasoned navigators became lost, people disappeared.

Virtually every culture on earth has a bogeyman; the most common, existing in peoples who had never encountered one another and lived tens of thousands of miles apart, was the man with the black sack who would snatch children. These stories, and the creatures within them, kept children away from dangerous areas when the parents were not around. Fear was a guardian. There were times, however, when it was not enough.

My mother continued to warn me, again and again, never to go to the Glen, and naturally I was irresistibly drawn there, regardless of how many imaginary bogeymen she placed there as sentries, and regardless of the actual bogeymen who roamed the place. Advertisements on the television supported her. Dark cautionary tales of foolish, arrogant children playing near whirlpools in flooded quarries or attempting to retrieve snagged kites from pylons. The Grim Reaper stalked these commercials for mortality, between adverts featuring the Michelin Man and the Jolly Green Giant.

It did not stop me. I knew people dumped things there: junk that I could salvage. I asked for some money for the shop as a feint and then, after my mother had buttoned up my jacket and fixed my hair, headed in the opposite direction. The place was strewn with detritus. It was hard to believe this was once the "lovers' glen," given that it had an air of wild desolation. A smashed television. A charred mattress. Porno mags, which I didn't really understand but was intrigued by, stuffed in bushes. There was a burned-out car that I and my friends had once pretended to drive but that was now too rusted to sit in. Certain words of my mother's stayed with me—to never climb into an abandoned safe or fridge, to never swim anywhere, to never accompany any stranger. There was always a "wee boy in England" who came to a sticky end. I began thinking it was the same character to whom every misfortune was meted out, on a perpetual loop: a sort of modern version of the medieval Wound Man. None of the cautionary tales held me back, though. I was on an important mission: to find salvage. It was a vocation. Mainly I'd find electrical parts, circuit boards, the insides of machines, and bring them back and take them apart quietly, covertly, in my room. Then, when they'd exhausted my attentions, I'd paint them silver and play with them as if they were spaceships and satellites.

I went to the Glen because it was dangerous, not in spite of that. Learning to lie in advance and on my return. Deception being the first sign of individuality. I avoided the nettles, hawthorn bushes, and great reams of hemlock, the devil's bread—somehow knowing it was poisonous—unaware that those weeds grew where buildings once stood. It was different when I went there with my friends. We would lie on our backs on the damp grass; gaze at the changing shapes of the clouds and the slowly dissipating contrails of long-passed planes, the color altering with the sun; and talk, always about what we would do, who we'd become. It was not uncommon to see a rabbit or a fox, which would ignite us into rowdy chase, startled that they existed surrounded by buildings, but they'd always evade us in their concealed labyrinth of warrens.

I had to be doubly careful on my own. Trebly careful. Making sure not to twist my ankle on the uneven ground. Stepping over the little winter-borne streams that dried out in the summer. Keeping my distance from any figure, and looking as if I were going somewhere in a hurry. Sometimes I'd bring my dog, Patch, the bad-tempered but unflinchingly loyal Jack Russell, who'd follow by my side everywhere, and who made for a noisy deterrent, snapping at ankles.

I found the cassette tape unspooled in the trees, wrapped around and draped between the branches like the kiting of spider threads. Part of it had snapped free and was fluttering in the breeze. I wondered how it had ended up there. It looked like the scene of a Mass rock, where priests had secretly undertaken ceremonies in the times of the persecutions by Cromwell.

Such places were now pilgrimage sites where people left relics and keepsakes, tied ribbons to trees, for good luck and blessings from a two-millennia-dead mother of a murdered child from the Levant.

I followed the tape to the cassette. The writing on its label was too faded to read. It took me half an hour, shimmying up the trunk, to unknot its length and wind it round and round. I placed it in my pocket. I did not know what was on it, and thus it seemed magical. Something from the past was on this tape undoubtedly. Perhaps someone now long gone. It was nothing but a broken cassette, except for the time travel and perhaps clairvoyance of listening to it.

Glass Eye

More than thirty-five hundred people died in the Troubles. How many went down in one night on the *Titanic*? Half that. Fifty-five hundred Ulster loyalists died on the Somme. Twenty thousand Austrian troops drowned in one river at one time in the First World War. Numbers alone say little. Conflict, like suffering, exists not in blank numbers but in hours. The hours of incarceration, of anxiety for all involved; the hours of the sentries fearing attack at any second; the hours of the mother whose child is gone; the hours of a kneecapped youth crawling to be found; the hours of blindness and burns and rehabilitation and brain damage and paralysis—all the unlived hours. All conflicts are measured in hours, and only those outside it all think otherwise.

My aunt worked as a nurse in a burns ward. She knew of the hours people spent in agony, long after the headlines had passed. Tubes in throats and veins. The hours of waiting for test results, 4:00 a.m. coffee from a machine, the squeak of shoes, howling down the radon-lit corridor. The shrinking hour as a dying RUC man, his voice destroyed, wrote messages to his wife and children. The time spent matching a glass eye to the color of the sightless eye that survived.

People hung on for weeks in pain, seemed to get better, and then died of a flu that a well-wisher brought with their flowers. An individual suffering twenty years of paralysis, unable to talk beyond weeping, died from blood clots. Others survived, but trauma played on them as they aged. Phantom-limb syndrome from a nightclub bombing twenty years earlier. Being taken to the toilet as a forty-year-old man. All those unseen hours. The hours of the view of nothing from a hospital window.

Toy Soldier

A t nine o'clock I would be shuffled off to bed and my sister would be read a story in the room across the landing. Once our mother had gone downstairs, deceived into believing we were asleep, we would wait the requisite ten minutes for our parents to settle in. It was curfew time, and our parents would play music and carouse with friends; neither were really drinkers, but it always sounded like a party. My sister and I would meet above the stairs, stepping lightly on the floorboards, squinting in the dark to see each other. Then we'd creep down, holding hands and urging each other to be quiet, all the while giggling giddily, to stand in the stolen light from a crack in the living room door. Then we would listen in to things we could not understand. We were trying to peer into the blinding light of adulthood at the gap in the door, but our senses could not acclimatize.

My parents and their friends never did small talk. It was

always some esoteric topic (ancient Egypt, outer space, the Celts). From time to time, religion and politics would rear their ugly heads and the talk would turn dark, but voices were rarely raised. They were hippies, and though radical politically, they were pacifists, taking us on "Ban the Bomb" protests and campaigning to save the starving children of Biafra, much to the derisory amusement of kids at school and their parents. My sister and I listened in, trying to prematurely hack into the future, desperate to live it now before we were fully equipped, but the conversations were always too muffled, the music too loud, the laughter too lingering; and we'd grow incautious and make a mistake, a creak on the stair, and give our presence away and be chased off, laughing, up the stairs with feet as fast as cartoon feet, by one of our parents, trying to scold us through a smile. I would go to my room at the back of the house and sit in the dark until my eyes became accustomed again, and I'd form caves and mountains in the bedclothes and play at what I thought was life with plastic action figures. I wasn't allowed toy soldiers, as they were figures of violence and oppression, but I'd secreted one from a sweet tin full of them at a friend's house. It had a flat green base and its face looked melted. It had a rifle pointed out from its shoulder, shooting at something—anything—unseen, out there in the dark.

Skeleton Key

There was a persistent rumor that you could somehow go beneath the city into a system of tunnels and emerge in any area, in any house. It was one of those urban myths that came about in many places around the world, but it was lent credence in Derry because there *had*, supposedly, been underground tunnels and basements during the Siege days. My friends and I heard it from an older kid, who also claimed he had a skeleton key that would open any door. He had, as his credentials, an earring, a learner driver's license, and a set of turntables. One day Gareth came running breathlessly up the street. Our gang had found a gateway, with rusted bars, as if leading to an infernal dungeon or the underworld. I had reservations, partly due to self-preservation, partly due to bookishness; terrible things were always down in the depths of those books. Fictions came back to haunt me, and, not for the last time, my mind conspired against itself.

There were other, more practical concerns—tetanus, rats, mere drowning—but we pressed on, not for plunder but for the treasure of access and peer pressure. To go and to see.

It was dank and dark. The sound echoed in an unnatural way, like the angles were all wrong. Sounds too close and too distant. Each step was treacherous, the moss shifting underneath so that even standing still felt unstable. Stale water was dripping from the ceiling, and the dark contained the sound of torrents. It was difficult to see where it began in the murk ahead, and we pushed one another as we edged forward, becoming more enveloped in the dark and the sound until both were the same. The other kids were at the gate, lit blindingly from behind in the distance until all there was were silhouettes, threatening to lock us in, but we kept going, knowing that if we showed any fear, it would seal our fates. And there underneath the earth I found a river, moving unseen beneath the roads and houses. People above completely unaware. I would find out only later that this forgotten river was the one my father had played and swum in as a boy, driven underground, its name stolen away.

Gas Mask

My father would find buried things in the course of his gardening. He'd bring them back and wash away years of clay and silt under a cold tap in the yard as my sister and I stood waiting politely to see what would be revealed, like watching a photograph developing. Our father would always date the objects, without identifying them. "From the forties, I reckon." We'd always have to ask what they were. Our mother would answer, "That's a water pump," or "That's a clay bottle," or "That's a rubber bullet," and add jokingly, "Derry women used to send their men out to catch them." We didn't have a clue what she was talking about. We'd fixate on the objects. Not just to play with but to inspect from every angle. We knew instinctively that all the objects found were invested, or had once been, with some kind of meaning. They were worthless, of course, at best the kind of bric-a-brac you see hanging from shelves in rustic pubs—sentimental value, as antique dealers would say—but there were within them, instilled by the passage of time, souls. Even the songs you hated seem more interesting in time. Even mundane places fascinate from exile. Left in attics, aura seeps into the bric-a-brac like damp.

My father had dug up the gas mask while planting, its insect eyes fixed with cracked, dry soil that crumbled at the touch. It looked evil. Satanic. Postapocalyptic. I was simultaneously fascinated and repulsed. "It's from the war," my father told me, handing over the gas mask. I wondered, "Which one?"

There were other Derrys, all of them marked with violence. I read about them, trying to place where each incident happened in a city of motorcars and billboards and supermarkets. On a day like this in 1213, Domhnall Ó Daimhín is assassinated at the door of the local monastery, near the pub where football fans congregate after the match. In 1567 English troops are occupying Templemore, the old church of Saint Columba, where there is now a sports center and pylons and parking spaces. The soldiers took it over with little respect for the hallowed ground, deconsecrating the church into a gunpowder store. A sentry holds up his burning torch at the gate, surveying the night. He throws the torch into the dark and walks back into the building. Unbeknownst to him, his trusty dog retrieves it and follows him in. The detonation destroys both of them instantly, and much of the settlement. In 1600 the English return in force and kill "man, woman, child, horse, beast, and whatsoever we found." Twenty-one priests are killed during a Mass. In 1607 the Gaelic aristocrats flee. The following year the rebel O'Doherty exacts a terrible doomed revenge, putting the occupants "to fire and sword." Then came the Plantation of Ulster. The famine. And the real trouble began. All here, in this unassuming town.

Sometimes I'd think that the view of progress is all wrong:

the view that we sit at the top of the great scrap pile of history and survey all that has happened in the past from our vantage point. We might equally say that we're actually beneath the great staggering scrap pile of history and we're scrambling to get out from under it, to clear a breathing space, to get some clear perspective of where we are.

Either way, the past had not passed. We lived merely in the most current incarnation of Derry. Who knows what versions are to follow?

The long glow of an arc of fire in the night street remains when you close your eyes, like the mark on your skin after sleeping awkwardly on a train, or the sound of a nightclub in your head while lying in bed afterward. It has a half-life.

The old guard of the British Army, the ones who'd fought the Nazis, had largely been discharged by the early sixties. Instead there were grunts led by those who'd been in Kenya fighting against the Mau Mau uprising, where extrajudicial measures were commonplace (castration, rape, outright murder). They were ill prepared for peacekeeping on the streets of a—reluctantly—British city. Chasing rioters into a house in Derry, they made no distinction between those who had trespassed and those who lived there, bludgeoning the family within. The father, Samuel, stood up to stop them and had his face smashed in. His son had to prevent him from choking on his own blood and removed broken teeth from his mouth. He died three months later, and that was that. Nothing was the same again.

Having been too evenly matched in overalls and nightsticks, the security services tooled up with body armor and rifles and gas masks. It made them look inhuman, identity-less. Faces replaced with horse skulls. Flames reflecting in what appeared to be eyeless visors. As the balance of power turned against the rioting youths, they were forced to improvise. Milk floats were raided to provide the bottles for Molotov cocktails. They used the height of the new brutalist Rossville Flats to drop projectiles from. Grown men were photographed with slingshots and marbles. Teenagers recycled ancestral relics: the helmet their granddad survived the Somme in, the gas masks their mother had clung to at the time of the Blitz—all used them as protection against the army that had issued them.

People didn't need to choose to become explicitly involved. They already were, by geography, class, and genealogy. Tear gas entered living rooms, kitchens, and bedrooms like miasma, the bad airs of a man-made plague.

There was rage on both sides but, if the truth be told, exhilaration too. It was a chance to appear heroic or just to appear: local boys would wear their finest treads, fix their hair, show off in front of the girls. Not everyone had a gas mask, and those who did found they were uncomfortable and restrictive, as I did trying it on, so handkerchiefs soaked in vinegar were used against the searing fog of tear gas. When civil rights marches were banned or attacked, crowds began to head down to the bottom of William Street, where the Bogside met the city center. This was Aggro Corner. Rubber bullets shot through the air were answered with arcing half bricks. From time to time a whistle would be blown so that girls or old people could walk through the melee, coming or going into town. Rioters would go home for dinner and to watch *Doctor Who*, returning, once satisfied, to wage war with their own imaginary Daleks and Cybermen. A note is left out for a milkman: "No milk, but leave 200 bottles."

Tattoo

On his knuckles, on each hand, was the word *love*.
On my father's arms, a panther, a harp, a bearded
Oriental figure like a Confucian philosopher or a
samurai, and some letters.

I realized early on that my father was an enigma that language could not quite broach. There were other ways, of course, to read a person than mere words. I had always been fascinated by the tattoos covering his arms. He had them inked at a time when it was neither fashionable nor profitable to have marks on your skin. Jobs could be lost over them then, certainly at the interview stage. You kept them covered. They were the markings of outlaws and ne'er-do-wells, transient types, strangers, outsiders. Signs of villainy, underground codes, nautical languages. Other paths than the pious life. Religious folks said a tattoo was the mark placed on Cain, the first murderer.

They didn't look like other tattoos, either; they had faded

too early or were much less dark to begin with. They had a rough, unprofessional edge to them that made them seem even more mysterious. I never asked him what their meaning was, or where he got them and when. I never even really looked at them directly, but rather through side glances. They were more than cryptic. They were hieroglyphs that possessed some meaning I did not quite wish to disturb, but nevertheless needed to understand.

When I was old enough, I would look through books for clues and was drawn to tales of carny folk, Maori tribesmen, and Siberian prisoners, but none could illuminate these particular markings. In the Gulag, for instance, tattoos denoted attitude, past deeds, and hierarchy. A marking of a monastery or epaulettes on the shoulders meant a problem with authority; a rose on the chest meant they became a man behind bars; a ship on the sea meant escape, not just from prison but from everything. What they confirmed was that signs have meanings, resonances, contexts. They told stories to other inmates, to the guards, to themselves. I found myself again a translator without knowledge of the language.

My father was always distant, even when he was there physically. He never said hello or goodbye. It was like, in his mind, he was living somewhere else. I had a book titled *Phenomena: A Book of Wonders* that fascinated me. Spontaneous human combustion, will-o'-the-wisp, bleeding statues. Astral projection illustrated with Victorian women soaring over Victorian London. Sometimes it seemed my father was able to project himself elsewhere, away from us. He was physically present but somehow absent.

Cracks deepened between my parents. The loudness of my mother, always a formidable matriarch, would increase in proportion to my father's quietude. Once, she lost her patience and threw him out of the house, hurling the dog out after him. The two of them stood across the street as my sister and I waved tearfully at them from the window. He walked away and returned an hour later with presents for us. It was like watching a silent movie. Eventually my mother relented and dragged him back in, looking frantically left and right, muttering, "Get inside before the bloody neighbors see you."

Da didn't go drinking or to the bookies all day, like other dads in the street, but he went jogging every night. Pounded the streets for two hours, like clockwork, then hit the weights, in a little gym set up in the corner of my parents' bedroom. A bar across the door that he'd do pull-ups from. He circumnavigated the two bridges of Derry in a great arc while jogging. He drank the most infernal protein drinks—tuna and strawberry powder and raw eggs. He quit only when his Achilles tendons started to give up after years of vibrations against the tarmac. He became even more withdrawn after that. More . . . *elsewhere.*

Fool's Gold

The bus hissed as I walked down the steps, my mother gripping my hand and my sister's. We walked through the depot and the arcade out to the front of the Europa. "The most-bombed hotel in Europe," taxi drivers would boast, with more than a hint of pride. We walked into the student area, past Queen's University Belfast, up toward the Botanic Gardens. When we reached the gates, I was mesmerized by the sight of the museum, with its neoclassical facade merging into a brutalist extension. It seemed to be transforming before my eyes.

My mother let us play in the gift shop, running from shelf to shelf, thinking *that* was the museum. Something sparkling in a tiny glass case caught my eye. She glanced over my shoulder. "Would you like that?"

"What is it? Is it precious? Gold?"

"It's fool's gold." She lifted the tiny case and read the message. "Iron pyrite. Millions of years old. It was used in firearms, flintlocks."

She bought it for me. Handing over a couple of coins. I could not understand how it was even possible to buy such a thing. It glistened in my palm. It had existed for millions of years, traveling all that way to my hand. I examined every mark and indentation as if it were a tiny, newly discovered planet. I kept looking at it, almost the entire way around the museum, ignoring the exhibits, pausing to look up and nod only when my mother or sister pointed something out, then turned my attention back to it.

Only one exhibit caught my attention. My mother told me in advance, entering the room, "You'll like this." There was a long glass box, lying horizontal. It took a few moments to decipher, but when I did, I took several steps backward toward the door. Someone was *inside* the box. I approached slowly as my sister excitedly knocked on the glass, jumping on the spot. "It's a mummy." The mummy's skin was black, leathery. I gazed very closely, enchanted, at her fingers, her eyelids, so incredibly real, compared with the painted figure on the wooden casket next to her. Her name was Takabuti and she had lived thousands of years ago. Another lady, Tjesmutperet, had also been discovered, but had disintegrated into dust when she was unwrapped. Possessions, grave goods, of Takabuti were placed beside her, for her to use in the afterlife. Jars of makeup. Food. Jewelry. A lantern.

I was still thinking of her, all through the mile-long walk back into town. We were stopped by soldiers at the doors of the CastleCourt shopping mall. Our bags, even the children's, were customarily searched for explosives. I held the fool's gold tightly in my fist. The soldier noticed. "What's that you got there, mate?" He leered down at me, grasping my wrist. My mother, visibly nervous, burst out, "Leave the fuckin' wee 'un alone," and the soldier startled, glowered at her, but let us pass. I smiled up at her, but she kept looking forward, striding us along.

I kept the stone next to my bed for several years. Imagining it was a comet, imagining where it had come from, imagining what the earth had looked like when it was formed. One day I brought it into school, and it was passed around the playground and went missing, but I was too shy to tell anyone, and "snitches get stitches," and its trajectory through time, having drawn parallel to mine for a while, spiraled away.

One day my father was cycling from our home up the hill toward Creggan, where you'd have to stand on the pedals to get leverage against the gradient, when he was suddenly struck from behind by a car that accelerated and drove on. A hit-and-run, they called it. My father returned to the house like a wounded animal hobbling somewhere private and familiar, like a dog going somewhere to die, bashed up and badly grazed. The bicycle was unrecognizable and beyond repair, all tangled metal. His face was drained of blood. He looked nothing like his usual self—the bodybuilder who would mimic the Incredible Hulk ("You won't like me when I'm angry"), to our shrieking delight. I opened the door to a premature ghost. It had not occurred to me, even in times when my little sister and I would playfully taunt our father, that he wasn't invincible. It was the discovery of another element for me; the discovery of kryptonite.

Mass Leaflet

I hated Mondays with a fear that made me sick, metaphorically and literally, every Sunday night. I struggled to get to sleep and would arrive at school with bags under my eyes. The reason was that my teacher, a pious gorgon, would line up the children and question us about the weekend's gospel to see who had, and who had not, gone to Mass. She could sense fear and would zoom in accordingly. My parents were agnostic at best; the story was that my father was expelled from school for proposing that God was a "spaceman." He was a freethinker, without much fanfare or the smug pomposity of the phrase; and my mother, if she believed, did so quietly and individually, being extremely cautious of the Church. She'd prevented me from becoming an altar boy because she'd more than an inkling about what was going on in the Church. Indeed, what happens when power is conferred on institutions without transparency or accountability and with blind deference. She understood what went on behind locked doors, in rooms with names like "sacristy."

So we didn't go to Mass, which was a cardinal—if not mortal—sin in my teacher's eyes. My classmates would rarely share the secret of what the gospel had been, though I'd offer them bribes to reveal the truth; even my friends enjoyed watching me sweat, enjoyed having some fleeting power, cackling along with the relief of the absolved. Once exposed, the transgressor would be humiliated by the teacher, who would punish the miniature person for their heathen family, in front of the baying class. Some would be reduced to tears. I never was, but I felt profoundly anxious on a weekly basis. I would beg my parents to take me to the church anytime in the day, in the hope that a leaflet was left in the pews that I could take into school as evidence. None of it seemed anything to do with Jesus, not the Jesus I had read about, at least. He seemed like a decent, kind man, one who perhaps belonged amid my father's plethora of heroes, and who had warned that whoever harmed a child should be cast into the sea with a millstone around his neck. I did not recognize this other Jesus, in whose name the priests and teachers spoke.

Nothing in the teachings fit what I had read in the Bible. The clear was made opaque, and the opaque was never made clear. Derry had only the first stirrings of a class system—virtually every Catholic was one generation away from peasantry, if not still there—but because of this, it was transparent, even to me, who was social-climbing and trying to set myself up above others. In a way, it made it more pronounced, given that people were so desperate to be above one another. It was still a friendly, down-to-earth place where people said hello (or rather "Alright?" in the street), and there was still a degree of solidarity in being in the shit together, but tiny differentiations were starting to be used as symbolism and leverage. Where you lived, how you spoke, how you dressed. I could see it emerging. The teacher was a case in point. There wasn't much of a genuine middle class in Derry—perhaps a handful of doctors, solicitors, an architect or two—but there was a desire for it. And so many people, who were two paychecks away from destitution, began to perform the role; and to perform it meant not only displaying one's feathers but also subtly pecking at others' throats.

My teacher was one such soul. The ritual was not about the gospel, which was just a means to an end and often contradicted the meaning of Christ's words entirely, but about the humiliation. Her harangues were symptomatic of the authority figures that we would face. Once, she read us the lesson where Jesus states that it is easier for a camel to get through the eye of a needle than for a rich man to get into heaven. Then she went on to state that the eye of a needle was a metaphor for a gate in Jerusalem, and therefore it was actually very easy for the rich to pass into heaven; indeed, they were at the front of the queue. I didn't know much then, or now, but I knew bullshit when I heard it. She would claim that "Jesus died the worst death it is possible to die," and so anyone who had cancer or any terminal illness should embrace their pain to be one with our Lord. It was a sadist's gospel, or at least vicarious masochism.

I kept reading the Bible, enchanted by it, but never really found its connection to the Church. Except for a fleeting moment in the iconography of the saints, but then it was lost, like light through stained glass. When a priest arrived who was genuinely Christian, who would talk to me about crises or intricacies of faith, I knew he would not long be in the job, the priesthood, or, indeed, in some sad cases, this life. When I asked other priests about matters that had stayed with me—the Tower of Babel, the Book of Revelation, the flaming sword that kept Adam and Eve from returning to Eden, the immortal soldier who'd pierced Christ's side—I was stonewalled. It seemed as if they had read another book, or no book at all, and instead made up stories to suit their unfolding neuroses. At the same time, I mistrusted the puritanism of Protestantism, which seemed pinched and judgmental and austere. Life-negating. I came to regard Catholicism—the ecstasies of Bernini, the animal-human evangelist hybrids of the Book of Kells, the strange mystic idiosyncrasies of the saints—as some vast, glorious outsider art project that I was party to, but which was very different from the Church that housed it. Perhaps even its antithesis.

There were things I could not believe, though I wanted to. One was the Resurrection. Even when I was a child, I could see the apostles for the scared, hunted group they were. They were right to be scared, given their fates. Shell-shocked that the person they believed in had been flayed and then nailed to a tree and died, doubting God himself. I saw the need for the Resurrection, the desire for it, the metaphor, but also the danger of believing in it. Doubting Thomas appeared not as the flawed character I was taught but as a real one (as, too, did Judas). No one was coming back to save any of them. There was no king sleeping in the mountain. If there was any saving to be done, we must do it ourselves.

My parents, out of habit and expectation, took me to the cathedral to be baptized as a newborn baby. Upon hearing that my name was to be Oisín (a close second after Rory), after the mythological poet-warrior of Celtic Ireland, the priest refused to baptize me. It was a heathen name and the priest would not let it pass his lips. Young and flustered, my parents plucked my name out of the ether and, suitably chastened, they bumbled through the ceremony. There was no room for poetry in the world of the Church or in histories that departed from the one true path. There was probably not even room for the mysteries of God.

Christ was incidental to such followers. It seemed arbitrary that this story of a Bronze Age Galilean fisherman was the one that took hold. It could have been so different, and they would still have been adamant believers in whatever the new religion was, because it served a purpose for them. It allowed judgment of others, chastisement, even banishment. I started to read beyond, into biblical ephemera, and found out there was another figure at the time of Jesus, a rival messiah called Simon Magus, who undertook magic tricks, which seemed synonymous with miracles. Other failed messiahs followed down the centuries. There was Cyrus Teed, who preached that the earth and sky exist inside a hollow planet under a mechanical sun; Arnold Potter, who, believing he would ascend into heaven, leapt from a cliff to his death; the sleepwalking divine Jacobina Mentz Maurer; Mad John Thom, the bulletproof Cornishman; Tanchelm of Antwerp; and Moses of Crete. It seemed merely historical chance that I grew up in a society dedicated to one messiah and not any number of other candidates. Their teachers were incidental. In those parallel worlds, men would still kill one another, using the split hairs of doctrine as excuses. And crones would still torment children over scripture, simply because they could.

Disaster, however, always loomed welcomingly on the horizon for the teacher. Something in the emerging news of impending climate change—at that stage the stuff of fairly obscure scientific studies and environmentalist polemics—chimed with her millenarianism. The ozone layer is disintegrating. The tide is rising. Acid rain eats the statues of our holy ones. She talked

about it with a kind of satisfaction. She was one of the chosen, she'd clearly decided, and so the Rapture was something to
look forward to, even accelerate.

I tried to imagine what the sea rise might mean. The docks
would be inundated with water. The Bay Road would become
submarine. The Bogside would return to its former life as a riverbed. The city center an island once more. Returning to the
state that the rifts in the landscape have always perhaps been
nostalgic for. We were lucky in terms of the number of hills in
the city, but that meant there were also valleys, and these might
become waterways. The future was an archipelago. I would
wander around the Glen and think, with a sort of future nostalgia, that I was looking at a landscape of heather, gorse, and
wire that would one day be coral.

I wondered if war was the same. Incremental. How it came
to a place. If it was sudden or creeping. You always imagine there
is an announcement over a loudspeaker, a chilling siren, a sudden explosion, a declaration, but perhaps it's more chaotic and
plural. It happens everywhere and nowhere. People leave and arrive. Sightings are reported. A tank enters one suburb, while in
others people are drinking coffee. People sit in rooms reading already out-of-date papers while other rooms are shelled. Perhaps
sometimes it comes as mistaken protection, full of promises and
garlands, soon to be discarded.

The teacher snapped me out of my daydream, with the edge
of a ruler across my knuckles, and I turned back to my sums.
I already knew what the teacher wanted—it wasn't an eternity
singing celestial praise, but to be elevated to heaven in order to
have a view of the damned below.

Inventory

The news gave the names of victims, their religion, their profession, where the killings took place. Little else was required, but every single one was a story, from multiple perspectives.

A petrol bomb hits an army Land Rover. Those inside spray fire extinguishers on a colleague they believe to be on fire, and he suffocates. A soldier is telling another about his newborn child, whom he is due to see for the first time, when the other's gun fires by accident. A man seen swinging a nail bomb is shot, and the bomb, in what will become a common occurrence, is nowhere to be found. Three Scottish lads from the Royal Highland Fusiliers, two of them brothers, are found dead on a hillside. They'd been off duty, out drinking, and, enticed by local women, headed off, pints still in hand. They were taking a piss in a row in a desolate spot when they were shot from behind. Their bodies were found by boys, playing in the morning. A suitcase with a smoking fuse is dropped in the reception of a police station, and a paratrooper is in the doorway, shepherding people out, when it goes off. A young man is shot trying to grab a helmet that was knocked off, and another is shot trying to come to his aid, bleeding out in a car on the way to a Donegal hospital. A schoolboy is beaten to death and dumped in a sinkhole. A terribly injured musician, his bandmates shot to death or blown apart around him, crawls across a field and notices a crescent moon in the sky. A middle-aged man has a heart attack as his windows are shattered. A workman's van backfires and a soldier shoots him through the throat; his workmate, dragged into the barracks, emerges later, injured. In Ballymurphy a gunfight ensues, and a private and an IRA volunteer are shot. Then a thirteen-year-old boy, throwing stones at the army, is shot through the face. Then a fifty-year-old mother of nine children. Then a priest helping a wounded man, waving a white onesie from the ground. Then a man who went to help them and had taken off his shirt to stem the blood. Paratroopers run a sweepstakes on who gets the most kills, a veteran later claims. A young man lies dying by a stream. A father of ten is riddled with more than a dozen bullets. A security guard is perforated by a nail bomb in his factory. A seventeen-year-old is shot in Ladybrook. A fourteen-year-old is shot dragging an injured priest to safety. A man with a prosthetic arm, which looked "unusual," working with a priest repairing a church, is shot in the head. A young secretary survives a bomb in her work and dies from another in a pub. A seven-year-old girl tries to lift her dead eighteen-month-old sister, killed by an IRA sniper's bullet. A fourteen-year-old schoolgirl, collecting rubber bullets as souvenirs, is shot by a soldier in Abbey Street. The army releases a statement: "In neither case was there anyone else in the line of fire. In the first case the gunman who had fired at the soldiers was seen to be hit." Swabs are taken from the hands of the dead and dying, for traces of lead. If none is found, the soldiers are commended for firing before the victims had a chance to fire from their imaginary weapons. A man panics, having stolen fishing waders, and runs and is shot dead. A driver mistakenly thinks a hand gesture to halt is one to drive on. Inquests and coroners. Regrettable outcomes and tragic incidences and promotions.

A Royal Horse Artillery soldier is shot dead at Bligh's Lane army post. A soldier firing tear gas at a crowd from a sentry post is shot dead; he is found by his brother, a fellow serviceman. Later that day a random civilian walking by is shot from the same post. A worker gets sloppy and takes the same route two days in a row. A furnishing store is bombed, killing two babies when a wall falls on their pram. Soldiers kill a man at a disco as a priest pleads with them not to. Three Pentecostal worshippers are killed as they sing "Are You Washed in the Blood of the Lamb?" A boy with a toy gun is shot while playing "jailbreak." The Star Pub is bombed. A girl is shot standing at a bus stop. A cop car is ambushed from multiple streets, trying to speed to the relative sanctuary of Rosemount station. A soldier is shot at a burning timber yard. A pub hosting a Bloody Sunday commemoration is bombed, the customers falling through the floor into the cellar. A chaplain, a gardener, and cleaners at the Parachute Regiment's base are killed in an explosion. Members of the Parachute Regiment, it is claimed by one of their own, use part of the skull of a slain Catholic civilian as an ashtray. Fantasists, seeking adventure and claiming "involvement," disappear. An eleven-year-old girl sees her father shot three times in the head in the hallway. A man with an incriminating mess card is found dead in the snow. A woman burns in a petrol-bombed bus. A seventeen-year-old is called over for directions. An eighty-six-year-old man is shot while standing at his window. An eleven-year-old boy is shot with a rubber bullet. An eight-year-old girl is shot in the heart.

Bombs blow up on their handlers, paying heavily for using rudimentary triggers of clothespins and rubber bands. A sailor is stabbed to death for wearing a crucifix around his neck by one of the loyalist Tartan gangs, dressed like the Bay City Rollers. A traveling salesman shares his samples with his murderers. A young man walking home with a fish supper for his family is shot by an army sentry from the Derry Walls. Five workers for the BBC are blown up by a booby trap intended for the army in their Land Rover, driving up to Brougher Mountain transmitting station in the winter. A bomb-disposal officer's last words are "What a wonderful find" before the mine explodes. A civilian is shot dead from a Saracen in retaliation. The IRA commit Bloody Friday with twenty-two bombs, in less than two hours, across Belfast. They kill nine in the village of Claudy, outside Derry, when they can't find a functioning phone to call in the warning. A civilian working for the army winds down his window and says hello to his killer. Two men with the same name are shot in Derry: one dumped in a coffin in a car at the border for informing, another shot by the army. A constable is shot in the back with a submachine gun while tending to a road accident. A mannequin placed in an army observation post overlooks two postmen being riddled to death in a drive-by. A nine-year-old, playing cowboys and Indians in his back garden, trips a wire next to a landmine set for the army by the IRA. A postman finds him badly maimed. "Help me, mister. I'm hurt." A twelve-year-old is shot dead by a corporal, who says, "Next, please." The judge laments "a momentary lapse in [his] normally high standard of discipline and restraint." The boy's father drowns himself in a canal the following year.

At a Derry army post, a package is handed in and explodes on opening, killing a second lieutenant and blowing the hand off his captain. Whistles are sounded to clear areas, three in succession, but civilian deaths still occur. A fourteen-year-old is shot in the cross fire of an IRA sniper. Two soldiers are shot on the ninth floor of Rossville Flats. Fire is returned on a hijacked taxi carrying a teenage boy and two teenage girls. A Catholic who works at Ebrington Barracks takes a colleague out for a driving lesson, with a bomb under their car. Informers are found dead in liminal places: garages, quarries, coastal paths, woods. Police and soldiers on guard duty are sitting ducks. So, too, are those called out to random reports of break-ins or fires or suspicious activities around derelict buildings. Some areas are too dangerous to investigate. A parcel left on a bridge, a helmet left on a motorcycle. Cars drive with no headlights on. Men die because ID cards are left idly on tables or a tattoo is thoughtlessly on show, however briefly. Things are seen. Words are said. Calls are made. Accents are deciphered. A man is asked directions from a passing car. Four soldiers are invited to a housewarming party by a group of girls, at a house where no one lives. Two brothers walk home with takeaway for their bedridden mother and never arrive.

Death lists are made. Both sides deny their bullet went through the four-year-old's head in the cross fire. Men die on the way to place obituaries in papers, and to place bets. A Protestant woman is shot for living with a Catholic. Someone sees a man staggering after gunshots and does nothing and he bleeds out after five hours. A politician and a ballroom dancer, who'd appeared on *Come Dancing*, are carved up by a future politician. There is a trend, a fashion that comes and eventually goes, of hanging victims. A woman burns to death on the upper deck of a bus. A man is shot by loyalists alongside his pregnant wife, who tries to shield him, but they finish him off; his father has a heart attack at the news and they have a joint funeral. A man, engaged to be married shortly, walking to buy a paper, is blown through a shop window. A soldier handing chocolate bars to colleagues is shot in the head. A last phone call is made with garbled shouting in the background. A man sits opposite a man in a pub who's been following him; others see but decide not to tell him. Bus drivers are shot in front of their passengers. A teenage soldier bursts into tears after getting separated from his patrol and having his gun snatched; a group of women take pity on him and try to shepherd him away, but he doesn't trust them and freezes, and he is pushed into a garage and shot twice when the IRA arrive on the scene. A son goes missing in 1969, his father spends the next four years looking for him in Belfast, day in, day out; the son is never found, while the father is found hooded and bound, shot in the head, for delving too deep and asking too many questions.

New faces in pubs are determined a threat. IEDs lurk in pipes under roads. Remote-control watchers operate from nearby hills and woods. Loyalist bombs in pubs are described as premature IRA ones. Family homes are taken over on operations. Code words are used to confirm real threats and crimes, as opposed to trolls. "Collaborating" women have their heads shaved, or are tarred and feathered and chained to railings. Ambushes are common. A man is shot playing darts in the pub. Bombs go off in moving vehicles. Cars are riddled with bullets. A soldier with a sniffer dog approaches a suspect milk churn; the dog survives. A sailor docked in the port, walking back from a party, is shot; they match him to his ship because his clothes have German labels. A group of men leave the scene laughing. A farmer and his wife are shot; their two-year-old son is shot four times but survives. A young man is bundled into the back of a car, while returning home from bingo with his fiancée. A man goes down to check on a noise in the night and staggers back into the bedroom. The pregnant wives of soldiers have to be sedated on hearing the news. The pregnant wives of soldiers' victims, likewise. Debts and drunken fights are claimed as sectarian and then revenged.

This is just a fraction of the opening years of our Troubles. If ghosts did exist, they'd be everywhere.

PART TWO

Da's Folks

Ink

Everyone knows where they were when Kennedy was shot. My grandfather was drowning. I had heard the story or, rather, listened in on fragments of it. It was part of the secret mythologies that all families have. Joseph had staggered drunkenly off the docks and, despite being a strong swimmer, was weighed down by his clothes and the drink he'd taken and the shock of the cold. The rusting ladders of the docks remained just out of reach. An unidentified would-be rescuer threw him a life buoy, which struck Joseph on the head as he struggled and, knocked out, he disappeared into the depths, thrown from this world in a slapstick silent-movie farce. In Texas, Kennedy's limousine was cruising down Dealey Plaza. "Mr. President, you can't say Dallas doesn't love you." "No, you certainly can't." In California, a bedridden Aldous Huxley, on the edge of death, wrote one last message to his wife—"LSD, 100µg, intramuscular"—and she injected him accordingly and he exited via an internal exploding cosmos. In Oxford, C. S. Lewis was lying on his bedroom floor, shallow-breathing. It was November 22, 1963. Just another Friday.

I would hear the story of my grandfather's demise many times, but never directly. It was spoken of in the spaces between, in sighs and as asides within other conversations. Early on, I'd found the yellowing cover of the *Derry Journal* in an envelope in a drawer. At the bottom of a page emblazoned "PRESIDENT KENNEDY IS LAID TO REST" was the news of a Derry man having drowned in the river in a tragic accident. Knowing somehow that it was intensely personal, I hastily put it back, as children do when they have upset some covert equilibrium, naively even wiping it for fingerprints. I had no idea where precisely on the quay my grandfather had fallen in, or how they retrieved his body. I had no idea what Joseph was doing there in the first place. I had no idea who Joseph really was. For many years I did not even know his name and hesitated to ask, for fear of stirring up matters that were best left undisturbed. I had no idea why both of my da's parents had drowned in that same place. All I had was a single photograph of my grandfather, proud in a British Army uniform.

The auguries were bad for '63, right from the beginning. The year was born in the coldest winter. The river froze. The sea froze elsewhere in Britain and Ireland. An earthquake in Libya. A volcano in Bali. A hurricane in the Caribbean. Mine explosions and train crashes in Japan. A theater fire in Senegal. The USS *Thresher* imploded at the bottom of the sea. An African American church was bombed in Birmingham, Alabama. The Moors murders began.

Even his loved ones did not recognize Odysseus when he returned home, so changed was he by his experiences of war and roaming. A hero fit only to slaughter the suitors he spied upon. Joseph was no Odysseus, if ever such a man existed, but my grandmother Needles used to say cryptically, "He had gone to war a total gentleman and come back, at his worst, an animal." At the very least, Joseph returned a drunk—an alibi perhaps, which would lead him to his untimely end. Scanning old wartime photographs of Derry, Da discovered, with an electrical jolt of genetic recognition, his father in the background of a picture. Joseph was behind a Pied Piper recruiting sergeant, handsome and full of juvenile hubris, staring at the camera with the same exuberance that had taken men into the threshing machine before and since. There was no mistaking the face. Da had it and so, increasingly, did I.

What happened after my grandfather signed up was much less clear. Joseph had enlisted well into the war and so had missed Dunkirk, which his two brothers had barely survived. He'd made it from Normandy to the collapsing Reich by the end of the war, but his path across Europe was obscured. I gazed over maps and wondered what he'd seen, been involved in. Operation Overlord? The liberation of Paris? Shadows moving in the Ardennes? The horror show of mortars and splintering trees in the Hürtgen Forest? Coming up against machine guns at the Siegfried Line? Or the boys and old men in what had once been Berlin? The Northern Irish had fought through the *bocage*, the woods and hedgerows that hid snipers, Panthers and Tigers. They'd liberated Caen after a prolonged bloody fight and had run up against the Germans' last-ditch offensive, Operation Watch on the Rhine. What path did Joseph take, beyond simply surviving?

When I was younger, I was morbidly fascinated by death masks, the last photos of doomed ship or air crews, photos of Franz and Sophie Ferdinand waving from their motorcade. Above all, I was fixated on pictures of the figures at Pompeii and Herculaneum frozen in death poses millennia earlier, some cowering or crouched, others as if they were sleeping, mothers cradling their children. I learned later that these were not the fossils of individuals, but actually the outlines. The searing pyroclastic flow of the eruption, superheated molten rock, had burned and buried them all with pumice and ash, which had solidified around them. The bodies inside were incinerated and were lost, but the silhouettes remained. They could identify the person from where they ended. I tried later to build up a picture of my grandfather through this method; trying to decipher substance from the outline of his absence. The negative space. But traces from other people blurred the point where he ended and fiction began, rendering it indistinct. Stories had been written and rewritten until they were only a palimpsest of text, and the facts were indecipherable from the conjecture that followed. How many times could a story be told, and by how many people, before it began to change? At what point did it lose resemblance to its origin? The one thing that all the stories shared was that Joseph had ended up in Berlin, at a time when that obliterated city was being rebuilt with secrets and lies, before returning home.

My grandmother and grandfather had known each other before the war and after. I thought of Joseph writing to her from the continent, her weighing every word for significance or change, wondering what lay behind the black censored blocks of ink, but in truth I did not even know if they could read or write to any significant degree. She had waited for him, that much was certain, even after he died. In Buddhist countries they speak of hungry ghosts, but the restless dead still exist, even here, even now.

Camera

In the Doge's Palace in Venice there are portraits all around a vast hall in which every footstep echoes on the polished floor. Visitors gaze at the myriad faces, bearded and bald but all festooned in magisterial purple, of the leaders of the Venetian Republic. Few, if any, names are remembered. Except one. Marino Faliero. He is the one people are drawn to. Precisely because he has no portrait. He is obscured by a black veil. Denied representation because he attempted to become dictator of Venice and, after a failed coup, was beheaded on the steps of the building. The sentence was death. The sentence after death was *damnatio memoriae*. To be damned from memory. It backfired, however. The effort to obliterate Faliero from existence—from having ever existed—only draws attention to him.

Growing up, I had that single photo of my grandfather Joseph. It was treated definitively, totemically. He was there in a British Army uniform, handsome and proud, and that was all that needed to be said. I did not yet know that things could be concealed in clear sight, but I still had a feeling that all was not as it seemed. You could not—I thought then, as now—sum up a life in an image; there must be some degree of distorting and condensing at work to make that seem possible. You can hide things in symbols. And that single truthful and misleading photo hid a life more complicated and troubling than I'd ever imagined.

Wedding Dress

All the front doors were left open then. Only the porch doors separated homes from the street, and these were never locked. Looking back, elegiacally, it could be seen as some sense of community, now largely disappeared. Da would joke it was because no one had anything worth stealing. Perhaps solidarity flourished only when everyone had hardly anything, save a common adversary. Keeping the doors open also saved on a new lock and doorframe when the army showed up, looking for something or someone. My grandmother Needles's home was raided continually then. Her floorboards ripped up. Doors wrenched from cupboards by boys young enough to be her sons. Needles kept a little stash of money in her mattress and under the lino for the omnipresent rainy days, and it would invariably go missing. Her girls were searched and manhandled. Her boys carted off in handcuffs. It always happened at dawn. Four or five in the morning, before the neighborhood awoke, but gradually the local families would congregate as the hours passed by. The raids were thorough. Eventually, through routine or briefing, the soldiers would come to know her by her first name of Margaret. They would tell her that her sons, with whom she had little contact, had hanged themselves, lying their balls off and sniggering like schoolboys as she went into hysterics. They'd pass on their derisory respects. "It did her nerves no good," my mother noted.

Once, the army raided the day before the wedding of her daughter, who was barely out of her teens. The troops forced the family into the living room. One of my da's younger brothers, who was due to be best man, was lifted and taken away. The soldiers held up my young aunt's wedding dress, dancing around with it, laughing and insulting them. Needles lost her temper. She pulled down the picture of her dead husband, in his British Army uniform, and smashed it on the floor, saying she was ashamed of it now. One of the soldiers immediately struck her in the face with his rifle butt.

Da's older brother was interned. His younger brother convicted. Another fled to London to escape it all. His sisters were dragged into it. One, aged seven, was caught throwing stones at the police, and was carried off over one of their shoulders. She remembered being sat in front of a blazing fire at the station and given a large bar of Dairy Milk to eat. The pleasantries did not last. As a teenager, she was arrested, kept awake for days and beaten, with open palms so as not to leave bruises. They dropped her off, without shoes, in the no-man's-land of a full-scale riot, with bricks raining down around her.

I thought of Needles again and her house, the one they'd finally been allocated by the council in Rosemount, with her and the children sleeping in the early hours and the front door suddenly bursting open, startling birds on the rooftops, and the army and police storming in. I wonder how lonely the world felt to her. She was alone through the war, and she returned to that state during the Troubles, waiting for Joseph to somehow, impossibly, come back and protect them.

Ghosts are memory incarnate. And they are impossible desires. I used to wonder whether the dead remember the lives and people they've left behind. In Greek myth, the dead drink from the river of Lethe and forget their previous life, before going into the underworld. They drink of it, but the living do not, cannot, will not.

Pen

War happens simultaneously. It happens within days of the week and once-familiar places. It happens while shops are open. It happens on routes to school. It happens while people are in hospital, while others are falling in love. I wondered where Needles was, what she was doing, when Joseph walked off to sign up for the army. If it was a long-pondered-over decision or an impulsive moment, ill-thought-out and designed to startle and impress. The beginning of my grandfather's involvement in the Second World War was unclear until that reprinted photograph from the local paper's archives. He appears there as a figure in the crowd, heading off for an uncertain future. He must have known he would have a hard time of it. His brothers had barely made it back from Dunkirk a couple of years earlier, with their eardrums blown in by mortars and strafing Luftwaffe, wading into the water with their clothes on and weighed down by their equipment for some attempt at safety. They hauled themselves onto one of the flotilla boats in what was named—optimistically, for a desperate retreat—Operation Dynamo. It was a rare occasion when the English had borrowed the Irish penchant for glorious noble defeats. One of the uncles actually lived with Needles's family. My da remembered him well. He dropped dead one day in Bishop Street in the 1960s, still nursing his injuries. His daughter had been sent off to live in England and was never heard of again. So the story went. Entire lives end up as the marginalia.

In the photograph, Joseph is marching, almost strutting, in a proud column behind a commissioning officer, from the Labour Exchange on Bishop Street down through the city via Abercorn Road. One of the brave. No one knows the depths of their courage, the shallowness of their goodness until tested, until really tested. He'd passed billboards and signs for stout, Wonder Bread, Wings for Victory; reading "Give all you can to Mrs. Churchill's Red Cross Aid to Russia Fund" and "Careless talk costs lives." He walked across the bridge over the river. I wondered whether there were any doubts in his mind, if he could just have slipped off on a side road, almost willing him to. Instead he kept marching to Ebrington Barracks with its sign at the gate: "Warning: This area is patrolled by armed sentries and dogs. Halt when challenged." Perhaps Joseph was sick of hustling for work, the shame of poverty and the performed gratitude involved, and saw something that, whatever the risk, had purpose, definition. Some kind of certainty. The ritualistic aspects of poverty weigh heavily, and perhaps a chance to disrupt them, even as destruction beckoned, seemed tempting. Shame and pride, in such conditions, seem the same thing.

Joseph is one of the few men in the parade, by choice or necessity, not wearing a hat and is the only one staring directly at the camera. He is smiling a rakish grin, marching with an almost piss-taking enthusiasm. There were dangers no doubt, but he could handle himself. It would be an end to small-town boredom. Just like in the movies. He is guilty of the sin that had man thrown from Eden, as Kafka put it: impatience. Joseph is young, but it is no Children's Crusade. He was a Jack the Lad. A young man who knew the way of the streets, who knew a scam or two, who could handle himself. Slippery and charming. You could tell in that photograph. The others look already hard-bitten, as people did then. My father recalled seeing Bernard McGuigan, father of six, killed on Bloody Sunday and thinking he was an old man. He was forty-one. Age was older then. Maybe it was fashion or diet or photography. Maybe youth is an illusion we have gotten better at maintaining. Joseph looked like he'd already won, like a soldier coming back victorious from war and not about to be thrown into one. The unlucky ones ended up failing the medicals, the physical and mental tests, or were deployed at home on antiaircraft batteries. My grandfather, the poor proud bastard, was lucky.

Ink is made from carbon black or lamp black or furnace black, which emerges from the burning of coal tar, which comes from coal, which itself comes from ancient plants compressed into the earth. The carbon particles had traveled all that way, all that time, underground and above, to end up dispersed onto paper in different shapes, signatures. Some of the men could barely hold a pen, some could write only their names and nothing more, some scrawled an "X." Some were too young to sign up, some too old, casting doubts onto their precise ages when they went to their deaths.

Stamp

There is a feeling, *saudade*, that does not exist as a single word in English. It expresses the yearning of someone who is apart from someone at sea. A mix of heartache, nostalgia, homesickness, and grief. I wondered if Needles had it. Maybe she was relieved, in Joseph's absence. I thought of her, and many like her, living their lives, walking around town, in the absence of their men.

The gray and red brick. The color of adverts. "You're never alone with a Strand." "Lovely day for a Guinness," with a toucan on a weathervane. "Ask for Blues." India Tyres. There were horse and carts and omnibuses on Shipquay Square. There were rusted iron rings embedded into the walls to tie the horses to—and not boats, as I had once thought. Bread carts. Sacks of coal. The RUC patrolled in long, woolen double-breasted coats. They looked shiny, smart, and black. It was a surprise to see them in photos with individual faces, even in photos when they were guarding de Valera's visit or Spider Kelly's boxing homecoming or stampeding into St. Patrick's Day parades with their batons swinging. They'd always seemed a faceless, malevolent force to me, but of course they were individual men with names and birthdays and first loves and appetites.

It might be thought that a solemnity would take over a city engaged, however remotely, in war, but Derry was a different sort of place. The dance halls boomed. Phone numbers on slips crossed palms in cloakrooms. Lights shone on the portion of halls not taken up by shuffling feet. The clubs had wallpaper. The cafés were filled afterward by desperadoes. In the daytime, nursing hangovers, regrets, or longings, the women would pass workmen excavating iron railings and gates to melt and redistribute over German cities and into German bodies. Perhaps Needles nursed an ache for Joseph through all this, imagining him, smoking under a streetlight, hair slicked, standing in a pawnshop suit due to be returned come Monday, the cock of the walk, forever that age, forever before.

Time is the spreading of ink on a page wet with rain.

No letters between them survive. At least not to my knowledge. Paper was not yet cheap, but if words were exchanged, they do not remain. After reading, maybe they were discarded, or perhaps cherished and found later and then thrown away by someone else, shorn of context and meaning. One person's precious object, divested of memory, is another's junk. Yet there's always the possibility of a letter's existence out there, hidden in the city, in some obscure vault or lost somewhere along the way, by the postal services that brought messages back from an expanding front. There must have been moments when Needles thought, "Please, God. Let him survive and come back to me," and then in terrible retrospect, "Be careful what you wish for."

Sundial

Beneath the Derry Walls, below the picturesque, oddly pastoral St. Augustine's Church, where the birds always sang, built on the site of the original church of Derry's patron saint, Columba, there were streets that have now disappeared. My grandfather and grandmother had actually grown up in the same part of Derry before their marriage, before even their courtship, a place almost entirely gone now, on the steep slope leading down to the Bogside, where the housing looked like it was sculpted from the earth, under a blanket of low-hanging soot. In surviving photographs it seems a Dickensian rookery with an industrialized charcoal city in the background. In time, pictures of it are more remote from us than NASA shots of the Martian landscape. Part of the rift between then and now, them and us, is the fact that these images came before the invention of color photography. The blurry black-and-whites seem older even than paintings that came before them.

This is, of course, an illusion. The camera always lies. Outside the lens, life cascaded on in every direction and every hue. The world was not black-and-white. It still isn't.

Joseph and Margaret (before she received her nickname) were neighbors on Walker's Square, in the triumphalist shadow of Walker's Pillar, which moved like a sundial with the changing light of the day. Governor Walker was the hero of the Siege of Derry, the great victory of Protestantism over Catholicism, when the rebels had held out against a tyrannical British king (the history of the North is basically an exercise in ignoring the huge complexities, nuances, and contradictions). Much of Walker's greatness was the result of his knack for self-publicizing in a book that wrote out other heroes like Major Henry Baker and Colonel John Mitchelburne, and the really daring, gun-toting figures like Captain Adam Murray, who died in obscurity and penury. The pen was, in the long term, mightier than the sword. And he who could rewrite history owned history. The governor was a curious case. A self-aggrandizing preacher who was not much loved or followed, but who gained, as often happens in Ireland, a colossal projected authority in death that had eluded him in life. When King Billy, the bisexual Dutch monarch so beloved by puritan Unionism, heard of Walker's death at the Battle of the Boyne, shot while comforting the dying Duke of Schomberg, he is supposed to have said, "Fool that he was, what brought him there?" The dead, however, become everything they, and we, could have been. They have their uses and assume grandeur in proportion to the function they offer the living. So they raised a pillar in Walker's name to tower over the superstitious papist peasants kept outside the city gates.

They built the pillar with a spiral staircase within: 105 steps to the top, one for every long, brutal day of the Siege. The statue brandished a Bible and a sword, which supposedly fell when

Catholic emancipation was achieved. The truth was, it blew down in a storm, given that the statue was exposed at its height to not only a multitude of sunsets but the winds funneling off the Donegal mountains from the Atlantic. Every statement is a challenge. One night an anonymous figure climbed the pillar and tied an Irish tricolor to the top of the statue. On another occasion, someone launched a half brick at it and knocked its finger off. Eventually it was toppled, mimicking the fall of Nelson's Pillar in Dublin. The IRA planted explosives, and in the dead of night there was an enormous explosion and it collapsed. Only the plinth remained, and empty cubes of once-inhabited air above it. It existed now as a different symbol. A monument of a disappearance.

My grandparents lived within spitting distance of the walls. The curfew bell sounded into the 1960s. Catholics were reminded they had to leave the walled city at 9:00 p.m. and were forbidden to reenter until 9:00 a.m. They were banned from owning property within; even the bishop had to use an intermediary to buy a house for a nunnery on Pump Street. Outside, the ghetto was a destitute but lively place. There were pubs nearby, shebeens really: the Steamship Inn and Willie Devine's. Larmour's shop piled junk and antiques up against the masonry of the walls. Performances were given at the Oak's and Emmet's Halls, the latter named after the "Great Catholic Emancipator." The basements of the houses on one terrace all ran into one another—a tunnel without partition. They set up a boxing gym there. I could see it in my mind's eye under a flickering, swinging light bulb. A montage of films I'd seen, and probably nothing like the real thing. The streets are obliterated now: Nailors Row, Friel's Terrace, and so on. Not only have all the people and the events that happened there vanished, but so, too, have the very sets and stages of the streets on which they took place. It exists now only in books, photos, memories. Instead there is a grassy incline barreling down to the Bogside. My father regularly cut the grass there for the council; he was on the cover of the local paper doing so, bare-chested, to my mother's embarrassment and secret pride, under the headline "Make Hay While the Sun Shines," on the unmarked site of his parents' young lives. The places where they slept and ate and dreamt are invisible. We tend the soil under which our ancestors lie.

Medal (Royal Army Medical Corps)

Needles must have known something of war. Secondhand. Its shadow. There were medals from her father in a drawer somewhere. He was in the Royal Army Medical Corps in the Great War— "the war to end all wars," as the utopian pessimists put it. A stretcher bearer. He carted men down trenches and across no-man's-land to behind the lines. Dreading the smell of cut grass, which was the first sign of deadly phosgene gas. Many of those he carried were ruined forever, whether they lived or not. Boys with jaws missing. Horrible fractures. Amputations without ether. Infections. Parts of their young bodies gouged out or shot off or mangled. What was once a face covered with a porcelain mask and a flat, motionless painted eye. Bionic men with legs and arms of wood and hooked wire. "Broken gargoyles" they called them.

In France a million countrymen had died. Double that number had returned home disabled. They marched at the front of the French victory parade to say, "Here is the cost," but few, if any, knew what it had been for, and people would subtly or unsubtly turn away in daily life. Afraid of staring too much, they avoided all looks. The government paid off Needles's father, and his memories and nightmares, at the end with a token sum. His medals for bravery lay in a drawer when my father and his siblings were growing up, and they would play with them and inspect them, holding them up to the light. No one knows where they went.

Pocket Mirror

The ink was faded on the forms but still discernible. It was written before he was even a father, let alone a grandfather. "Full name: Joseph XX Anderson. Date of birth: 20th March of 1925. Trade on enlistment: laborer. Next of kin: Sister—Miss Mary Anderson. Address: 33 Walkers Place"—an address that no longer existed—"Londonderry. N Ireland. Religion: RC. Single. Industry group: ZE. Occupational classification: L485. Hometown: Omagh, County Tyrone."

Omagh? I wondered if that's where Joseph had genuinely come from (no one had ever mentioned it previously), if it was a mistake in processing, or if he was covering his tracks from the beginning, trying to set them on the wrong path, give himself a head start. According to the forms, he was transferred immediately by train from Derry to Omagh. They place him there at the beginning of March 1943. He disappeared on March 8.

They notice his absence at one minute to midnight, at the nightly head count. He is missing for five days.

The Blitz spirit existed, of course, and crime rocketed, of course. It was a golden age for shysters and opportunists. Ration-book fraud, smuggling, rape, theft, looting. For someone who'd grown up hustling, prowling the edges of the underworld, the allure of safety and perhaps the chance to make a buck or two outweighed valor.

At that time Convoy SC 121 was struggling across the Atlantic in icy, gale-force winds. It was becoming increasingly dispersed and the crews became worried. The wolf packs of the U-boat fleet prowled toward it. The *Guido* made a break for it and was torpedoed southeast of Cape Farewell by U-633 (itself rammed and sunk two days later by the SS *Scorton*). Ten of its crew were taken to the ocean floor. The stragglers *Empire Lakeland*, *Fort Lamy*, *Leadgate*, and *Vojvoda Putnik* (formerly the *Kerry Range*) were gradually picked off. The next day the *Bonneville*, *Malantic*, and *Rosewood* followed. The next day the *Coulmore*, the *Nailsea Court*, and so on. Hundreds of tonnages with hundreds of sailors lost to the sea. The German submarine U-156 was sunk by depth charges off Barbados. A life raft was dropped for the handful of survivors, who climbed on board. They were never seen again.

On land, the Czechs and Soviets were slowing the Wehrmacht at Sokolovo, while 7,240 Jews were transported from Yugoslavia to the extermination camp at Treblinka. The Kraków Ghetto was declared officially liquidated. On March 13, 1943, at the Nazi Werwolf bunker command network in Ukraine, Major-General Henning von Tresckow asked a colleague accompanying Adolf Hitler to take a case back to Berlin with them. It contained two bottles of Cointreau, which, he explained, he'd lost in a bet with another general. Inside was a plastic time bomb, designed to explode midflight, killing the dictator. The Condor plane took off and the fuse wore down, but, due to the temperature in the cargo hold, the bomb failed to detonate. On that same day, at 12:30 p.m., Joseph was apprehended in Derry. He was punished by being locked up, was forfeited five days' pay, and was ordered to pay back the cost of his now-missing kit, which he had cashed in or lost along the way.

Joseph returned to his regiment, resumed his training. They didn't let him forget what he'd done, and for a few weeks trained an eye on him. He kept his head down for a month. At one minute to midnight, the time of roll call, on April 22, as the Germans burned the Warsaw Ghetto to the ground, he was found to have vanished again. The roads and railways between Omagh and Derry, and his old haunts in both, were searched, to no avail. He was declared a deserter on May 13, 1943, the day the Axis forces in North Africa surrendered. It was not until June 15, 1943—perhaps when he'd gotten complacent, thinking he'd escaped them for good—that he was arrested by military police in Derry. Two weeks later he was sentenced to eighty-four days' detention and forfeited fifty-four days' pay. The sentence was suspended so that he could continue serving, to be reviewed on September 30, provided he changed his ways.

At one minute to midnight on August 1, the day of the execution of the Martyrs of Nowogródek, Joseph vanished again. He was found five days later, forfeited five days' pay, and earned himself six months' detention at the prison barracks at Carrickfergus. It was a place where those who'd committed acts tantamount to treason were kept. They held German prisoners in the nearby Sunnylands and Italians at Sullatober Mill. Joseph's record was repeatedly marked "Struck off strength," signifying being kicked out of regiments and sent to others. He would not have received a pleasant welcome. "Close arrest" was another

recurring term, assuming imprisonment with continual surveillance. His sentence was annotated "IHL"—imprisonment with
hard labor. They sent him to a psychiatrist, for medical tests,
and then on to the place where they would break him.

In '44 Joseph was shipped to England. Chorley detention
camp. He'd have been imprisoned with a mixed bunch. Everyone
had fucked up in a different way. Nervous shell-shocked wrecks.
Explosive hotheads. Spivs. Paratroopers who'd frozen in flight.
Conscientious objectors. They worked outside in all weathers.
The guards were sadists. It had to appear worse than war. A
disincentive. There were beatings. Denials of access to water.
Isolation cells. Humiliations occurred on the parade ground for
the others to see. One lad was battered around the ground by
two commanding officers. When he complained of being unable to breathe, they throttled him and laid into him with their
fists. They gave him a savage beating, which he did not long survive. They got a manslaughter charge. The judge began, "I am
extremely sorry to have to sentence two men with the records
you two have . . ."

Joseph outlived the war. The price for that would prove to
be a heavy one. He was placed back in the army, supposedly re-
formed. He had leave in 1946, went back to Ulster, and did not
return once more. He was marked AWOL on July 14. He was apprehended by police in a night bust, 3:55 a.m. on July 31. What
did he do in those days and nights of clandestine freedom? Did
he hide completely or in clear sight? Why did he not just cross
over the border to the Irish Free State (as it was then called),
go on the run, as many had and would, and construct a new
identity? What brought him back to Derry, again and again, a
small place where he'd easily be seen, where people would talk?
Perhaps it was her? Perhaps this was a love story, after all.

On August 10, Joseph was shipped to northwest Europe. On

the twenty-ninth of that month, he was ordered to make good the sum of nineteen pounds for the loss, by neglect, of his kit. On September 19, he was found guilty of going AWOL again for over a fortnight, forfeited seventeen days' pay—the time he'd absented himself on the continent—and was sentenced to one year's imprisonment with hard labor.

"Was he a coward?" I wondered. Perhaps. Perhaps he was terrified of things he'd heard about. That the conflict would swallow him up. Yet cowardice didn't seem to ring entirely true. The military prisons were places of great shame and fear. Joseph could have kept his head down in the army, tried to get through it all alongside his comrades. The path he took, though, was willfully intransigent. Continually bashing his head against his own army, continually escaping, continually caught, never changing. It seemed not the act of a coward, but that of an inveterate dissident or a maniac. Had he fought and lived, he'd likely have been out in '45, but he was stubborn, stubborn as a mule, fighting perhaps himself.

At the beginning of 1948, Joseph is listed as a member of the British Army of the Rhine, an occupation force of Germany. He was based at Sennelager, Paderborn, North Rhine–Westphalia. There's still a British base there. It was called the Theatre Barracks because it had one at its center, altered into an Army Kinema Corporation cinema for newsreels and flicks for the troops. On R&R, they'd sneak off to local pubs like the Pupasch and Danni's Bar on Danziger Strasse. After less than a month there, Joseph is "tried in the field" and charged with "whilst on active service, disobeying a lawful command given by his superior officer, in that he at Theatre Barracks, Sennelager, did not leave the dining hall when ordered to do so by LSM Day." He was found not guilty. "Military conduct—very bad. Testimonial—not assessed." Charge 2 was simply that "he was drunk," of which he was found guilty and sentenced to six months' imprisonment with hard labor, to be followed by being discharged with ignominy. He was sent to His Majesty's Prison Shepton Mallet. The "glasshouse." Infamous for its hangings of soldiers who'd committed rapes and murders, most of them black kids in dubious convictions. One took twenty-two minutes to die. The last execution by firing squad took place in the courtyard, one Benjamin Pyegate, who'd stabbed another soldier in the throat during a brawl. The gallows were still there as a warning. Brutal places. Sadistic guards. Atrocious food. Poor hygiene in earlier years caused diseases to run riot. It was the oldest-surviving prison in the country. Ominous. Stone so thick they kept precious books there during war, protected against bombs: the Domesday Book, Magna Carta, the *Victory* logbook, the Olive Branch Petition. Just a few years after Joseph's stay, the Kray twins had served out their time here, after a spell in the Tower of London for the same crimes of AWOL and ill discipline.

The deserter's tale is one that goes largely untold. Personal, familial, and societal shame have a silencing effect, even today. Who wants to read of the cowards, the weak, the self-righteous, the mutinous? Except that there were one hundred thousand deserters in the British Army alone. An awful lot of secrets to keep.

During the First World War, Joseph might have received the death sentence: two hundred thousand soldiers in the British Army were court-martialed for various offenses. More than three hundred were shot at dawn for desertion or simply freezing in action; twenty-two of them were Irish.

Joseph came back to haunt his own life. Perhaps he was already damaged, and the war made sure of it. Perhaps my grandmother was being nostalgic when she said he went away a gentleman and came back a monster, but perhaps she was being honest. There was no chance of him getting a job in anything to do with the state, or with anyone who knew his history. He was a marked man. He would no longer have the anxiety of being uncovered by the military police and forced back, but in its place came a shame that was inescapable, that rumbled always in the background, that seemed to exist within the slightest glance from others. It turned the victory celebrations to ashes in the mouth. The temptation would have been to nurse your grievances, like a devil locked in frost, and then to silence them with drink and false tyrannical certainty. He wasn't the same person as the one who'd left; and the person he was now, the person others saw, he could not evade. Joseph had ruined his own name and his own face, and he could do nothing but continue to wear them.

For some, it would have been better to die than to live in disgrace. To those who believed in preordination, perhaps avoiding the war was to cheat God, to betray not only the army and the populace but destiny. Maybe some people survive past their chosen day. No one wanted to discuss the war that soon after it, but reminders were everywhere: they had rations until the 1950s, and the army—even the U.S. Army—remained until the 1960s. There were veterans everywhere, hobbling along with war wounds. One gentleman from Nailors Row had even lost an arm to a Japanese bayonet in Borneo. The psychological damage was generally unseen, in public at least. It tended to be housed in pubs and homes, behind closed doors.

All drunks are sentimentalists. They are mutually reinforcing conditions. It is easier to live in the past—especially a romanticized past that never existed—than to confront the present and face the future. If finding yourself occupying a narrowing sliver of what your life had been or could be, the temptation is to expand it through fictions, boasts, bolstered by the temporary confidence of intoxication.

After the war, most people wanted a quiet life, stability, a modicum of luxury. To forget, even if others could not. Gradually tales of the war did creep out, distorted by being contained for so long. The fog of war, the many perspectives, could hide a lot of inconvenient truths from strangers, but not from themselves. The mirror, however, was merciless in the precision of its reflection.

Jukebox

Fifteen years passed. Joseph and Needles had children. Seven of them, which was a relatively modest number for Catholic families at the time. The kids grew up and became teenagers; Derry, like all provincial towns, enacts an imitation of the big cities. Jukeboxes came in. Big bands modified from schmaltz to rock 'n' roll. Youngsters dressed as teddy boys and girls. The churches condemned the youths as being in the grip of sexually rapacious communists. Effigies of Elvis were burned. Shows were picketed. Denunciations boomed from pulpits about the dance crazes of impressionable youths, as if the Twist were the danse macabre. They were still sending young mothers to work as serfs in the Magdalene Laundries, but this baby boom endangered the power they'd accumulated. The churches risked being swamped in a liberated tide, or rather, drained of congregations and influence. The fear, functioning so well for so long, was threatened by optimism. The *Londonderry Sentinel* declared that rock 'n' roll was "endangering civilisation as we know it." A mass jitterbug to Little Richard's "Tutti Frutti" threatened to become a riot. A song came on the radio, "Pledging My Love." "Why can't you listen to nice, wholesome music like that?" Not realizing the singer Johnny Ace was already dead from a back-stage game of Russian roulette. Joseph would sing songs quietly to himself. The words and melodies of which go unrecorded.

Thimblerig

In the daytime our little family had only one regular visitor. Needles. She was small and quiet, with dark, dark hair. Her daughter Rosie said she wore scarves around her head with rollers that made her look like the queen. She'd call me over and sit me on her knee, ruffling my blond mop of hair. I was always intrigued by her, but a little reserved. Her features were sharp and pale, her skin a map that made her look older than her years. She looked the way witches did in my picture books, and I wondered if there were good witches.

There was a story, less a story than a rumor, that Needles once read palms. She foresaw the future for a living. In a religious society, where everything is part of God's plan, that plan—the future—could conceivably be uncovered in advance. Yet it was heretical, for it was subverting God's will and it had the stench of free will. Nevertheless, people tried to find out what was to come, through signs in the environment: the way birds flew, patterns in smoke, the ripples from a stone cast on water or sand, ideograms in clouds, the paths that water took through the landscape. Invariably they tried to find out the future so they could change it.

It seemed, however, that the rumor had been garbled. It was not fortune-telling that Needles had performed at traveling fairs, but "find the pony" or thimblerig: placing a ball under cups, a sleight of hand aided by stooges planted in the crowd. It was a confidence trick, centuries old—older even than Christianity. It was, in a way, its own form of subversion. There in the rabble days, six of them occurring annually in late spring and winter, among the spectators, stalls, quacks, salesmen, pickpockets, trick-o'-the-loop men, dentists, blood-letters, and army recruiters, Needles staked her place, shuffling cups and talking the talk. She learned to be tough, to talk tough, to face down anyone in that crowd, should they turn nasty, and to do it with charisma, to keep the other patrons laughing.

That was not to say Needles did not try to foresee the future. While raising her children, she discovered she had breast cancer. The treatment was traumatic. The perception then (until fairly recently even) was that cancer was a death sentence. People could not even broach it directly in words. It was referred to as "the Big C," as if saying its name would invoke some kind of curse, and those who mentioned it would somehow become afflicted. It was like the black death in folk memory. To look too intently at it could bring no good. Such was the fear of wasting away or being eaten from within. I could never understand, as a child, how the word *cancer* also referred to a star sign in astrology. I did not know its origin in the Latin for "crab," which originated in the shape of veins around tumors and the thought of claws digging in, directed by soulless eyes. There was a body horror to it, like the beauty of pregnancy inverted into something obscene. Something growing inside you. Needles dreaded the cancer ever returning, with a biblical fear, and it seems, from insinuations toward the end, that she thought it had returned. Death perhaps was her way of escaping dying.

I didn't remember the last time my mother and I saw Needles, though the memory must be in there somewhere. Where else would it go—the things we experience but forget? Lost in the heady dream of childhood that nothing will change, that everything will remain and there will always be time, I did not keep track, or know to keep track, of what was happening. Every time I thought of Needles, I pictured her in her house. The bare walls and floors. Weird little things. A carved Brian Boru harp on the windowsill. All the brambles in her back garden. The sun on the front door. A riotous assembly of children always gathered around. Yet I could not retrieve that last memory from the banks in my mind, even though it was later than the rest. There seemed no logic to the storage. It was like trying to recall the end of a dream, having only just become aware that you are awake. Scenes were spliced together. They were missing sections, or ones were at the wrong speed or with the wrong voices. Most often they faded into nothingness so absolute and formless that it was not even a discernible void of black or white, but true nonexistence.

"We spent most of the time hiding in a room at the back of the house," my mother said. "Needles was bruised. She didn't look herself. I couldn't look. You know that waxwork look they get? It was worse than that—a lot worse. I wanted to remember her how she was. It just wasn't her.

"There was this horrible fog over us all. I've always hated wakes. All the whispers. How crowded it gets. And awkward. When do you get people to leave? What do you say? And the keeners; well, they're not keeners anymore, they don't get paid as such, but you know those old biddies who turn up, having barely known the person or actively disliked them, and they take over and hold court. Vultures. Plus the family, as you well know, are reserved. It made it more distressing. They weren't ready for it. It wasn't fair. Everyone coming in and out was overwhelming. We just stayed out of the way together until she was safely buried."

Suddenly I remembered something. Not the last time or viewing the body, but being in a room while the wake happened next door. A memory that I forgot I had. Reading a book while people came and went, the sound of sobbing and talking through the walls, people checking on me occasionally. I read a book on how, by 2020, cities would be built on the ocean floor, illustrated with people swimming around with fins and gills. And I looked at objects around the room, thinking how strange it was that they survived when the person who owned them was now gone. That a useless object could outlive its owner.

What powers grief seems to be the proximity to before, so close but so unreachable. It is the torment of Tantalus. The world of before is within sight. It is just a few days, even hours, earlier. Everything looks almost the same, and yet it might as well be a thousand years ago, such is the change. It gives the continuing world an unreal, uncanny feel. When they say that time heals, it doesn't. It just extends this proximity, like watching a ship sail away as you float in the sea. The past is irretrievable, but so, too, is the future that could have been, had things just kept going.

I was not old or close enough to really feel grief's force, the intrusive waves of thought that sweep in out of nowhere, the torturously pleasant dreams that they were still here. My abiding memory was a kind of silent, gnawing terror, the dimensions of which I could not fathom and was too afraid to inquire about. It terrified me, the mix of paralysis and puzzlement, the fact that contrary to everything I had previously assumed, no adult had an answer; they, too, were all stricken, all the fundamentally strong characters. No one knew. For a year or more after her death, I noticed that the light never went off in my parents' room at night.

"Why was she called Needles?" I asked.

"Well . . ." My mother sighed. "She was needle sharp, and she let everyone know it. When she felt like it. She gave me a desperate time at the beginning. Called me 'princess' 'cause I came from a 'fancy' part of town. Didn't matter I was from a council estate. I gave her a wide berth for a while, at the start. I realized though, eventually, that her bark was worse than her bite and she'd gone through a lot in her own life. And then we got to talking. I grew to like her very much."

Everyone had nicknames. There was an aversion in Derry, maybe in all working class cities, to calling people by their actual names. There was my da's younger brother, who was called Skin. And Budgie, who was raised with my father as one of his siblings but was technically my cousin. Everyone had a nickname, whether they wanted to or not. I was called Andy by my friends. Most of the time the nicknames were affectionate, but there was still a degree of coercion to them. If someone was to insist, however politely, on being called their real name, the reaction would be one of derision. It would be taken as a sign of arrogance and snobbery. Who do they think they are, insisting on having their own name? A lot of the time nicknames had a cruel wit to them. A kid with polio was called Big Shoe. There was a guy who walked around with a disability that meant his neck was crooked, and his face permanently looked upward diagonally. They called him Birdwatcher. It was merciless. Mahogany Shoulder was a frequent funeral attender. Micky the

Moth was notorious for finding house parties at night by their lights. Some nicknames were amusing, no doubt, but they could be vicious too. I hung around with one kid who stressed out his younger brother so much, with taunts and nicknames, that the kid's hair started to fall out. There was a point where keeping people's feet on the ground became trying to nail them into it. I didn't know if my grandmother approved or disapproved of the name Needles, but it clung to her.

"She was different. Needles had what was called 'bad nerves' back then. A lot of people have it now, and you'd get tablets for it. She called herself an alcoholic, but she'd only ever sit with a single bottle of stout, two at most. She was a slight wee thing. Just a coping mechanism or habit, I guess. A kind of veil.

"Towards the . . ." My mother paused. "Well, she started to come more often, down to our house. I'd keep her a bite of dinner, then some lunch, supper. She'd stay longer and call earlier. And she started telling me stuff. Your da denies it, but as far as I'm concerned, she said what she said. He wasn't there and he doesn't want to know, but she told me all this stuff . . . about the hiring fairs. Those were auctions in the town square where girls and boys would be sold off to go and work seasonally for farmers. There was a lot of stigma back then that's still in people now, however modern we seem. They're still horrified by it. The workhouse and everything. We forget that lasted until after the war. She was really, really poor. They used to have the fairs up at the Diamond. 'The Rabbles' they called them. You were hired out for months at a time to work. They'd barter for them. She used to talk . . . insinuate . . . about the troubles she had with them."

She paused thoughtfully. "She opened up more and more towards the end. Needles was obsessed with him. Her 'Joesy,' she called him. Fool that I was, when I was young, I thought it was romantic. In fact it was terrible. She couldn't move on. She was stuck in time. She couldn't go back and she couldn't go forward without him."

I suddenly recalled that photo of my grandfather, and a line or a paragraph from a book I'd read somewhere, on how Aborigines forbid photos or footage, or even the naming of the dead. Maybe they had a point.

"She'd come down on Sundays. Perch by the fire. I'd feed her homemade vegetable soup. That was her excuse, but I knew it was to see you. The only thing I ever saw that got her off the sofa was you. She'd stoop down to you, and you'd be playing there with your *Star Wars* toys and your *A-Team* van. 'Don't let him be an only child,' she said. I'll never forget that as long as I live. The last time we saw her must have been up at her house on Osborne Street. She came out to give you a big hug on the wee path. I always remember her, leaning over that last time, saying to you—and you with your blond curly hair—'Bye-bye, wee darling. Bye-bye.' None of us ever saw her again."

Needles left no note, or at least none was ever found. Nothing to take comfort from or fixate on. She just left. "Death by misadventure," the coroner typed, out of kindness perhaps, given the lingering Catholic idea of eternal limbo for the lost souls of those who took their own lives. She was slight, and it was conceivable that a sudden gust had caused her to lose her footing on the quay's edge. She'd visit the docks every week, like clockwork. A bus driver regularly saw her on his route, kneeling at the place her husband had drowned. Maybe she went there to talk or to weep, or just to sit and look at the water. It's believed that Needles followed her husband, twenty years later, into the river at the very same point. I tried to imagine her there, as the driver saw her in passing, but her face—seen fleetingly from behind—is always obscured.

In truth, there are many ways to drown. The Chinese poet Li Bai died trying, in ecstatic drunkenness, heroic and idiotic, to hug the moon's reflection in the Yangtze River. The American poet Hart Crane climbed over the railings of a Caribbean cruise ship in his pajamas, believing himself to be "quite disgraced," and leapt and was last seen swimming for the horizon, impossibly far out to sea. Virginia Woolf waded into the River Ouse with her pockets full of stones, believing her mental instability was returning and seeking permanent respite: "I feel certain that I am going mad again. I feel we can't go through another of those terrible times. And I shan't recover this time. I begin to hear voices, and can't concentrate. So I am doing what seems the best thing to do." The Japanese general Taira no Koremori, who preferred reading to war, drowned himself after fleeing a battle at the sound of a flock of birds, and having been fooled by flags and fires that larger forces had amassed. We search in complex fates for single notes that will chime with us. Suicide, however, is a plural thing, even in the death of a single person.

My mother and I were the last to see Needles, or rather, the last to see her who knew her well. It's certain she passed many on her journey from Rosemount, through the town, to the river. Those who walked past her in the street were unaware that here was a lady who would never exist again, on her way to exiting the world.

Coin

The train line ran alongside the river. We used to place coins on the tracks as kids to flatten the queen's head. "Our part in the revolution." The train passed Gransha Lake, a backwater or slough behind the tributary. It was set in the proximity of the "big house," the local psychiatric hospital. While it was no longer accepted that the planet Saturn exerted a melancholic influence, people still spoke of the influence of the moon on matters beyond tides, matters of the mind. A person was "wired to the moon," as the saying went. There were woods there, and the deeper you went in, the more it turned into marsh and the less you could count on the ground being stable. We had ventured over there as boys, deep into forbidden territory. I don't know what we had expected to find. What we did find were rusting beer cans, porno mags stuffed into the bushes, undergarments scattered without explanation across a forest floor. Solar systems of sunlit midges existed there in rooms of light under the canopy. Vernal ponds, depending on the time of year and rainfall, that made a person further mistrust the land beneath them. I did not tell my friends back then why I paused at the train tracks or crossed them, as they larked around up at the giant graffiti-strewn pillars and added their own scrawls. I did not tell them this was where my grandmother had been found.

In the time before black-box recorders on planes, they would have to put together the pieces to understand how a crash occurred, trace the clues back, reanimate the dead.

The train tracks continued on a long arc toward Waterside station, passing woodland that merges treacherously into reeds and wetland, an area called Rosses Bay. The western end of the inlet was once called Troy, the eastern the Crook. My maternal grandfather, Anthony, a fisherman, knew it by the name Otter Bay. Others, much earlier, had called it Port Rois. At the time of Genghis Khan, the sack of Constantinople, and the Fourth Crusade, there was a sea and land battle between rival clans on this obscure corner of Christendom. The McDermotts launched a doomed ambush on thirteen ships of the O'Donnells and were routed. The surrounding land remains named Caw, from the Gaelic for "battle." Language remembered what people had long forgotten.

It was around Halloween, as my family remembered it, a time of tempestuous weather, when Needles washed up on the edge of Rosses Bay. The Foyle Bridge was not yet built. The train driver saw her from his passing cabin. She lay there with her hair, black as a raven, black as the Morrigan, black as the Egyptian night, unfurled on the shoreline. I thought of the long, wispy water-silk tresses I'd seen in streams. They found her money—not much—stuffed down into her pop socks when they recovered her.

I had this recurring thought of Needles, a cruel and kind thought. She is there on the shoreline and she is walking, she is walking somehow, somehow back from the river.

Roll of Microfilm

Joseph's original background was rural; from Donegal, as Derry folks tended to be. His people were from Stranorlar. Not long ago I hitched a ride down there, with a trucker who talked incessantly. It wasn't much more than a widening in the road. An ivy-shrouded hotel, a church with rusting scaffolding, an almost-bleached poster for an Easter Rising commemoration, and a sign to the Drumboe martyrs execution site, where four republicans were marched into the woods and killed by their former comrades. Along the road was a boarded-up Art Deco cinema called the Ritz. The town merged into its twin, Ballybofey, across the river, but once they had been strictly segregated, with Catholics forbidden to live there. The river was the Finn, which merged farther downstream into the Foyle. The river led my grandfather to the city. Genealogy followed topography. The village was on the edge of the wilderness. The road signs changed from old people and children to leaping deer crossings. The road led to a mountain pass through the Bluestack Mountains, huge boulder colossi and scree on either side. The pylons went from metal to wood, like antique oil derricks. The trees turned to pine as the soil thinned, a skeleton of stone beneath a skin of moss. It was a place where the wild lucid stars could be seen, where snows fall in unlikely months, where lakes freeze, where rivers begin.

The machine hummed into life, causing heads to turn in the otherwise quiet library. I unraveled the microfilm, carefully threading it under the tight panes of glass, as if examining microscopic organisms or biopsies. I wound the ends around each spool. The negatives appeared enlarged on the screen as it wheeled along. The light needed adjusting, the alignment, then the focus. Reeling back through their life-spans, headlines accelerating past. Now and then a photograph or an advert would catch the eye and the reel would stop. "EXPLOSIVES: If you know anything about terrorist activities—explosives, threats, or murders—please speak now to the CONFIDENTIAL TELEPHONE LONDONDERRY 262340." They used to have the same message sprayed in stenciled yellow print on the sides of army Land Rovers. It was even printed on the backs of bus tickets, with the added line "in complete confidence." I tried calling it now, out of curiosity. Three beeps and the phone line went dead and then disconnected. I wondered who'd called it when it worked. Informers, curtain-twitching neighbors, paramilitaries setting up ambushes or setting themselves up for ambush. Back then, nothing was as it seemed.

The newspapers zipped past, faster and faster, taking us back through life, younger and younger until we all shrank and became embryonic, then disappeared into the death before life and kept going into the prehistory before we existed. More than a century of local papers were kept like fossils: fraying cardboard boxes in filing cabinets. Each reel contained six months in a city. The mechanisms whirled and the text and blackened images passed on the electronic scroll. I felt like a character in a cold war spy novel, even though the papers were everyday information. Revelations hiding in clear sight. One of the reels was labeled incorrectly and I ended up a decade early. A priest columnist railing against juvenile delinquency and gutter comics and the godless English. A golliwog in an ad for Rigby's Reflection Rum. A resolution passed for the playing of the national anthem at all dances. "Dublin Clerk Dead in Gas-Filled Room." "New Prohibited Area in Kenya." "European Women Kill 3 Africans." "Briton Stabbed to Death in Canal Zone." "Food Shortage in Poland." "Tenants Squat After Killea House Collapses." References to Mau Mau "clean-ups." The search was on for missing radium after a Belfast air crash. "No fixed address" again and again. A call to add prayer to the nuclear arsenal. "Fight Mouth Acid and Save Your Teeth." "Panic Grows as East German Purge Continues." In the autumn of 1961 Hurricane Debbie had hit Ireland after bringing down an airplane on the Cape Verde Islands, blowing the rooftops apart and laying waste to houses. Fourteen died. Exactly a year before my grandfather's death, a forty-thousand-ton Spanish ship, the *Mirto de la Esperanza*, taking seed potatoes to the Canary Islands, had run aground in the Foyle.

I moved forward toward 1963, the year I'd been seeking and avoiding. On May 10 a child watching the submarines at the quay fell onto the USS *Headfin*, bouncing off and disappearing into the river. A quick-thinking mariner, Victor Campau, leapt in after him and saved him. The docks were already slowly dying then, the Derry-to-Liverpool and -Heysham cargo routes closing in October. I wound my way forward to November. I tried resisting the urge to find portents of what was to come, but it seemed far too tempting, although the text remained resistant. "Wanted Button-Holer." A performance by the Vampires Showband. Much talk of bazaars and the letting of lands. When tragedy occurred, it appeared deceptively innocent. A thirteen-year-old Boy Scout, searching for a seagull's nest, falls from the cliff face at Horn Head. I edged through the days, page by x-rayed page, through a past as dumb about its future as we are about ours. All the unread footnotes that every city accumulates and buries.

The day my grandfather Joseph died, the main story in the paper was the dire weather: "80 MPH Gale Gusts Hit North-West" and the "worst flooding for 60 years" in the Glenties, Donegal. Further into the issue, "Honour Springtown Camp Pledge, Corporation Is Told." Further again, "Powder Trap Laid for . . . Thief." There was an opinion piece on "Irish Saints on the Continent"—chiefly Cataldus, the miracle worker. An ad for Bushmills: "That's the Irish for you." That evening the Odeon was showing *Blood Money* and *Madame*. The ABC was showing the Miss Marple mystery *Murder at the Gallop*, the *Western Guns of Wyoming*, the Sinatra comedy *Come Blow Your Horn*, and *Night of the Prowler*. The City went with *Reprieve*, "the most startling true story ever filmed." The following night—a night Joseph would not live to see—the Miami Showband would be playing ("dancing 8–12"). They were twelve years away from being murdered, massacred by members of the Ulster Defence Regiment and the Ulster Volunteer Force, the most innocuous advert seen back through the dark prism of knowledge of what was to come. I wondered whether Joseph had read the paper earlier in the day, propping up the bar perhaps; if he felt anything different in the air, anything of unusual significance, any portent of what was to follow. The sad thing was that none of it was preordained. Any number of things could have happened differently. I pressed the Forward button and the paper sped through sports sections and classifieds and then petered out into the blinding white screen between editions.

With the high tide, the river spills over onto the land. Flood warnings go out too late. People are still queuing at the U.S. military base, next to a ceremonial guard and a mini Stars and Stripes, to sign a book of condolence for John F. Kennedy. The sailors go to Mass in their uniforms. Lyndon B. Johnson is already president, sworn in on Air Force One, next to a stunned Jackie Kennedy in a pink Chanel outfit stained with her husband's blood. There's a disconcerting note of small-town pride in the paper: "The news of the assassination at Dallas in Texas was flashed to the United States naval station at Clooney Road at 6:50 on Friday evening, about half an hour before it was heard on television. Londonderry probably being the first place in the United Kingdom to have heard the news. The Londonderry US naval station is the link through which Service and diplomatic messages to and from Western Europe are channeled. The flag at the US Naval Base was lowered to half-mast and will remain so for thirty days." A bakery and flour mill closed until twelve noon in honor. JFK is already ascending to sainthood, a millenarian one perhaps, given how close the Cuban crisis had taken us to the apocalypse.

The paper tells other stories. Chess leagues and sheep grading and dances and amateur boxing. The Sophia Loren film *Boccaccio '70* had been banned from Derry by a single nationalist vote. Men were apprehended taking scrap metal from the river's edge. The city's shipping traffic was decreasing. "Bring the children along to see Santa Claus in the enchanted forest" on the third floor of Austins. "Tennent's lager makes a thirst worthwhile."

The storm dominated: 87-mile-per-hour winds and "driving heavy rain" felled a ten-ton, forty-five-foot-high scaffolding at a zebra crossing on Guildhall Place, bringing telephone wires and a thirty-foot iron lamppost crashing down with it. At the site of the burned-out embassy (the "smart ballroom for smart people"), three workers were huddled and only narrowly survived, two dodging the collapsing structures and the third crawling out of an excavation trench, miraculously unhurt.

Then, in a small box column—smaller than those for butcher's ads or liturgical formalities—"Foyle Drowning Tragedy: Thirty-nine years old Joseph Anderson of 128 Springtown camp, Londonderry, was drowned in the river Foyle at Derry on Friday night . . ." The unionist paper, *The Londonderry Sentinel*, offered a fraction more detail. Every word seemed stricken with weight, and yet it would have been passed over in a cursory manner by almost all who read it. "When he was seen in the river, a life-belt was thrown to him but he was unable to grab it and went under. He was brought from the water near the Guildhall a short time later by a RUC Constable and a Harbour Policeman. An inquest will be held."

Drownings are romanticized in folklore, just as much as they are feared in life. Of the floating, singing Ophelia in the Millais painting, "Her clothes spread wide, / And, mermaid-like, awhile they bore her up," before they dragged her under. The corpse is only beautiful from far away. There is no desperate thrashing, no last gasp or reaching for the light, no sense that a person can die from an accident as surely as from a grand tragedy. No bloated, unidentified bodies washing up.

Thirty-nine, he was. Strange to think of being older than your parents or grandparents ever were. How would that work in the afterlife? How would that work in this life?

45 RPM, Single, Mono (Electrola, 1962)

There are worlds where Joseph caught a wound to the head and ended in a French ditch; where he died in childbirth, as many had then; where any of the links and accidents, which led from the birth of the universe to these words, turned out differently.

One night Joseph steps onto the bus, a Green Massey marked 151, bound for Springtown. He fumbles from his pocket a crumpled return ticket or the coins to buy a single. He's tired or he's skint or the pub threw him out, or he just wants to get back to see his family or to sleep it off. The weather is rough and he takes a seat next to the window, the lights of the city multiplied by the raindrops on the pane. And I'm writing this half a century later thinking, "Stay on board, stay silent, put your head against the window and dry off; just stay on board and get home to your wife and your wee ones." But he doesn't. He never does. Instead he starts singing, and singing in German.

Drunks are sentimentalists, and sentimentalists—however charming—deal in the past and future at the cost of the present. Songs, in Derry, were often their medium.

They sang on the buses. Young lads. Scottish songs. Musicals. Rock 'n' roll. Wannabe crooners. They are laughing and joking and giving each other shit. Joseph was older.

Huge matters of offense can come down to tone. Perhaps my grandfather swaggered down the aisle to the back seat, knocking against the rows, and took one look at his fellow travelers, sat in a swaying throne, and began an embittered provocation, the German anthem "Deutschland Über Alles" or the Nazi "Horst Wessel Song." Maybe it was innocent or a botched joke, a cabaret turn of "Puppenhochzeit" or "Seeräuberjenny." "You'll Never Walk Alone" was number one in the charts. There was something musical, theatrical, in the air. Perhaps he had leaned his head against the vibrating window, a streetlight reflection of his face like a doppelgänger next to him, and sang, without even consciously realizing it, "Schön Ist Die Nacht" or "Lili Marlene," with genuine nostalgia for someone he had once loved and lost, in an age where *goodbye* meant goodbye for eternity. What song it was goes untold.

My father remembered two particular things about his father. He "always had his head in a book" and his favorite song, which he sang over and over, was "Where Have All the Flowers Gone?" Pete Seeger's folk song reflecting on those who never came back from the war. Joseph had come back when others he'd known hadn't, but what good had it done? Perhaps he hadn't really come back at all from his experiences, his failures—not fully.

Something made me check back through the records. I vaguely knew the Seeger song. It must have come out in the mid-fifties, late fifties at a push. Then I noticed a German version, by Marlene Dietrich, released the year before Joseph would die. Its name "Sag mir, wo die Blumen sind." Single. B-side "Die Welt war jung" ("The world was young"). A radio in an Irish town, at the edge of Europe, tuned to Berlin. Perhaps that was it. Perhaps that was the song he sung.

Joseph sings in German, and a man stands and confronts him, and he continues to sing. It is not yet two decades since the war. Feelings still resonate. Troops are still in the city. War wounds reanimate in the winter cold, the broken bone, the bullet or shrapnel never removed. The man returns to his seat, but just as he is about to sit down, he straightens up again and walks to the driver's cabin. Joseph Henry is still singing, a fraction louder perhaps, intentionally or obliviously; it no longer matters. The bus slows, a glance in the mirror, and the bus stops. Words are exchanged. "Get this fucker off the bus" is one line remembered. A scuffle ensues. Joseph is escorted off and onto the road, still within town. The bus leaves toward a home to which, without knowing it, Joseph will never return. He is almost blind drunk. Half-seas over, as the old saying goes. He watches the lights of the bus disappear, then maybe he curses and staggers off toward somewhere. Perhaps he is still singing as he staggers off the edge.

There are other worlds. Worlds where he did not sing, or sang another tune. Where the offended man did not rise. Where the bus did not stop. Where the earth did not rotate. Where the things undone could be put together again. Where he is still alive and the echoes are all different.

Joseph looked like Tony Curtis, Needles always said. The spitting image, if he'd cured that curl in his hair that most of his descendants still have. He always had his head in a book, it was agreed. Maybe all those old classics that I had consumed like oxygen as a boy, which had directed my life toward writing, for good and ill—*Kidnapped, Journey to the Center of the Earth, Around the World in Eighty Days, One Thousand and One Nights*—were his. He had a swagger in his step. He carried a toothbrush at all times in his back pocket, Needles remembered with a smile. And he had green eyes, she said, not blue, like others claimed.

Bottle Top

My father would share his childhood memories, or lack thereof, only once he'd had a drink or, rather, lots to drink. His recollections were almost all of the outside. There were almost none, he claimed with only a degree of sadness, of the inside of the homes they'd made in the abandoned military camp. Da remembered the actual interior with ragged curtains pulled as partitions, between the two or three families in each hut, but what took place there was not significant enough to burn into his mind, or was too significant to retain. He remembered being bathed outside with his siblings in a tin bath, with the water heated in a blackened kettle over a fire. Ma teased him. "Tell them what your mum used in place of a cot?"

He tutted. "Would you give it a rest?"

"She used to put them in different shelves in a chest of drawers."

My father laughed. "Happiest years of my life."

On occasions, I would listen to my father and an uncle from Cork exchange notes over their relative poverties, like the "Four Yorkshiremen" sketch, but the stories that stayed in the mind weren't the deprivations so much as the small details: an admission, for instance, that a favorite children's television show was *The Clangers*, but how it would be watched in silence through strangers' living room windows.

There is the city and there is the environment. There are demarcation lines, boundaries of what they once called—with iron in their irony—the Liberties. Except this is known to be false. The city is not apart from the environment. It is an environment and its overlap with that which surrounds it, its reliance, the symbiosis, is always there, fluctuating like tides on the land. I thought of my parents as intrinsically city folk, urbane, cosmopolitan. Only later did I realize they had lived in the overlap, the edge lands, the shifting borders between urban and rural. The places called liminal, as if clear gateways and transitions still existed. And they, in different but related ways, had been pushed out there.

To speak of Springtown Camp is to speak of the ghost of a ghost. Where it once stood is now an industrial estate, the sort of characterless place where only the obliged go, to eyeless warehouses with names like Tradeforce and Budget Energy and Möbius-strip roads, empty enough to be used as a training space for those who'd never sat in a driver's seat before. No one else visits these roads, bar delivery vans and disgruntled workers, and even they are a rare sight out in the open. The greenery is immaculately maintained. Springtown's afterlife, physically at least, is a limbo. Its past lives exist now in memory, paper, and film.

It was built, the story goes, before the official U.S. entry into the war, as an American military base (others were scattered around the city at Creevagh, Lisahally, and Holcomb, the last taking over the mansion Beech Hill). It had long Nissen huts of corrugated tin for the troops to bunk in. There was a barbershop, a laundromat, a sick bay, and a cinema. The library stocked Zane Grey westerns and Dashiell Hammett pulp novels, maybe Pearl Buck and a Hemingway or two. There were pinups above beds, some real, some fantasy, hometown girls and Hollywood icons in suggestive poses. The canteen had a soda fountain and a milkshake machine. You could get American beer and genuine Coca-Cola. They'd play cards for matchsticks, checkers, chess, acey-deucey, bitch about the omnipresent East Atlantic rain. Paths on the parade ground led to, and encircled, a raised U.S. flag with forty-eight stars (Alaska and Hawaii would follow later). The noise of synchronized boots and "The Battle Hymn of the Republic" would trace the paths in sound waves. They were here to save the locals, first from the Nazis, second from themselves.

They had marched off their ships, from Hoboken, Brightmoor, Metairie, and into a world where priests organized the official entertainment. They trod carefully, initially. Local girls would be invited for tea dances and glee clubs. The Church, knowing that absolute power was arbitrary, forbade riding buses to dances, but the dances themselves, though immoral, were permitted as a necessary evil. They knew betterment when they saw it. The dreaded military police would drive around in jeeps, patrolling for commotions and misadventures. The mail back home was censored. Words, places, names, and plans lost behind those redacted blocks of ink. When they left, many with local wives, they took their machinery with them, the loudspeakers and projectors and generators, and left the camp as an empty carapace, waiting to be filled.

Springtown was beyond the pale. The corporation, as the council was known then, offered them little, as it was dominated by rich unionists and had gerrymandered the vote to keep it that way. The families were forced out beyond the official city boundaries, where the distasteful things that made the city function were located—rubbish dumps, the slaughterhouse, soap boilers, charcoal burners, saltworks, tanners, the hanging tree. Rendered nameless by history, the only woman I came across who had been executed in Derry (outside of the Troubles) was burned alive as a witch outside the city walls on what is now Bishop Street Outer. The details did not state if she'd undergone a trial by drowning, in which if you float, you burn, but burn her they did. Her child had inexplicably died, in what would probably now be diagnosed as cot death, and she followed, undocumented, exiting a cruel world. The authorities pushed their crimes, their guilty secrets, outside and nursed their myths within.

The families moved in, climbing through the fences, in the summer of 1946. Hitler was still regarded as missing. Traitors were still being executed; the wheelchair-using former prime minister of the Slovak Republic, Vojtech "Béla" Tuka, was hanged. The suddenly aged former prime minister of Hungary, Döme Sztójay, was tied to a wooden post in front of sandbags in the courtyard of the Academy of Music of Budapest and riddled with bullets. Rioting in India killed ten thousand people in a single day. On August 22 a column of families moving into the 302 rusting arcs of tin was understandably subsumed. A footnote in a local paper. Yet everywhere is local.

Everything was recycled back then. There was no scrap. Rubbish was unlucky. Only objects cursed were thrown away. Anything that could not be put to use was remarkable in itself and was avoided. It's hard to imagine now, so deeply immersed in a culture of convenience and disposability, that things were retained and endlessly repaired. In photographs, taken by visitors, the camp looks one hundred years older than it was. Isosceles of washing lines. A bonfire. A pet goat. A rag-and-bone man, whose very existence was predicated on reinvigorating broken things.

You choose what to remember to some extent, at least until trauma. And times of stability, even when you're near destitute, might seem like a golden age before uncertainty comes. My father remembered pulling his coat over his head trying to catch encircling bats at twilight, to inspect them or try to keep them as pets. He remembered continual walks over Sheriff's Mountain, exploring the woods, playing "Last of the Mohicans" in the oaks and pines, climbing up onto the ramparts of Grianán, the "rocky place," playing blissfully alone as boys, with a view of granite mountains and four counties of Ireland on a clear day, where chieftains had earlier stood and divided the island between them—the terrible contingencies of power that still reach us, regardless of whether we know or not.

From behind the Collon Bar, my father collected discarded bottle tops as a boy, because of the colors and designs. A burn ran past the rear of the building, all the way from Bridge End to Pennyburn, named after the amount once paid to cross the toll bridge. The stream had, at one stage, built up enough force to power a watermill, but had died down by my father's youth. It passed, within sight of the camp, the remains of an old railway bridge. The boys, aged eight or nine, would dam the burn in the summer to create a small lake. They'd dive in or spend hours catching little fish, hypnotizing them by tickling their bellies, then flinging them onto dry land. My father swam in it from the age of three. "Nobody drowned." It is mostly underground now, emerging in sputters from a pipe into the river.

The place I had gone underground as a boy was the burn that my father and his friends had swum in, redirected and driven underground, flowing every second of every day since into the Foyle, below unwitting roads and buildings and people.

"Was it difficult there?" I asked. "Springtown? As a place to live?"

"You didn't know any better. It was a continual adventure, being out at the edge of the city and the beginning of the wilderness. Why would you go home?"

Da always avoided the word *I*, using *we* and *you* instead. I couldn't tell if it was an act of including or distancing. I was a little skeptical of my father's idealism, seeing it as too romantic, celebrating a bygone era of solidarity when no one had a pot to piss in. Yet it was hard to remain cynical. Da told me a story that when his uncle had dropped dead and they had no options, his neighbors had said, "Put him in with our relatives." That was real solidarity. No performance. No bullshit. That was the loss he lamented.

As my father and his friends scrambled around hills they'd conquered, the radiographer's van would pull into Springtown, to x-ray the lungs of the children in the camp during breakouts of TB, as much to protect the city populace from infection down the line. It was a slum essentially, known to people in town as "Greenhell" or "Hutland." "Tintown" lay nearby. The authorities sent out a party to examine the site: 304 huts in various states of disrepair, 90 percent of them corrugated tin, 10 percent wooden. Sending in the police to clear them was deemed counterproductive, so instead they left it as it was and posted out rent books, charging them to squat. Five shillings a week was due up front, per hut. There was one door per hut, and though they were potentially death traps in the event of a fire (especially given the use of braziers indoors), it was the damp and cold that carried off the infants who died there, as well as being surrounded by swampy land full of miasmas. Eventually stoves were added for heat. Outside there was a toilet and tap for two hundred people, a firepit, a coal house, and a sink they referred to as the "jaw box," as people would gather round it, chatting as they washed. The corporation made slight improvements, but no attempt to rehouse them. It did not go unnoticed, time and again, that single people and childless couples of Protestant backgrounds were getting houses elsewhere. Questions raised at council meetings were greeted with silence. When the mothers of the camp spoke up from the public gallery, the RUC were called in. Occasionally there would be a heartwarming story, like when the Hollywood star Jane Russell jetted in and back to the United States with a newly adopted Springtown son. These were largely distractions.

The camp went on for twenty years, lasting well past "You never had it so good" and well into the days of Swinging London. Alienation brings conspiratorial thinking. So, too, do conspiracies. A protest march of two hundred residents dressed in their Sunday best, or the best they could muster, had signs reading, "We Are Nobody's Baby," "No Future in Tin," "Springtown— Derry's Little Rock," "I'm Good Enough to Serve in the Army but Not Good Enough to Have a Home for My Children." They joined up with other civil rights marchers and protesters and the stream became a torrent. Though there was no single origin for the Troubles that followed, this was certainly one early tributary, especially when it was blocked. They tied their struggle to the black civil rights movement under Martin Luther King, borrowing the same tactics, singing the same songs. In response, all hell was unleashed on them. "We were born into an unjust system; we are not prepared to grow old in it," declared the activist Bernadette Devlin, elected an MP at twenty-one.

She was right. Many didn't grow old. Justice would be sought before peace. For a long time, neither would exist.

The study light glowed on the window, replicating itself off on a bend into infinity. The photographs show a landscape that would have been unrecognizable today. A sepia army base on a flat plain of scrub, with mountains that could just as well be the Atlas or the Caucasus in the distance. Dirty-faced children and proud adults, posing for perhaps their first or last portraits. I flicked through the records until a spark of recognition came with their names. Margaret and Joseph H. Their hut had been allocated an address, 128 Springtown Camp. Next door, or perhaps next to them in the same hut, were my father's cousins, the Scanlans and the McBrides. Sheets hung between them for privacy. In the next entry, Margaret and Joseph H. are listed again. By the 1964 register, it's just Margaret.

She was still there in '67, with her brother James staying with them. By that stage, the camp was in collapse. Many families had finally been evacuated elsewhere. The streetlights had died one by one, and the roads were riven with deep potholes. The rent nevertheless increased. Looking at the photos, I thought of the old military bases at Dunree and the ghost towns farther south that we'd explored as teenagers, attracted to the captured time in decaying rooms. The attraction lay partly in the fact that you got to leave at the end of the day. Romance exists only with the prospect, or certainty, of escape.

The huts were green and black, with gray walls inside. The windows were small. The floor was stone. Those—the vast majority—in the tin huts envied those in huts of felt and wood, given the rust, though the wood, too, would eventually rot in the rain-sodden climate. The rain fell metallic on the dome, running down the ridges. Panels would blow off in storms. Shocks from deteriorating wires were not uncommon. Wind and rodents, nocturnally flitting at the corner of vision, made it through corroded holes that would be closed off with whatever was at hand. There was a bus stop at the gate and a phone box beside it. People would call it at prearranged times.

The children, right down to the youngest, were born in the huts. They were bathed in a tin bucket. There was no hot running water or washing machine, so women spent interminable hours constantly cleaning, while their husbands absented themselves under the guise of seeking work. Six of my father's siblings were in nappies at more or less the same time, given the twins and the rapidity of their births. A child every year for a decade was not uncommon, happening on both sides of his family. There were always bands of children hanging around, but they'd soon be scattered away like pigeons or would venture off themselves into the landscape. The deprivations for my father were balanced by access to a rough pastoral arcadia, and doubtless his later occupation as a gardener sprang from his immersion in nature then. Da learned a love of the earth the hard way. They raided orchards and watched weather fronts coming in over the land from the ocean, being the first in Europe at times to see them. All the fallow fields were named after now-forgotten owners. There was even a Priest's Lane, where a minister had once been hanged. You still found Mass rocks in hidden places around Donegal, where priests surreptitiously celebrated the Eucharist on tables of natural stone when banned at the point of death from doing so.

Home was grim then, but it's easy to forget it came as a desperate temporary measure for those dwelling there. Slums are not an absence of planning, but rather an improvisation of it by citizens when the authorities have abdicated responsibility. They were hated and looked down on, naturally, because they

reminded people of this failure. Rather than face the guilt behind it and those who profited from the status quo, it was easier
to blame those who barely scratched out a living in the consequences. Their very existence and their visibility were affronts.
You did well not to make people feel guilty.

Handkerchief (Bloodstained)

"What did you do when you were young?" I asked my father.

"We threw stones at the police. Then petrol bombs."

"What about when you were really young?"

"That was when we were really young."

The day before Bloody Sunday, an army sniper shot two young men huddled on the corner of Abbey Street, one in the shoulder and the other in the back. My father was there, right next to them. He was fourteen and was cornered, too, and thought, "This is it," but it wasn't. Not for him. Not yet.

At two o'clock, twenty thousand people marched from Creggan to the city center in protest against internment without trial and non-jury Diplock courts, demanding a return to the rule of law. They reached the army barricades at William Street. A water cannon with purple dye was employed at the burned-out cinema. Plumes of CS gas emerged from canisters, kicked back to army lines. Barricades of burned-out cars at St. Columb's Wells. Rolls of barbed wire. The Parachute Regiment, with their maroon berets, badges with wings—the best of the best—who marched to "Ride of the Valkyries" and "Pomp and Circumstance" from their base in the Presbyterian church, were let loose on the protesters and bystanders. The shootings began at four. They lasted half an hour. They've lasted more than forty years. A sixteen-year-old boy was the first. He was standing in the courtyard at Rossville Flats, laughing at the sight of a running priest. He suddenly keeled over. The priest, the future Bishop Daly, knelt over him. "Am I going to die?" "No," the priest replied and gave him the last rites. The priest will be filmed leading the way for the men, who look like they've come from a greyhound race, only dazed, carrying the sheer weight of a dying boy, waving a bloodstained handkerchief. A young man was shot in the spine crawling along the ground at Rossville Flats. A young man cried, "I'm hit," dashing from the flats to rubble. A middle-aged father waved a white handkerchief on his way to help a screaming injured man lying on the Fahan Street steps. His last words were "Don't shoot," before the bullet entered his eye. A young man was executed on the ground of Glenfada Park. A young man was shot there in the stomach; a girl from the Knights of Malta trying to help him was shot at. Fourteen dead in all. Two young men ran for the doors of the flats together: one made it and turned to find the other was not there. Fourteen dead. The coroner would recall how the dead had Sunday dinners undigested in their stomachs at their autopsies.

The killings occurred in a meticulous vertical spread from the bottom of the now-demolished Rossville Flats along a four-foot rubble barricade across Rossville Street, to the alleys turned kill zones of Glenfada Park. "We've had a pretty good bloodbath here this evening," a republican spying device in the army base recorded. The aim was shock and awe. To knock the wind out of the civil rights and civil disobedience movement. To make an example of "ringleaders"—mass murder on the streets of a British city. In the old days they'd do it with dead bodies in public places. There was the local case of Brisland, a peasant who talked too loudly about making a stand against landlords and the authorities. His body was hung in a gibbet at the quay, having "brought on his destruction by his own folly." Little had changed.

My father, and boys like him, reeling, were lucky to return home. The world before that event was still visible, just hours or days in the past, but it was gone forever.

PART THREE

Ma's Folks

Lighthouse Bulb

A quarter mile off the coast of Moville, a fishing village north of Derry along the river and over the border, there is a pile lighthouse forty-three feet high on stilts. Its lights can be seen for four miles. It's unmanned and automated now, but back then a lighthouse keeper would row out at night and spend the hours, often battered by the elements, in the watch room.

The last time I saw my maternal grandfather, Anthony, he was confined to a sallow box room that had the feel of a renovated bunker. There was a bed with white plastic handrails, a flat-screen television permanently tuned to football, and a toilet annex. From the windows, nothing but a view of a wooden fence, a clothesline, angles of telegraph wires. It was a waiting room, not uncomfortable or ill equipped, for the afterlife. *Death and the Miser* double-glazed.

The river was now treated as just a backdrop to the city, but

Anthony had known it when it was a living, dangerous thing, and he was one of the few who knew that it quietly remained that way.

Bedridden, he still loomed large, despite hitting eighty. Generations of hard-living Donegal peasants had put granite in his DNA. Lantern-jawed. Barrel-chested. He had hands like shovels and commanded his bed like a throne, the remote control his scepter. The weather used to perpetuate from this place: storms would formulate above my grandfather's house and radiate outward, great cumulonimbus towers, an Ian Paisley–esque voice that boomed now only over telephone lines. His power dissipated as he got older and his children, the focus of his force, became parents themselves.

It felt like he was already mid-monologue when I arrived. I sat by the foot of his bed and let him talk. His stories were long and tangential. They very often had no conclusion and no intentional punch line or moral. Anthony was talking for the journey, not the destination. At times he would delve into riveting tales of seafaring, but they seemed entirely arbitrary; you could never be sure what direction he would veer off into. He had no capacity for editing or any desire for it. He would go on for extended passages, beating against a headwind by zigzags, then reveal some fleeting, utterly gripping secret and just move on. If you interrupted the flow, he'd become irritated. When I'd inquire about the origins of a particular word he'd said— "the hounds" of the mast, for instance—he'd pause, not at all for comic effect, before thundering, "Well, how the fuck do I know?" and then resume his rambling stream of consciousness.

He told his stories simply because he was still here to tell them, unlike so many he'd known. The BBC had been tipped off that he could spin a good yarn alongside his oldest friend, an Italian ice-cream-making patriarch called Sonny Fiorentini, whose father had moved over in 1912. The reporters had come from London to interview my grandfather about his days smuggling on the Foyle during the Second World War, from the Free State to the North. After a day's recording, they found they couldn't edit any of his lengthy spiels into coherence. He had a natural aversion to the sound bite. You were not hooked by what he said so much as pummeled by it, witnessing lucid moments whizz by.

Under cover of darkness, Anthony often sailed across the invisible border on the river out to the massive American naval vessels moored there. He'd shout code words to sentries to prevent them from firing on him and ask them to get the canteen officer, knowing that the way to men's wallets was through their bellies. "You'd have boys hanging out of the portholes, shouting requests." They'd be sleeping or up playing cards. There was a game called able whackets, where if you lost you got hit with a knotted cloth. Anything to pass the time. Sometimes they'd shout down requests for tartan paint or glass hammers, acting smart, but they were always hankering after something real. Anthony and crew would hoist up crates of eggs, precious after long stretches at sea with only egg powder. He'd supply chickens, butter, fresh cream cheese, porridge, vegetables, and lamb. In return there'd be lowered cigarettes, always cigarettes, Camels and Lucky Strike, lots of tea (chests of it), dollars and pounds, chocolate bars (the Americans called them "chicken bait" in derogatory reference to local girls), silk stockings, cosmetics, chewing gum, even comic books. My grandfather talked *at* the interviewer, bombarding the poor sap for three or four hours. It never made it to broadcast and was presumably filed away in a library in the depths of the Corporation; perhaps it lurks there still, or was taped over, joining the lost world beneath other recordings.

History multiplies if you follow leads into the undergrowth. Who were the individuals he was interacting with, these figures in passing? The war brought a beguiling number of sailors from all over the planet to this backwater. Men from the occupied Lowlands, boys from the landlocked forests of Alberta. New Jersey, Louisville, Gdańsk, Visakhapatnam, Honningsvåg. There were even ships full of Chinese sailors who found themselves on the other side of the planet, thousands of miles from Nanjing and Shanghai and Marco Polo Bridge. They kept to themselves, Anthony remembered. I wondered what they made of this place, from one edge of the world to another. Anthony didn't query why—the grand scheme of things—or contemplate that the goods he hoisted upward, ascending onto the decks, might be the basis of a last supper for some of those sailors.

Having read and reread books like *Moonfleet* as a boy, I was excited to find out about my grandfather's smuggling days. It was not, however, respected at the time. The authorities in the Republic frowned on it, administratively and personally. It was not just a question of taking chocolate or cigarettes or dairy or meat from the South to the North. It was not about lost revenue. It was a point of pride. And other things—guns and ammunition for other purposes and later use—could be smuggled too. The local guards would curse Anthony as he passed, saying they knew what he was doing and would soon snare him, "the bastard," but they couldn't, even standing on the shore, because Lough Foyle was legally British waters.

The smugglers were nevertheless looked on with envy and spite. It was thought they should do something useful, like pilot boats in through the channel, but some of them already did and were simply moonlighting. The market would always be there, just as laundered-fuel smuggling now dominates the borderlands. Supply and demand. It was not pretty or romantic at all. It meant the keeping of unforgiving hours, and sometimes unsavory activity and the possibility of sudden violence. Anthony recalled that as they made their way back from one of the ships, a sociopath on one of the decks started firing at them. Anthony was convinced he intended to do them great harm and missed only because of the sea conditions at the time, the rocking of the boat affecting his aim. He never found out who it was or why he fired.

Smuggling on the land was often a dirty business. There was less room for chivalry or sea fevers, especially at border crossings where the officials, some of them "iron arses," couldn't easily be bribed. Goods were therefore placed inside prams beneath swaddling babies, but even these were soon checked. I had heard of a fake funeral passing over the border with a coffin filled with bootlegged items. Another time a horse carcass, allowed to ripen for a few days so that closer inspection would be avoided, was taken over in a cart, its rib cage filled with whiskey bottles.

Accepting the existence of smuggling was one thing. Acceding to it was another. The authorities and rival sailors baptized them "bum-boat men," denying them the legend of the word *smuggler*. They were the bottom-feeders, the groundfish in the demersal zone, of the sailing world. You had to be a canny operator, though. The guards couldn't catch Anthony with his black-market goods because he knew the river intimately. He knew secret caves and coves around Shrove. He knew sandbanks and times of day when the tide would ebb and you could literally stand on ephemeral dry land, surrounded by the river. Shell Island. The Slob. The Tons. There was one notorious for wrecking ships, before permanent lighthouses. Inexplicable lights and sounds were witnessed there. It was said to be the dwelling place of the Celtic sea god Manannán mac Lir, who, when offended, dragged ships into the depths. They didn't offer sacrifices or throw votives into the river to appease the vengeful deity. They only did this, it seems, in bodies of standing water like lakes or ponds. The river gods, always moving, protean, could not be placated with gifts or bribes. These were casually swept into the sea and could not be retrieved in times of need, like pennies in a fountain could.

Anthony struck a deal with the lighthouse keeper to store his goods there, palming him off with bounty. As the police racked their brains for his hiding places, they were there all along, for all to see, with a flashing light on top, mocking them across the water from the entire town.

I thought of those nighttime journeys out to the ships. Where they hid their boats. How they covered their tracks. What risks they took. Equally, though, were thoughts of what they had literally experienced. The weather at night, the fall of moonlight or darkness across the water, the sound of the waves, of anchors dropping, the sounds that came from the ships as they cautiously approached. Along the shore and in the quays, the familiar sound of objects dangling from the boats, clanking like bells when the wind stirred. Sounds that might alert and sounds that might betray.

During the war, the closer to the city you went, the more ships had amassed, until they were legion. It was said, maybe apocryphally, that you could cross the river by stepping from deck to deck. The naval base was encircled by silver barrage balloons, helium airships that rose one hundred feet off the ground, attached to steel cables that created a forest of metal that would shear off the wings of any low-flying enemy aircraft. For those old enough to remember, they would have set off recollections of the much-feared German zeppelins during the Great War. Now they were protective angels rather than avenging ones.

There were air-raid shelters, not just in underground bunkers, but overground. They had no windows and seemed more like concrete tombs. Brutalist machines for dying in. No one would actually die in them, at least not here. More hazardous were the large open-water tanks erected to provide water for the expected incendiary bombings, in which at least one child was drowned, mucking around. Downstream was the much larger menace, so colossal it suggested the infinite. The gate to the ocean expanses, sublime and monotonous and treacherous. Corvettes, sloops, destroyers sailed into the unknown and, in numerous cases, the next life.

Even the way I thought of this scene is predicated on what followed, and not just emotionally. When I pictured all this, I did so from a bird's-eye view, the consequence of growing up with airborne photographs, soaring films shot from helicopters, digital maps. It was a view that would not instinctively have occurred to my grandfather, given that in those days flight was rare and a leap of the imagination. Anthony's view was sea level, sometimes within the waves. The development of technology has subtly, almost unnoticeably, changed the way the world and the past are viewed. Memories and imaginations are edited from without. There were many hundreds of men on those ships, most of them asleep or near sleep when my grandfather visited. There must have been some who were glad to be there in the relative sanctuary of the Foyle, and others who cursed the place; some who were itching to fight, and others terrified but hiding their fear. All counting the days. They must have dreamt too. Of home, the past, the future. A degree of fiction seems inevitable in considering them. Rows of men in rows of beds, in rows of rooms in rows of ships out on that now-empty river.

In the daytime the scene would have been different. There were men painting ships on swinging rope platforms. Loading depth charges onto cranes. Idle banter in barbershops and laundromats, on a steamboat that took them back and forth across the river, bitching about Irish food, celebrating the girls and the drink. Radio chatter in code swam like unseen spirits above their heads. There was life and color beyond the monochrome of photographs.

Ill blows the wind that profits no one, and "the Emergency" was one such time. That's what my grandfather, and others like him, called a war that had claimed more than sixty million lives. I used to think it a disrespectful, delusional term, but I no longer do. The war had many names (the Great Patriotic War in Russia, the Phony War for the first year in the West, the Continuation War in Finland, the Second Sino-Japanese War in China, and so on), and its boundaries appear clear only in hindsight, if even now. Did it begin on the Polish border? Or the Czech? Did it begin in besieged Madrid? Manchuria? Versailles? The Belgian border? Sarajevo? Braunau am Inn? Or much earlier and from many sources? "The Emergency" suggests something undefined by singular meaning or limits. At the time it was entirely unclear how it would all pan out, especially early in the conflict. The near future would have seemed a place of immense threat. At the same time there was a distance, however illusory, in Derry. The deaths are barely imaginable now. A death on average every three seconds; twenty-five thousand every day, for six years, but for the moment they happened in places with names in other languages. The destruction occurred just over the horizon. Those boys sailed off or flew away toward it.

Speculations were rife, not just when an invasion force might set off for mainland Europe but, especially in the early years, when an invasion force might land in Ireland. German spies were a continual talking point, exacerbated by the fact that there were both willing collaborators and steadfast anti-fascists

in the republican movement. As it turned out, Ireland was so in-
sular and parochial as to prove almost impregnable to the Germans who parachuted in. They filed messages back to the Reich
that Irish society was maddening and their mission hopeless.
Everyone seemed to know everyone, and no one could keep
their mouth shut.

The invasion nevertheless was being planned and even had
a name, Operation Sea Lion. That it is a curiosity now is down
only to the contingencies of history. Had the Luftwaffe continued to destroy radar stations and decimate the RAF, Britain
might have folded in months, perhaps weeks. The Royal Navy
still posed a formidable threat, but without air superiority, it
would have faced a bloody, unassisted fight. Ten thousand German paratroopers were to be dropped along the south coast of
England to seize key installations and ports. Others would come
in at Romney Marsh. Once bridgeheads were established, the
Panzer armies would be brought over, and the race to outflank
the British Army would begin. Einsatzgruppen would follow
in their wake. There was a list, the Black Book it was called, of
three thousand people to be arrested immediately, interrogated,
and executed. Virginia Woolf, Paul Robeson (who'd already
left), Sigmund Freud (who'd already died), Aldous Huxley, Ber-
trand Russell, H. G. Wells, and so on. Rebecca West sent Noël
Coward (both on the list) a telegram saying, "My dear—the
people we should have been seen dead with." It's easy to laugh
now, but back then the future was, terribly, open.

The country, it was rumored, once London fell, would have
been run from Senate House. Death squads would be set up
in the capital, Bristol, Liverpool, Manchester, and Birmingham, seeking collaborators not just in Mosley's British Union
of Fascists but in the existing police and security forces. The
royal family would be en route to Canada, with the Duke of

Windsor returned from the Bahamas to reassume his regency. Resistance would take to the Highlands, the woods, the valleys. Germany would turn to the east with its plans for colossal German colonies, mass starvation of the Slavs, Moscow ceasing to exist under a huge reservoir. Rewriting Poland and Russia and the Jews out of history. No longer existing. No longer having ever existed. Berlin replaced with Germania, with a dome so vast that empty clouds would form inside it. Hitler leaned over the model city that Albert Speer had built for him like a model railway set in an attic.

The foolhardy nature of the saying "England's difficulty is Ireland's opportunity" would become apparent. An enemy of an enemy is no friend. Following Operation Fall Grün and the Nazi occupation of Ireland, beginning with a beachhead at Waterford, most Irish people would probably have fallen into line, as they did elsewhere. The topography would have aided whatever resistance was mounted. Flying columns that existed in the Anglo-Irish War and Civil War would have resumed against the occupiers and their collaborators. The likely outcome would have been low-level guerrilla warfare, with colossal reprisals against the civilian population. An authoritarian Catholic client state would probably be set up. Though he was pro-British, seeing which way the wind blew, Anthony would have changed his smuggling habits perhaps, selling to the Germans. And perhaps my father and his brothers and sisters and the generation to follow would have taken up arms against the new occupiers.

Pack of Lucky Strike Cigarettes

The peripheral nature of Derry's docks to Europe was the reason for its unlikely reinvigoration. When Europe fell, one blitzkrieg after another, the insignificant islands in the sea remained free. With the opening of U.S. Naval Operating Base Londonderry in 1942, the city became Base One Europe. Naval vessels and their men were sent out from here for patrols or attacks. They returned for repair and protection or to take stock of their losses. They even sent out war pigeons with messages from here, probably the ancestors of the birds that skittishly flapped around as they laid waste to the hangars. Derry transformed during the war. Industry, the matriarchal shirt factories, had been the first catalyst from essentially an indentured-peasant age. The war was the next. The Americans brought ideas, technology, an essential otherness that remained familiar, that suggested you could do it too. After the war there was no question of shutting the future closed again. The genie will not willingly return to the bottle.

The establishment was temporarily deposed. The loyal orders and the Church, while still throwing their weight around and not definitively uprooted, subsided somewhat. It was a reconfiguration. The old oppressions—the overbearing, life-negating tedium of it all—were briefly reprieved. Magee College was taken over by the British Navy. A secret bunker was built under the lawn in front of it. If Luftwaffe spy planes were overhead, they disguised their position by playing games of baseball on it. Talbot House became the U.S. Navy base. The country house of Beech Hill was occupied by U.S. Marines. The ammunition was stored at Fincairn Glen. A hospital was set up at Creevagh. The soldiers were housed at Beech Hill and Springtown. A thousand-foot-long timber jetty was erected on the river in six months by eight hundred Americans and two thousand locals at Lisahally. It was built from Oregon pine. It now lies in braille, an ogham script of ruins, the remaining tall posts covered in barnacles.

In the Victorian age the transatlantic telegraph was envisioned as angels walking on the ocean floor. Now messages came beneath the waves continually. Even after the war, it remained that way. The nuclear hotline from Moscow to Washington allegedly ran through the city. Benbradagh, near Dungiven, was riven with telecommunications aerials during the cold war. Derry's local saint, Columba, wrote in Latin of living at the world's edge. What had seemed a place of isolation, or at best liminality, became an advantage when the center was overthrown.

Kids stood up on window ledges to watch the U.S. Marine marching bands. Watchmen were posted on rooftops to look out for fires and spot enemy planes. American and British planes were named after girlfriends, good-luck mascots, and favorite sports teams. Nose-art on the front of aircraft became a specialty, like maiden-heads bringing fortune to ships or to ward off the evil eye of the flak-gunner's aim. It seemed almost normal to send groups of boys into the thundering sky. Second World War Carter sirens stood prominently on rooftops for those who looked up. They resembled futuristic spindles, with a surrounding wooden frame casting shadows like gallows. Testing them gave passersby the creeps, as if howling backward from some apocalyptic future.

Ships were stationed from all over the world. The flags of a multitude of countries fluttered in the wind. There were dozens of warships in the Foyle and their guides: corvettes, destroyers, and frigates. The Atlantic convoys zigzagged across the ocean to evade wolf packs of U-boats. There was a 50 percent death rate at one time. The tankers and aircraft carriers had to remain in the lough rather than in the river. Anthony remembered unnamed Indian vessels, the *Black Ranger*, and a French ship, the *Petrophault*. There was a large troopship, the *Manilla*, and he'd watch them play hockey on the deck. Once, Anthony was trawling and thought he'd unearthed a defunct copper wire that would have made their fortune to sell on the black market, until they realized it was an actual functioning transmission cable. As they held it, messages were pouring through it about the war. Swordfish planes were dispatched from Maydown to protect convoys and try to obliterate the prowling enemy subs. The camouflaged dazzle ship USS *Alexander Dallas* (DD-199) escorted the Atlantic fleet into safety. HMS *Foxglove* was the harbor guardship, years after rescuing people from the doomed SS *Hong Moh* on the White Rocks in the South China Sea. HMS *Bayntun*, HMS *Loosestrife*, HMS *Loch Dunvegan*, and other U-boat killers with their successive weapons systems (with intriguing names like hedgehog, squid, and limbo) ran out of Derry. They turned the hiding place of the sea into a tomb of water. There was a turning point in the war when the hunters became the hunted, resulting in a 75 percent chance of death on board the U-boats. They became metal coffins, and what occurred to many of them in their last instances we will never know, in this life at least. For all the legends of ghost ships, none have been seen in living memory.

Forty thousand sailors assembled in Derry; 140 escort ships. Innumerable supporting vessels with grain, coal, and timber. They accompanied convoys from the Eastern Seaboard, Iceland, Nova Scotia, Newfoundland on to the Lisbon run, and, even more dreaded, the Archangel–Murmansk route. It was a haven, or as much as anywhere could be then, perched on the continental shelf, with a long inlet that was difficult for enemy vessels to penetrate without guaranteeing their own destruction. That is not to say they were safe. When the decision came down the chain of command that the ships were to go out into or come from open seas, the sailors' lives hung in the balance. The *President Sergent* was sunk, en route south-southeast of Cape Farewell by the submarine U-624, which was in turn sunk by depth charges from a fortress aircraft. All hands lost. HMS *Black Swan*, *Scimitar*. Anthony was there as all this went on around him, like a character in the corner of a Bruegel painting.

The U.S. sailors and soldiers were the same. They came in off the ships on "liberty boats" to get pissed, have a feed, and try to get laid. Black markets grew up. In the South, because of neutrality, they took off their caps upon arrival and were free from the regime of military police zipping around Derry in jeeps. There'd be scraps, mainly between Americans and Canadians and both with the English. Rarely with the Irish.

The river was abundant with masts, like trees or spears

held in battle. And it was no bad time for fishing, given the amount of refuse that was thrown overboard the big ships and the shoals that congregated around them. There were always side effects. You lived in the side effects. The women of the shirt factories made uniforms for the boys and men who set off for war. The fabric they made ended up scorched, buried, shot through, floating in the sea. Occasionally a drowning, an accident or a suicide, would occur, ahead of history—just to prove, in the midst of overwhelming fate, that something resembling free will still existed.

The promise of safety was the real siren. Anthony recalled being out at night on a little boat, fishing with a colleague and his son. One of them spotted something up ahead, looming through the dark. A single light was held up. It looked like some kind of meteorite covered in seaweed, a floating globe with metal prongs. Anchored to the sea floor. A genuine magnetic mine. Modified ships and low-flying airplanes had electromagnets that were supposed to blow these up, but the sea was more vast than man or technology. There are fifty million munitions objects discarded in the North Sea and Baltic alone, rusting, waiting, occasionally unintentionally hauled up. Something stirred this one to the surface. After the war, my grandfather found employment on a trawler, sweeping for mines; it's exceptionally dangerous work, trying to find what others dreaded finding.

Small mysteries abounded. Insignificant, apparently, in the grand scheme of things. The ST *Leukos* vanished with eleven men on board. It was discovered only later what happened to them, in a single line of a U-boat captain's diary, having surfaced amid two ships: "I decided to give one of them a lesson with our gun." The *Ardmore* vanished with twenty-four men. The *Kerry Head*, and its twelve men, was last seen being bombed, by people on the shore. Similarly, the lightship *Isolda* was exploded under bomber fire with six men on board. The *Innisfallen*, the *Clonlara*, the *City of Waterford*, and the *City of Limerick* (the last filled with fruit) all went into the depths. The British and Irish Steam Packet Company ship the *Meath* was struck by a magnetic mine at Holyhead, sinking with seven hundred squealing animals on board. I imagined those who had dived or been thrown from their ships in the sea during the war. Those starlit last moments. The sea somehow on fire with burning oil. Some too close, some too far away. Under mute stars, they all lived their last unrecorded moments, hoping for a rescue that would never arrive. The thermoclines, agents of history, reached up toward them.

I wondered what it might be like to drown. Was there panic or release? I could not say. Some say the bodies of the drowned are found with torn muscles in their arms and shoulders, where they have been grasping out toward the light. Others say there is a serene sense of release, floating there, once the finite number of breaths in each life reaches zero.

Storm Lantern

I t is the night of April 15, 1941. Easter Tuesday. Everyone with any choice is sleeping. A cold wind is scything along the river, off Magilligan. A full moon is broken by racing clouds. Two stooped figures on board a boat. Darker silhouettes against a dark background.

"You hear that?"

"Hear what?"

"Cut off the engine . . . and the light. Now."

The engine wound down with a splutter. Anthony turned the switch slowly on the hurricane lamp, steadying it with his other hand. The only light was the spliced moon on the water. The waves sounded suddenly more pronounced.

"There . . ." His father, Dennis, pointed his finger upward. "There it is."

Anthony paused, weighing the air.

"An airplane. The Yanks, no doubt."

"That's a Jerry. Listen. You hear that engine? It's different."

Anthony stared at his father as the boat rocked.

"The Yanks and the Brits have a constant drone. You hear that? It's whirring."

His father had been in the British Army for many years. He knew.

"Christ, you're right. Where is it?"

They followed the sound echoing around the dome of the night sky. Due north, by any reckoning. It was following the coastline or the river, which meant there was one place it was bound.

"You see anything?"

"Not yet."

The clouds seemed to accelerate.

"Maybe it's nothing. Could just be passing. We're too far away for—"

And then suddenly the whirring became noticeably louder. They moved to the stern of the boat, bracing themselves at the gunwale, without taking their eyes from the skies.

"It's getting close. We should be able to see it. We should see its lights."

"There." Dennis pointed upward.

There were no lights, but it was there. A veil slowly consuming the moonlit clouds. It seemed to be descending and growing like black space, like a void even in the night. Before they knew it, the shape was roaring toward them, so low that they could look up, holding on to their hats as gusts rippled on the waves, and see the outlined crosses, the *Balkenkreuz*, on its wings. It bellowed past them and disappeared into a bank of clouds.

Anthony thought for a moment he had seen faces at the windscreen. Perhaps they had seen their faces. He would later wonder if he'd imagined it.

"It's heading towards the city."

"It's trying to."

They sat in the dark and waited. They may have blessed themselves, Anthony mimicking his father. And the seconds stretched.

The light reached them before the sound.

During the blackout the city tried to hide, but the plane followed the river, which betrayed the city and led them to it. Belfast was already burning. Harland and Wolff shipyards bombed. Workers' housing blitzed. There weren't many shelters for people. They protected the statue of Carson at Stormont, though.

Magnetic submarine mines floated down on parachutes. The aim was to land them in the Foyle, where they'd lie dormant until a ship passed overhead and would suddenly attach themselves to the metal and then . . . well, goodnight, Irene. It was a windy night, though, so two blew off course, onto the land. One seemed to have been a dud, or its fall was cushioned by the sandpit that it dropped into at Collon Terrace. Those people didn't know how lucky they were until later. The other landed right on a group of houses in Messines Park. The houses aren't there anymore. They are gone. Three houses with families in them. The chimney and the wall of a fourth remained, but everything else was scrap, piles of it, all caved in. Bodies covered in blood and plaster. Rescuers looked like ghosts, with the plaster dust. There was one guy who'd been blown clean over a fence, and his unaccounted-for body was found days later by a blackout officer.

They found one wee baby crying between its two dead parents in the bed. They'd pull away rubble, like digging into the ground, and they'd find beds, sofas, like they'd been under there for a hundred years. All the windows blown out in every direction. Tiles shorn off rooftops. What was once a piano lying in the crater. Strangest thing.

There was one guy that my uncle used to mention. He was blind and wore black all the time. Had shades on indoors, like Roy Orbison. He would turn up at dances with all the young ones. Sit at the side. They said he was standing up against the bedroom window, looking out, the night that bomb dropped. Last thing he ever saw.

My teacher said that the Virgin Mary had saved the church by deflecting the bomb onto the houses. It was a miracle.

A Key That No Longer Fits Any Lock

In the twenty years after the war, childhoods came and went. The place where my mother and her siblings had once lived, once grown up, once been happy, was no more. On the map, only half a century old, there are fields that are now streets, but more unusually, there are also streets that are now fields. Even Free Derry Corner is the gable wall of a vanished terrace of houses. I tried to walk in my mind the streets and alleyways and courtyards that have now vanished, to picture the vistas, to inhabit them, but the figures are faceless, the light is like that in a Giorgio de Chirico painting, unreal and filled with menacing shadows. History is discussed and decided at an inhuman scale. Yet history is really made up of the events that befall individual homes.

The area Shantallow, whose name came from the Gaelic meaning "ancient land," once had another name. A significant patch of it was called Bogs Lee. It is the site of a secondary school now and a housing estate, but in my mother's youth it was, they recount, a rural arcadia with a house, grown huge in their memories, at its center. Ma and her siblings grew up there in relatively idyllic surroundings. My da would roll his eyes when my mother told the tales of what they had and how they fell from grace ("my grandfather was the first person to have a car in Derry, a Model T Ford"), and while, no doubt, memory is deceptive, the incidental details give the tales a ring of truth. It was her grandparents' home originally, but it was large enough for all of them to live in. Ma would talk about it with a certain bruised pride that came from having lost it all through bankruptcy, and having been a young, disbelieving witness to that process. History was rewritten or simply rendered redundant; you lost your place, and certain people, certain places, were airbrushed out of existence or just faded with exposure to light.

There were no public phones in those days. Private phones were rare and precious things, but Bogs Lee had a telegraph wire connecting it like a tightrope to the switchboard. Locals and passing strangers would follow it and knock to make a call, and my grandmother Philomena, or Phyllis, as she was known, would let them use it. "They would always leave a coin, whatever the denomination, and she would always fret if they could afford it." Traveller mothers would call to the door to ask for milk for their babies and "she would never turn them away." I wondered how often they *were* turned away for this to be a sign of exceptionalism, but Phyllis earned a reputation for unassuming charity, and soon calls were being made regularly by impossibly exotic figures. To Ma, then a child, they had stepped out of fairy tales, with their red shawls and their covered faces, and the older ladies with their long silver hair. Phyllis kept money on the mantelpiece for them, and for the nuns who visited. The nuns offered a prayer in thanks. The Gypsies offered a curse on anyone who wronged her. One was as good as the other. Life was hard for the Travellers then. My father remembered, even in the sixties, families living under black canvas sheets in ditches by the roadside.

No idyll survives close scrutiny. The rainbow is easily unwoven. It was a huge house to the infant mind, but there were still five girls to one bedroom. Such was the size of the family (a typical Catholic family, at the time, of nine children) that the oldest and youngest barely knew each other, one leaving for university as the other left the maternity ward. Ma recalled mosaic tiles, reminding her of illustrations of ancient Rome that she'd seen in books. She remembered her mother, Phyllis, being glamorous. Always dressing in black and white, Chanelesque, with button-up cardigans with pearl buttons. She was a hairdresser, up to date with the modern fashions of the time, but she disapproved of hair dye, believing the chemicals to be toxic. No good could come of messing with nature. Ma recalled her grandfather's exquisite writing desk, how it was untouchable, and how she'd wait until no one was in the immediate vicinity and then pull a stool over and climb up to draw on it triumphantly; and how her grandfather was a real old-school gentleman, whom they all admired and loved dearly. By that stage, however, he was diabetic and would have fits; and they knew, seeing him "turn," to back off ("we knew, without being told, to get out of the way"), watching him malfunction in fascinated horror. He was an oil and gas man—an innovator of sorts, without realizing the damage it was doing.

For all their rural lifestyle, with the toddlers chasing around pigs and bantam chickens, their money was founded on industry, a reminder of which was the huge shed with oil containers and mechanical equipment from which they were all forbidden.

Naturally this stirred the interest of Ma and Tony, the more subversive siblings, and Tony soon found himself in hospital with his stomach being pumped and a mouthful of charcoal, having inquisitively sipped petrol directly from the tap.

Though he was formidable, Anthony was the weak link in the family. He was tall, strong, and broad-shouldered—ridiculously so for his time—next to the squat whippet of the average male. He looked more Nordic or Dutch. Not unlike Charlton Heston. He played football, semiprofessionally he fancied, as his frequently brandished photos attested. He was, however, an anomaly. He was full-blown peasant stock, for all the movie-star looks. He ate periwinkles with a pin. He brought home metal buckets filled with live crabs for the children to poke with sticks. By stark contrast, and hence the attraction perhaps, his wife and her two sisters were Fitzgerald-esque ladies with furs and hats and elegant poses. Perhaps she had been drawn to Anthony because of his physical presence. Perhaps because he had an air of disreputable arrogance, being a smuggler. Yet he was not a man to be relied on. He was strong only physically and in rage, and weak otherwise. He would take the business from his ailing father-in-law and it would fall to pieces in his hands. Perhaps she was attracted to him, and vice versa, because he did not belong there. He was, as my mother put it, a cuckoo in the nest.

My grandmother changes in photographs. Most of the time she looks eerily like my mother. At every stage of her foreshortened life, she is protean. She became her children. Certain looks and mannerisms. Always someone else. Her name, though, was Phyllis Doherty. In those days she was Mrs. Anthony McMonagle. That was how they addressed her when they told her the terrible news that would follow.

I could never imagine my maternal aunts and uncles all

together as children. They shared traits, echoes of their parents, but nevertheless were as different as star signs. Edward Gorey characters on separate pages, somehow surviving their escapades. One ate bluebells. One fell into a slurry pit (Anthony rescuing him at the last minute via a rapidly sinking plank). One got her tongue stuck to the freezer. One made mechanical wings and jumped from the garage roof, breaking his legs. The oldest were expected to fulfill their father's misplaced ambitions; the rest were jettisoned to an extent. They were expected to be identical, with their hair in bowl cuts, and resisted idiosyncratically. My mother wore her haircut defiantly. Once, while being taunted by a pompous irritant of a child between the boards of a fence, she launched a dart, intending to scare him, and had to rush in hot pursuit to wrench it out of his forehead before he made it, with the evidence still attached, into his house, bawling.

At the bottom of their lane was a standing stone their parents referred to as Billy Babbins's Grave. Anthony and Phyllis told them it was haunted, to keep them from wandering down to the thoroughfare, the Racecourse Road, where Thran John's pub stood. Except there really was a ghost, or a ghost story at least, attached to the area. The tale went that it was the specter of a jockey who'd fallen mid-race and broken his neck. He was doomed to wander the winds, looking for his horse. The great-aunt corrected the story that he had actually been a jockey who'd been murdered for his winnings, returning victorious from a race. Ghosts were placed there by guilty consciences. The kids would still venture down there, though they feared to after dusk. The main peril they encountered were two mad old sisters, whom they called the Talkers, who would walk the lanes talking in tongues. My aunts and uncles, as children, would hide in hedges listening to the glossolalia of the Talkers as they passed, trying to make sense of them, as if they were wandering, threadbare oracles.

Life was not easy for anyone then, but they had it relatively good. All it would take was for life to keep on going as it was going. Life did not keep on going as it was going.

It's a matter of some debate among her children, when, or indeed if, Phyllis ever found out she was dying. It was an argument that carried on for so long that no one could remember its source. There's a school of thought that it was immediate. Another that it was kept from her to the extent that she never knew, and died aware of her pain and the fact that she was sick, but oblivious to the terminal condition. Imagine dying and not knowing—the wondering you would do, how you would doubt the world and everything in it, how you would question your very body. Imagine dying and not knowing that others knew. Perhaps my grandfather thought it was a kindness that he was gifting her. They certainly never told her nine children, the youngest being only eight months old. They were sent away to other families, away from their mother, evacuated from the city, as if the skies had darkened with bombers once again, which, in a sense, they had. The median seems to be that she found out she was dying of inoperable stomach cancer after her husband did. It was deemed compassionate to tell her. It's unclear if Anthony was the one who did so or if he left it to someone else.

Anthony recalled that Phyllis had gone to have her fortune told in Portrush, one of those picturesque Protestant seaside towns that boomed when trains ran throughout the land and the seaside was seen as restorative to health—little England in rain-lashed Ireland. A holiday, then as now, was a kind of ritual cleansing from the grubbiness of work. To the sound of carousels, Phyllis asked for her palm to be read. The astrologer held her hand and examined it intently, then abjectly refused

to reveal what she had seen and politely asked Phyllis to leave.
She was naturally upset. Anthony always said fortune-tellers,
or anyone dabbling in "black magic," as he put it, were evil
after that. His superstitions and his religious beliefs were certainly that, were like a scaffolding on the wreck of a life. The
saints and the angels were things not remotely of wonder, but
of fear and proscription. A necessary masochism was involved
for him. In place of class, back then, there was faith. Anthony
did his bit to kiss the altar rails and have the monsignor, ancient
even then, over for tea, cowering the kids into obedience behind
closed doors, but he was never granted the social ascendancy he
sought. When the faithful of the new housing estate began to
show up at Thornhill Church for Mass, among the established
congregation, they were told by the priest that services would
no longer be offered and to walk into Steelstown, several miles
away. The following Sunday, at the beginning of their trek, they
looked over to see the priest greeting the rich of the congregation as they stepped out of their cars.

Anthony clung to his faith nonetheless. Its discomforts
brought him comfort or at least the semblance of order. He could
channel his madness through it. He'd leave a statue of the Child
of Prague outside at night in the yard to ensure good weather at
sea the next day. As with any ideology, life inconveniently kept
interrupting. As Phyllis lay dying, Anthony noted that a hedgehog had come scratching at the back door at night. He lifted it
and carted it down the road on a shovel, but it came back the
next night. So he drove it away in his van down the road. It took a
week to come back. Though it lacked the theatrics of the shrieking banshee or the eerie doppelgänger, he nevertheless took it as
an omen of doom. The Romans believed the owl to be a baleful
presence, a foreteller of shipwrecks, an emissary of the underworld sent to deliver us terrible messages, indecipherable until

they happened. To someone who believed that all was preordained in God's plan, then portents of what was to come might
well appear and be possible to interpret. The murmurations of
starlings, a single bird flying into a room, all the stages between
the butterfly's wing and the tornado.

There's still some mystery as to how cancer begins. It can be
a traumatic event—a rupture, an injury, something that upsets
the delicate genetic balance and creates a mutation that begins
to replicate. There might be a propensity already; Phyllis's was a
family inheritance passed down in the genes, but not helped by
having so many children in so few years. She would be feeding
one child, weaning another, with another on the way. Nine children later, she was physically and mentally exhausted. She had
once shared a ward with a Gypsy lady who had just given birth
and whose stitches were barely in when her husband stopped
by. The lady had begged the nurses not to "let him at me," saying that he insisted on getting her pregnant again immediately,
that she couldn't go through it again, not this soon. But sure
enough, in an age when a woman dared not turn a word in any
man's mouth publicly, he silenced them and pulled the screens
around. Phyllis, unable to see her own situation clearly, too
close and immersed in it, had told of her deep, resounding pity
for that woman.

She was diagnosed at the same hospital where she had given
birth to her children. When Anthony heard the news, the check-
ered floor turned into black holes as he collapsed trying to walk
down the corridor, along the walls, the building suddenly tilting,
suddenly storm-tossed by the words "too far gone." Mourning
her before she had died, or rather pitying himself. As she deteri-
orated, and it happened rapidly, the kids were sent away.

To a child, death is a collapse of gravity; you find yourself
falling off the face of the world and grasping to hold on. Noth-

ing that you took for granted is ever quite real again. Trying to find handgrips and footholds in a whirlwind. Ma saw her mother only in excerpts that made no sense, with a quality like waking up into a nightmare. Her mother was emaciated and bedridden. It didn't matter how much she ate or drank. She was starving to death. Phyllis had what my mother thought was a fireguard wrapped around her. In fact, it was to keep the blankets off her, given that anything touching her skin was unbearable. Her bones protruded from her skin. My mother remembered the antiseptic smell of the bedsore cream and the aroma of lilies, which her mother had once loved and asked for. For three weeks the children were scattered across the country in different houses, kept out of the city as if the Blitz or the plague had suddenly begun again. Some experienced kindness. Others were treated as impostors and impositions. All pined for home. Two years older than Ma, Caroline conspired to escape from her confines and successfully made it back to the house, where she ran in and climbed into bed to hug her mother. She was caught and brought back, where she immediately plotted her next escape. Most of them had no goodbye or explanation.

The ritual took precedence. Phyllis lay in her coffin at the wake, and Ma stretched to kiss her forehead when one of the old spinster keeners—professional mourners in Ireland at the time— talking about how she had suffered like our Lord and was thus blessed, while stuffing her gullet full of cakes and tea, leered at her, "Don't touch the body!" Ma was seven. She was gathered up into the hearse and driven through streets lined with people, so slowly that she could hear them talking. "She left nine wee ones." Ma, then tiny but feisty, said she hated them all, everyone who gave them pity. She hated the exposure. "I felt like a monkey in the zoo." All summer long her teacher, with parochial sadism, dedicated the class prayers to Ma's "dead mother." Ma resolved never to cry in front of any of them—her classmates, the teachers, the morbid baying audience—and fashioned herself an armor of burnished pride. She couldn't look at pictures of her mother for years. She hated that she looked like her. When she attempted to remember her, contrary to her siblings' memories of a saint, all she could think about was one occasion when her mother had protectively scolded her for playing with an electrical socket. Caroline would kindly give copies of photos of their mother to Ma, and she'd put them into envelopes and stash them at the bottom of drawers. They almost scared her to look at them.

A curious consequence of grief is the attempt to put more and more past between you and the lost ones, distancing yourself from what you miss, following the cold comfort that time heals all wounds. Ma felt abandoned by her mother for years, until she had her own children, and it hit her in a flood of emotion that her mother hadn't wanted to leave them; that as terrible as it was to them, it was terrible for her too, unimaginably so, to be pulled away, like Eurydice into the dark. As a girl, in the aftermath, unguarded by sleep, she would wake up crying and no one would come. Except her sisters. They became immensely close, joined together in the terrible presence of absence. All who had been children when Ma died went into caring professions in later life, what Jung called the "wounded healers"— nurses, teachers, social workers. "She was our mother and we missed her like the sun."

Soon afterward the family received a compulsory purchase order. It ordered them off their land in Bogs Lee. The council finally, partially, beginning to relent to the housing misery, was to build a housing estate there. Those who were left of the family were offered compensation way below the market rate. The decline in their fortunes was already well underway, but the insensitive manner and timing of the vesting order always seemed to Ma to have been a curse placed on them that finally broke everything. Their house, all the rooms in which they had grown up and their mother had lived, was bulldozed. For weeks before it was cleared, the children would return to the empty house, playing in the gardens, looking through the windows and trying unsuccessfully to open the locked doors.

If any trace of it remains now, it is under pathways and car parks. There was nowhere left to haunt, or rather nowhere physical. Anthony lost the gas business shortly thereafter, through mismanagement and bad luck and a propensity for extravagant gifts to women he was chasing. In fairness, it was said already to have been on its last legs, due to his father-in-law's sickness and the fact that he was too kind and wouldn't chase down the debts that people kept mounting. Anthony, by contrast, was out of his depth and too stubborn to admit it.

My grandfather moved the family to another area, one called Belmont, downsizing as they went. None of them liked it there. The oldest sister, Anne, had sleep paralysis, waking up thinking that someone was leaning over her. Their car got burned out inexplicably. My uncle Tony, my grandfather's namesake and nemesis, had bad dreams as a boy and they threatened to turn into bad thoughts, especially when he began to hang around the riots, so the decision was made to move again, far enough out of trouble, to the Woodlands. It felt even more remote then than during my childhood. There were no shops. They could walk to the pub, then called McKeels, and knock on the back door for peanuts or a Fanta—that was the height of it. There were fights every day getting on and off the school bus, when they were lucky enough to be allowed on it, given that one driver, nicknamed Mungo Jerry for his sideburns, wouldn't let any plebs with a bus pass onto his vehicle. The walk

home, when the sun went down early in winter, was pitch-black
without streetlights. Tony called it "the ghost run" and was always relieved to see the telegraph wires shining, meaning that
a car was coming, to temporarily light the way. They'd tiptoe
past Barber's Corner to evade a dog that delighted in sinking its
teeth into their legs.

The move out of Derry to avoid the escalating Troubles may
have been wise, but the violence spread to reach them. Before
the checkpoint was constructed, there was a single customs
man at Muff, always waiting for his shift to finish. Gradually
the family watched the checkpoint erected. Soldiers would drive
around the estate in a soft-topped jeep, scouting out the place
and the people. The soldiers used to call into the old guy opposite Anthony's house for tea and buns, as he was ex–Ulster Defence Regiment. He had a dodgy reputation, and the children
of the estate, regardless of religion, were warned not to darken
his door. Presumably he gave the troops a rundown of who was
who on the estate, because shortly afterward Anthony's family started getting grief. The soldiers weren't the worst—"you
could have a civil chat to them." The UDR were harsh, however.
They'd take your car apart at the checkpoint, literally wrenching off panels, or confiscate things you'd bought, like trays of
eggs, and then loudly make it look as if you were collaborating
and had gifted it to them. The UDR men were also quick with
their fists and boots if you said the wrong thing. Once, they
started roughing up my uncle and were stopped from delivering
a savage beating only by an MP intervening, telling my uncle to
get back in the car and fuck off. They were accidents waiting
to happen.

Farther up the back road, past the border-marking concrete blocks, sprayed with "IRA" and "Long Live the Baader–
Meinhof Gang," was a remote house where two old hermit

brothers had lived. They died suddenly, poisoning themselves unintentionally with gas or foraged mushrooms, if the stories are anything to go by. The rumors about that added to the feeling that the Woodlands were cursed. Terrible things kept happening there. Among the reasons for that, however, were its proximity to naturally dangerous sites and machinery; the place being a dumping ground for the city's ne'er-do-wells; and the people already there who thought they were sane but were just as crazy. If man made the city and God made the country, then the devil made the satellite village.

Barometer (Cracked at "Stormy")

Even before a certain slowing of the mind, Anthony's storytelling had peculiar quirks. He'd become bull-headed if you didn't intimately recall a fellow who had died thirty years before you were born. It was safest just to nod and throw in the occasional white lie of confirmation: "Aye, I remember Dinny McCartney from the Isle of Doagh, three generations dead—I remember him well." I paid attention for as long as could be deemed respectful and then, as he veered into some genealogical conjecture, stood up and began to idle around the room, still half-listening but ever curious at the objects, the little totems with which he'd surrounded himself.

All Anthony's relics, unsurprisingly, were nautical: flotsam from a life finally run aground as the tide slowly retreated across the fields, leaving him landlocked, close to the river, but out of sight and reach. He kept a large pink conch, a fossilized extraterrestrial life-form the color of damask and fuchsia, as a doorstop. It had chambers in it that resembled rooms, and, when I was a child, that made me think of Jonah wandering inside the whale. Banded flints sat on his shelf, with markings that looked like tidal bore lines. There was a broken barometer, fixed just shy of "Stormy." Sea charts with rocks, islands, rivers, tides, fluctuating depths, magnetic directions, and latitude lines, with bearings, corrections, and hazardous areas scrawled in red ink by hand. Different knots in rope framed in wooden boxes—Palomar, Surgeon's, Trilene, Hangman's—intricate as medieval script, knots that men's lives had relied on at times. Flies, of dazzling color and weights, like tiny sculptures. A ship in a bottle, its rigging delicate as a moth's wing. I could never work out how it was assembled as a child. The glass had somehow grown around the boat, a genie's vessel.

Something in the way Anthony was speaking made me pause. A certain doubt. Almost a stutter. The bluster of old that had seemed, at times, an elemental force was gone and in its place was a forgery of what he'd once unconsciously been. Something in him had changed. His legs had packed up several years earlier. He'd put it down to the lasting effects of a motorcycle accident years ago, but it struck me as more incremental. Off his feet, inactivity began to erode him. Time worked on him like frost to stone.

Anthony's empire shrank to a few landlocked rooms. The cyclone that whirled around his home had turned in on itself. To the unfamiliar, he'd have remained formidable, still Old Testament, but I knew him well enough. He lacked the telltale signs of the coming end that he'd seen in folks of his age, or younger even; the weight loss that left grown men looking like they were children wearing their parents' clothes, a hunted, hounded look in their eyes as the skin retracted and they had to maintain intense focus so as not to fade completely. These obvious features were absent. Bar the circuitry of purple veins in his hands and the speckled egg of his brow under wispy blond hair, he could have passed for a decade younger than he was.

The mortality lay in his voice. It was no longer an exerted bellow. It no longer crowded out all responses. It had a hesitancy that seemed utterly alien. As if something had profoundly shaken him. Anthony never disclosed what it was. This was something worse than the deaths of his wives or parents or his brother; this was something private. Age was a war waged on him, and this was collapse, disordered retreat, when all comes crashing down, but the motions are still gone through as some attempt at denial or comfort. He went through his old stories like an actor who had lost faith in the play, or his ability to know the impending lines. My grandfather's newfound weakness was mistaken by some of his grown-up children as a sign of mellowing, a hoping that he'd found inner calm and forgiveness. This was wishful thinking and understandable, given his dominance for so long. He had not, it seemed to me, found inner peace at all. He simply could not be physically as he once was and still wished to be. Gods have power only for as long as they are believed in. They become myth after that.

I asked him about the river and he obliged, talking me through a journey from the old docks out along the lough to the sea. "We'd follow the shoals. Head out at night."

"Did it ever get rough?"

"Jesus, Mary, and Joseph. Did it get rough? Did it get rough? Have you been up at Malin Head?"

"I have. I camped up there many's the time. It's on the shipping fore—"

"Aye, well, we went out for a few days up round Banba's Crown, right at the tip of Ireland, where you go north until you run out of land. It gets rough up round there. We knew the weather was taking a turn for the worse, but we thought we'd make the most of it and pick up what we could before heading back for Greencastle. The storm came on quick. I can still see the clouds racing over us. After an hour the waves were so rough that you couldn't tell one direction from the other. The whole world seemed to be rising and falling."

"Were you worried?"

"Some of the young boys on board got spooked. We started hanging on to anything that was tied down. We thought it would pass, but it got worse and we started to realize we were heading towards a rock called the Dutchman. Do you know it?"

I blinked back at him. "I don't."

Anthony knew the names and positions of hidden assassin rocks and treacherous currents, the vortexes and whorls that the uninitiated could not foresee.

"Well, it was just off the coast, which we were hugging. Rocks jutting out. It'd make mincemeat out of us, and we were headed right for it."

"What did you do?"

"Some of the lads were crying. Some of them knelt down on the deck and started to pray."

"Did you have life rafts? In case you went in."

He batted away my question with a withering glance. "You didn't go in."

"But what if you fell in? Could you swim to the shore?"

"None of us learned to swim. None of the fishermen did. It's bad luck."

"But if—"

"If you went in, it was already too late."

"You never went in?"

"You never went in."

I stared out the window. The light was changing. "What about the drowned? Mum said you used to help bring in—"

Suddenly, a large thud interrupted us. I thought for a moment that one of the neighborhood kids had thrown a stone at the window and tried to look through the gaps in the fence; but then, from the corner of my eye, I noticed a little bird sideways on the ground. It had not seen the glass and had struck it at full speed, mid-flight. My grandfather had noticed none of this and carried on talking, but his stories no longer quite made sense. He was speaking in orbits, narrowing spirals, tangents that went nowhere, but continually talking, as if in fear of a moment of silence, a moment of contemplation. Talking to avoid thinking. I could see it on his face, but he kept talking. I thought of the black holes on the hospital floor.

He had already shifted onto the subject of his late wife, or rather his later late wife, and memories within memories, wheels within wheels. Her name was Kitty. I had grown up regarding her as my grandmother, but she was, in fact, no relation. She was my grandfather's second wife and could not have children herself, but had come in and acted as a surrogate mother to nine kids who'd been robbed of their birth mother. In hindsight, she was just a troubled person who had been thrown into a situation that was beyond her capabilities. Nevertheless, she had fit the evil-stepmother role—designed for her perhaps in advance—rather well. She was prone to hysterical performative outbursts, throwing herself down the stairs, for instance. She kept padlocked a cupboard filled with Swiss rolls, chocolate, and biscuits. Perpetually hungry, the children managed to pick the lock and were caught only when they got carried away and didn't thin the food down gradually. If they didn't steal food, they went hungry, watching their otherwise beloved dog, Dino, be fed the leftover chicken and roast potatoes. Sometimes it was just thrown away, to teach them some deranged lesson. They joked about it years later, with genuine humor, but with that echo of pain that humor conceals and is often born from.

Kitty gave Anthony an alibi. It was Anthony who lay at the root of the problem. He had a rage in him and was intractable and narcissistic. His worldview did not extend far beyond his immediate desires. He was big too, and handy with his fists, provided it was to those junior to him, like his children. He'd have shat himself with an equal or better. He was clever, though, and he had idiosyncratic tendencies. Tyrannical power reserves the right to be arbitrary. It unbalances its victims. At times, he'd favor certain offspring at the expense of others (the older ones were particularly "blue-eyed"). At other times, his anger was more strategically chaotic, to divide and conquer, detaching itself from logic or cause and effect to keep them all second-guessing. You could get a hammering for peeling the potatoes too thick, or at other times too thin. The parameters were changed deliberately and without explanation so that nothing was safe and they were always kept in an unsettled state of anxiety.

At other times, punishment would be collective and disproportionate. He'd batter them with a strap at night when they were all in bed. They'd cower against the wall to escape the lashes, trying to push past one another, since the ones on the outside would take most of the force. Another method was to squeal loudest, in the hope he'd focus on the quiet ones. A lot of dysfunction begins as a form of functioning in desperate conditions.

Every word came with a welt. Every staccato syllable. "I'll. Teach. You. To. Do. That. Again." Threats were backed up with blunt force. "Don't you dare turn a word in my mouth." "I'll take my hand off your face." "By Christ, I'll knock the fear of God

into you." Or alternatively, "I'll beat the Jesus out of ye." All with
their own insane contradictory logic. Only once did I hear of him
coming into conflict with someone approaching an equal. Even
then, it was weighted to his advantage. He had been upstairs
when an opportunist burglar had broken into the house. Anthony knew, from the sounds, it was a stranger. Rather than go
down promptly, he stepped lightly onto the landing and took out
the shillelagh, a huge blackthorn branch fashioned into a decorative, ordinarily ornamental cudgel. He tested its weight in his
hands and then stepped back into the bedroom doorway, waiting
for the steps on the stairs to reach the top, knowing—like the
defender of a round tower—that to have the upper ground and a
right-handed swing downward meant everything.

He paused, recounting the story.

"So . . . what happened?"

"Well . . . he didn't tell me no more stories."

I'd no idea what he meant. And he just left the recollection
hanging cryptically there in the air. The shillelagh was mounted
on the wall like a trophy. There was no doubt he could have
handled himself; it was in the blood. His half brother boxed
in his time. He once knocked an opponent out so early that
the bookies insisted on bringing him round with smelling salts
so that they could begin the fight again and not start a riot.
On another occasion, he was on the warpath and a number of
guards locked themselves in their own station and had to radio for help. My mother remembered him, oddly, as a gentle
giant, who in opposition to Anthony used force only as a last
resort. Whatever the real history was, or the real person, had
fragmented into a series of contradictory stories.

Though he was proudly a teetotal "pioneer," Anthony had
met Kitty in a pub. He had called in for "a mineral," as he used
to put it. Anthony was a dry alcoholic. Little doubt about it.

He didn't touch a drop because his father was a mean drunk ("real bad," people would say without elaborating). Anthony worshipped his mother as a saint. It only came out in recent times that she, too, was a heavy drinker. His parents would fish and take their catch to market in Derry on a horse and cart, in soaked bags of rushes under a tarp. They'd sell them off and return with enough money to go on drinking sprees that would last days, coming round just in time to begin the process again, maybe even fishing in the drink-sodden overlap. Anthony was largely raised by a stern puritanical aunt but was close enough to witness what was happening.

In contrast, Kitty, by her own admission, had been a good-time girl. She would brag to my sister and me about how she'd been invited onto the naval ships, "whistled on by the chief petty officer, no less," beaming about her implied exploits. We were bemused. As teenagers, my mother and her sisters would do hysterical "rock the boat" motions behind her back, as she'd earlier reminisced to them, trying not to burst out laughing in her face. Notably Kitty remained in Derry, while many girls her age ended up in the States as the wives of marines. She no doubt felt that situation acutely.

It turned out that she was much younger than I had thought at the time. She hadn't had an easy time of it. As a young woman, she'd cared for her aged mother and her blind sister until their deaths, and then for my grandfather's children, but she had gone into freefall in her later years when I knew her. She had high blood pressure and obesity, which showed as strain on her face. Her eyes bulged, her veins were pronounced. Her body looked as if it was straining heavily, simply to continue continuing. She reluctantly took enough tablets every day, hand-fuls of multicolored pills, to choke a horse. She dismissed the doctors who warned her about her diabetes, her hypertension, in order to continue as she saw fit, in terms of diet and lifestyle. She was an arch-skeptic of modern medical practice.

At the same time she was superstitious. The version of Catholicism to which she was wedded appeared to me, even as a child, as intensely kitsch. She had shrines everywhere, to Padre Pio, the Child of Prague, Our Lady of Guadalupe. She had never been anywhere abroad except Lourdes, but she'd been there many times. She'd talked about it as if it was not in France but a foreign enclave of Ireland. At that stage the pilgrimages to Knock, Fatima, Jerusalem, Medjugorje, Santiago de Compostela (sites of Marian apparitions and Christ hauntings) were done on bus and ferry rather than on foot. She would not live to see them all linked in a pilgrimage network of budget airlines three thousand feet in the heavens. Kitty's pleasures always had a morbid, unearthly edge. She read obituaries in newspapers like they were horoscopes or poison-pen letters. "Aw, look here. Auld Agnes is dead, God bless her. I never could bring myself to like her." Her idea of helping, in any situation, was to light a candle for you in the church. She thought of it as a technology to petition an invisible civil service of guardian-angel bureaucrats. Eventually, housebound and unable to make it to church, but still thinking nothing was wrong, she'd reach over and light the candles where she sat.

A Sacred Heart picture nailed to their living room wall glowed in neon red. It seemed to flicker and hum continually, as if a wire was loose and too much or too little electricity was reaching it. It was fed with three rosaries a day. Initially I was terrified that it was alive. My first crisis of faith came upon discovering that the pulsing Sacred Heart was not illuminated by some divine connection, but had a cord that led to the plug, the socket, and the switch. God evaporated that day. In hindsight, it was a cheap import from a factory where bored workers made shoddy miracles on conveyor belts. Its Christ looked like Barry Gibb. Kitty spoke of Jesus as "the most handsome man who had ever lived." He was just one of many icons, Catholicism being polytheistic beneath the monotheistic image. Kitty took her religion as she took her tablets: a fix to counter her vices. In Germany they had *Schluckbildchen*, devotional pictures that worshippers swallowed.

Under her guidance, I began then to notice superstitions everywhere and all the time. People blessing themselves as ambulances passed. Holding their collars until they saw a dog. Never passing on stairs or under ladders. Broken mirrors and magpies and black cats. The fishermen had their own equivalents, never letting a priest, as Catholic as they were, on board the boats. Always take salt to sea, but never a watch. Always have an odd number of nets. Don't mention anything to do with land life while at sea. These were believed, or at least not worth risking. Later one of my uncles told me that Kitty was not religious at all. She'd wanted to be, no doubt, and had probably convinced herself, but if you watched closely, it fell apart. Faith is made of more than simply belief. To Kitty, it was habit, ritual, and grounding. It was character. It filled gaps. Those things she believed in. God was incidental. It was no big thing. There'd been popes who hadn't believed in God. As I grew older, such matters made me doubt my own atheism.

A copy of Leonardo's *The Last Supper* commanded my grandparents' bedroom. It always puzzled me how futuristic the room looked—strangely out of time. The original, painted on a wall with a flawed experimental method, has been crumbling away for centuries. A door was cut through it once; French revolutionaries hollowed out the apostles' eyes, and the hall in which it was held was bombed to rubble by an Allied missile. Yet the version that looked over my grandparents' room was airbrushed to a gaudy perfection. The disciples bulged in glossy three-dimensional relief. There was no patron saint of kitsch because all the saints were kitsch, at least in their holy-shop incarnations; all the trinkets and action figures and the plastic cherubs and ecstatic polystyrene monks. The strangeness of the actual lives of saints had been defused. It struck me that all the iconography was not a celebration but rather represented containment devices, as if the madness could be trapped in marble and glass, just as God could be contained in a cathedral and visited only once a week. It was a way of keeping them out of everyday life.

Kitty's was a world where the sixties had not happened. She listened to Perry Como. She kept a collection of music boxes. I liked her, in defiance of prevailing opinion and despite myself, perhaps because parental and grandparental relationships are different. One night she woke up suddenly and began vomiting all over the walls. I remembered the horror of seeing my grandfather weeping at the resulting wake, "What will become of me now?" and thinking to myself that no one was asking what had become of her.

The much-vaunted Catholic virtue of mercy was lacking in Kitty and Anthony. One Sunday my mother and her sister, then teenagers, had lain in their beds as a silent protest instead of getting up and going to Mass. Anthony reacted with the nuclear option. It had only been a matter of time, given that he had found other excuses for each of his children to be propelled into the world. This gave him the excuse he wanted, and perhaps they knew it was time for them to leave, deep down. It was still unpleasant. He manhandled Ma and Caroline down the stairs, opened the front door, and launched them onto the path. There was a pause and then a huge teddy bear that my mother had won in a raffle came flying after them. The door slammed so hard it almost splintered the frame. They began the long walk into town, trailing the bear.

After crashing on sofas, my mother was taken in by a kindly trainee priest, who later lapsed, being perhaps too Christian for the profession and complaining of being continually sexually harassed by other priests and trainee priests in Maynooth. Even though Anthony had banished my mother, he would still call round on unannounced visits to make sure she wasn't living in sin (he wasn't ready to let go of his dictatorial position), and my da would have to climb out the window and sit out on the roof, smoking, until the coast had cleared. Nothing existed in my grandfather's world without his express permission. His grip had been broken, however. It was a changed world. My parents had fun with their friends, enjoying their first taste of freedom, whenever they could. Playing music, putting up pictures, throwing parties on a budget, even flashing passing soldiers ("You'll get tarred and feathered for entertaining the troops" went the gallows humor).

Eventually, in the late 1970s, my mother and father got their own place. As a teenager, my mother had been sitting at the back of a rickety country bus, smoking and staring out, day-dreaming at the passing surroundings. They'd stopped to let a boy out at a blind corner. Another bus, roaring down the road, skidded into them. The glass shattered and the rear of the bus crumpled, her ankle along with it. She received compensation for the injuries, from which her father took a substantial portion for raising her. With the remainder she was able to buy a dilapidated council house between Rosemount and the Glen, but a house nonetheless, in the days when they were affordable. When she and my father moved in, my grandfather, fuming but powerless to stop them, had her banished from the family. When my parents married, they went to the local Chinese restaurant for their reception and could afford only starters. Ma's brothers and sisters were banned from attending, but Tony had escaped and turned up, beaming and wearing a duffel coat. Not long afterward he, too, was kicked out, after returning one of Anthony's punches. He'd been hit a welt that had left him seeing stars and had instinctively lunged back. My grandfather was outraged and stunned into momentary silence, then he began stammering and built up into threats that he'd call the police and the priests, and what was this world coming to that the young would strike their elders? Tony brushed past him, barely able to look at him, hurling a few choice insults. He made his way to London, sleeping on park benches back in the old "No Blacks, No Dogs, No Irish" days. Expected to sink, he learned to swim.

Even when time eroded the divide, Da and Anthony never got on. It was inevitable, with their temperaments—Anthony all sound and fury, signifying nothing, and my father a stoic with a certain militant streak. Irresistible force meets immovable object. Both stubborn in their ways, as I am too. When first introduced, Anthony had said nothing, then when Da left, he raged and fumed that Ma had married someone unbefitting of their status, which was practically nonexistent and thus important. He was an inveterate social climber, a skinflint who was mean enough to turn the engine of his car off when going downhill to save money, and who insinuated that he had a miserly fortune stashed away. Da was a godless heathen who could barely mumble the Angelus, the daily method by which the last professional Catholics marked the passing of time. He was an eternally curious agnostic. Added to this, the Church disapproved of long hair, beards, and poverty. So Anthony disowned his daughter and her children, my sister and me, returning only when I made it to grammar school and became useful in his ever-downward clamber upward in society.

Compass

A nthony used to say, "You people on land," as if he were a different species or one of the elect. He knew the coastlines intimately, from the sea's perspective, when the rest barely realized they were on an island at all: "You don't understand the lie of the land below the waves." There's another world down there. It isn't flat or singular. There are clefts, valleys, plateaus, chasms, and caves. He could visualize the landscape down there with a mapmaker's accuracy, as if the rivers and oceans had drained away and revealed the land beneath—new unfamiliar countries. He was convinced that is what took the dead so long to come back up. It was as if he believed they got lost down there.

Cautious because of his knowledge, Anthony stuck to what he knew, clinging to the coastline wherever he could and wherever it was safe to do so, venturing farther out under necessity alone. Curious about his incuriosity, I asked him once about places farther away. If he'd ever been tempted to sail off into what he'd called, with a hint of derision, "the blue beyond"? "Did you ever hear of Londonderry Island? It's in Tierra del Fuego. The land of fire. It was—"

Anthony stopped me with a look that suggested I was a gibbering maniac. After a pause, he reanimated with pantomime bluster. "Sure, what the fuck business would I have there?" He thudded the breakfast tray for emphasis.

I stared at the ceiling. "Fair point."

Anthony had no use for tales of the Horse Latitudes or the Doldrums or the Maelstrom, of sailors dressing as Neptune crossing the equator, or Hong Kong junks, or the genius of Polynesian navigation. He knew nothing of the mechanics of haloclines or that the sea was blue because the other color wavelengths were absorbed. All that mattered was finding the shoals and returning to land in one piece. He had a contract with the sea and to go further, to think foolish thoughts, would be a betrayal, a broken covenant. It would chance fate. This was not an idle game.

And yet he must have dreamt, knowing of places of threat and plenty, places he let slip in conversation—the Grand Banks of Newfoundland, the Nantucket Shoals—and even further, places that must exist in some dream world out of reach: the Cape of Good Hope, Deception Island, the Bimini Road, Bouvet Island, the Great Blue Hole. The matters he discussed were particular and practical. How two ships, having a certain gravity, will always collide if left near one another in a calm sea. How to "brace in" or "chapel" boats. Carrying the helm amidships in baffling breezes and raging gales. He was too busy surviving to entertain much wondering, too busy trying not to imagine horrors to imagine wonders. Faith was a kind of silencing for Anthony. It did not invite thoughts, surprise, memories, or the chance of being wrong. It kept guilt away. It enabled blustering certainty in the guise of modesty. Certainty was his wreck and certainty was his raft. As long as he could stay sure, the past could not catch up with him.

What he knew, he knew well. How to find his way back, by internal radar. The routine of the catch, by muscle memory. How to spot land when no land is in sight, from signs in clouds, water, or, like Columbus, coastal birds. The deceptive and revealing angles of light on the sea's surface. He knew the feel of the water, the landscape of the sea, with eyes closed: surge and sway, heave and yaw, roll and pitch. The trade winds and trade routes, where they mattered. Abrupt headlands and inviting but treacherous coves. Nothing if not superstitious, he would sail to Killybegs annually for the Blessing of the Boats to bask in heavenly protection for another year, vaccinated by the Holy Spirit against drowning.

He and his crew would sail around and between the isles of Donegal—Eighter Island and Inishcoo, abandoned in the 1960s. The "island of the white cow," Inishbofin, and the green cloak of Glashedy, with its huge cliffs and a surreal pasture on top. The "island of the hollow beach," Inishtrahull, and the red Oileán Ruaidh, formerly the "island of the prisoners" (identity unknown). There was mystery in the places we thought we knew, if you looked closely enough. Some were hard to reach or to dock at, fit only for passing or for guano; or for pilgrimages, in the case of Inishkeel, or refuge from pursuers in the more remote islands. They multiplied as if Ireland were shattering at the edges. Gola Island off Gweedore, Torglass Island off Gola, each island smaller and more rugged than the last, some dangerously concealed for sailors, others concealed enough to be sanctuaries during the successive invasions. The inlets in sea cliffs they call "zawns" were places to hide in the shadow of natural castle walls and to beach illicit cargoes. There were accidental bridges leading out onto wave-lashed rocks, half-collapsed buttresses and stacks, like Gothic ruins.

No one could ever be sure why Anthony took to his bed. He hadn't really lost his spirit. He could still give out hell, and for a long time commanded the family even when confined, trying to play one off the other through poison phone calls and calculated asides. Though he had been hobbling, it was a very sudden deterioration, and his inactivity only seemed to make the problem irrecoverable. Idly drinking coffee by the window one morning, I watched him limping along, using a walking stick with a handle, smooth and rounded as the heel of a Lourdes statue, and then I watched him run for a bus when he thought he might miss it and no one was looking. There was something performative in it all initially, until it became a self-fulfilling prophecy. You only ever destroy yourself, someone wrote. My grandfather could walk, but simply gave it up one day, as if under the influence of some diabolical counsel in his head that he'd mistaken for good advice. Eventually his newfound passivity—inertia—would kill him. Maybe even he didn't know the answer why. Maybe there wasn't a single answer, more of a dialogue that he decided to spectate at, even though it was his own life.

There was a tradition in early Christian Ireland of holy men setting off in boats without oars, to go wherever fate decided, never to be heard of again. You placed yourself in God's hands and at the sea's mercy. Later it became a punishment for those who had killed their brothers, an execution without spilling blood. They'd be sent out oar-less, tied to the boat, never to return or to be mentioned again. Where they went, no one knew or asked.

My grandfather had another brother, or rather a half brother. They shared the same father. He'd kept to himself and was known as something of an odd character. Anthony had learned that he was not faring too well, so he'd gone to visit him at his home in Quigley's Point, a stopping place along the Foyle shore. He found him there alone, gripping the blankets of his bed, prematurely old and already dying, between peeling wallpapers. It was the only night he spent there. Anthony remembered there were holes in the roof, letting in the elements. He noticed you could see the stars.

My grandfather told me this the last time I saw him, bedbound in his own starless room. He was talking and then he suddenly sat up, mid-conversation, and looked at me as if he'd just noticed me. He was not himself. Becoming less himself, but who or what he was becoming instead, I did not know. It unnerved me but I did not react, for fear of alarming him further. Instead, I shook his hand and embraced him and told him everything was all right, and to take care of himself and that I'd come back to see him. Except, of course, I did none of these things. I left him almost as he was talking, telling myself that I'd say these things next time. Little did I know that we had already run out of next times. The fog took him, too, along with our unsaid things. Age undoes all, at least for the lucky ones who make it that far. Then life just carries on without a person. Even meaningless objects remain. Anthony would have stopped the entire world when his life stopped, if he could. I'm certain of it. His last words, with hilariously extravagant misanthropy, were, "You're all just a shower of bastards." He had the tyrant in him, unquestionably. And yet I missed him.

I left, and not long afterward, my grandfather drowned in that airtight room.

All that is left of my grandfather's memory are the things he passed on, now that he has gone into the soil and is reduced to bones, the network of nerves and electricity in his brain shut down, area by area, like a city trying to conceal itself in the night.

Naval Insignia

Anthony kept a photograph of his younger brother Charlie, not on direct display, not framed, behind an ornament on the cabinet, but still there. Visible yet partially hidden, in some hierarchy that only he was party to. They looked almost like twins, except that his brother had chosen the open seas and signed up for the merchant navy. He was wearing his uniform in the photo. Spotlessly white. He was on board long enough to make able seaman in the deck department of several vessels. It was a hard life. On shore leave, he had recounted to Anthony an incident he'd seen on watch one night. Some of the sailors were playing cards, unwinding by escalating the tension, and an English fellow was beating a Scot, horribly so, in front of everyone. "He made an example of him. Laughing while he did it. Took a month's wages. The guy didn't know when he was beat." Eventually the Scot snapped and took a swing for the other. The cards and the chips went everywhere, and eventually the scuffle was broken up and it all died down. Or they thought it had. A razor was hidden in the back of a cap, and one of them pulled it out and you could see the sudden glint as he lunged at the face. Poor bastard lost an eye in one fell stroke. The crew beat the guy to within an inch of his life in retaliation. "They danced on his head," Anthony remembered his brother saying, word for word. The military police carted him away. They roughed him up so badly he ended up mentally disabled, according to Charlie.

Charlie looked simultaneously proud and lost in the photo, gazing somewhere beyond the camera. He was not destined to live long. That much was certain. Anthony had no reluctance about speaking of him and his early death, but the circumstances changed every time he related it to a new person. He had told my mother, cryptically, that Charlie had been "hit by a lift." He told my aunt Anne that Charlie had fallen into the dry dock of a harbor. I wondered if there was some sliver of truth in either tale, some surrogate story where he had been injured or someone else had died, and Anthony had passed it off for ease of mind, to himself as much as other people. Fiction was easier to absorb than inconvenient painful truths. Suspension of disbelief was easier than the demands made by the factual.

When the contradictions came to light, however, people started to pry. The great secret, the source of shame, for a devout Catholic at least, was that Charlie had committed suicide in his late twenties. He had knelt on the tiles of his London digs and laid his head on a dishcloth in the gas oven. It's not known whether he had left contact details for Anthony, but the authorities managed to get in touch through Bernie, my aunt. Charlie lived in Holland Park, that much was remembered. It turned out that he had married the love of his life and, having set off for sea for an extended period, returned to find that his bride was pregnant by another man. Upon learning this, Charlie's photograph seemed to change. He had become a tragic figure—if not a martyr, then certainly one instilled with melancholy and retrospective doom. A lost, and wronged, soul. The knowledge that he would be betrayed and ruined, and would never grow much older than he was in that photo, invested the image with a terrible haunting resonance. He became our familial patron saint of heartbreak. The weight of other people's experiences hung ungainly around his neck.

Much later, it would become apparent that the information they'd received was inaccurate. It was in fact Charlie who had cheated. He had gotten a teenage girl pregnant and, unable or unwilling to face a problematic future, had checked out. The saintly appearance of the photo would require another overhaul, and yet again it had not changed one iota. It remained exactly the same, as the dead do, while we the viewers are in flux. Anthony had traveled, in his best suit, alone to England to identify and retrieve his brother's body. I wondered what he was thinking on that ferry there and back.

In the days when he had rowed out on the lough, Anthony had approached a British four-funneled destroyer with sacks filled with contraband, as he had done many times before. He shouted up to the chief mate or the watch officer (the time of day or night goes undescribed), "Permission to approach the vessel?" and the usual haggling began. Reaching into a bag, Anthony was momentarily stopped in his tracks.

"Hey, McMonagle! Would you ever wind your fucking neck in?" went one recollection of the call. In another version he shouted, "McMonagle, are you up to no good?" Either way, Anthony heard someone calling him by name. He froze and turned to gaze upward, shielding his eyes, to see.

"How are ye doing, anyways?" the voice continued.

For once Anthony held his tongue, thrown by the voice. Eventually he let out, irritated by even saying it, "How do you know me?"

"None of your business, but I know you all right."

It was then that he recognized his brother's voice.

Charlie had vanished off to sea and somehow returned. What were the chances? They talked, the other sailors giving them a little space, but Anthony was unable to get on and Charlie was unable to get off. So they shouted back and forth. "I hadn't seen him in years," my grandfather admitted later.

Anthony told him to wait there. His heart was pounding and he set off rowing to the shore. He ran all the way home, bursting into the house, breathless with news for his parents that Charlie was back, rousing them to go see him. His parents were instantly dismissive. He begged them to come, but they fobbed him off. There would always be another time.

When you went away then, you went away for good. It was like grief. Families regularly undertook, for those setting off on the transatlantic crossing, what was called an "American wake" because they knew—regardless of success or otherwise—they'd never hear from, or even of, their loved ones ever again. Even London swallowed people up forever. Not a phone call, not a postcard. Yet his parents would not budge, even as Anthony pleaded with them.

It goes unrecorded whether he, or they, ever saw Charlie alive again.

Revolver

One day, long before I was born, my uncle Tony, who specialized from an early age in delinquency as a fine art, came home with a spring in his step. His God-fearing patriarch father, suspicious of any signs of joy, followed him through the house as Tony whooped and hollered like a cowboy, grabbing him hard by the wrist and shaking until he dropped what he was holding. It was a rusting revolver. Anthony was incandescent with rage, cursing, threatening to deal with his son later, before taking the revolver quickly and covertly—like it was a terrible omen that would curse the house by its presence—past the checkpoint's glare, down the lane, and launching it as far as he could into the river. It sank like other secrets into the depths, where it remains. Perhaps he was right: perhaps it was an omen, given what was to come.

PART FOUR

The Liminal Place

Nail

After Kitty died, my family left Cedar Street for the suburbs, or rather a council estate that was marooned in the sticks, a stone's throw from the river, the place where my mother had grown up. The idea was to be close to my grandfather to help look after him, which was like moving into a web to look after a giant spider. The area was waiting to become the suburbs, but was ten years from doing so. Not part of the city yet, or of the countryside anymore. Suspended animation. The streetlights petered out long before the estate, so it was surrounded by darkness. My mother had been wanting to move out of town for some time, convinced that Cedar Street was going to hell in a handcart. Drunks had wrenched the guttering off their wall, and on another occasion smashed the back window of the tiny Renault 5 that she and Da had finally saved up to buy. Building work had stirred up the earth and caused an influx of rodents. A bristling rat in the attic, keeping us awake at night, was the last straw. So we left. The excuse was to help a grief-stricken Anthony, keep an eye on him and make sure "he didn't do anything silly," so they moved into a house recently vacated.

The local teenagers took umbrage at my presence from the beginning. The distance from my old gang was insurmountable in those pre-digital days, with a haphazard bus trundling past once in a blue moon. I watched the local youngsters in the fields. They'd buy beat-up old cars from scrap dealers in order to run them into the ground. The fields were like spirographs of deep mud tracks. Then they'd sit around in the carcass when it finally gave up the ghost, before a fiery Viking funeral. The younger ones would gather up golf balls from the rough and sell them back to golfers. I let my shyness get the better of me, and the brief window of opportunity was missed. And I didn't endear myself by hanging around alone or with the local girls, for whom I was a novel, and not unwilling, plaything.

Once, I foolishly invited old school friends over. They were trouble at the best of times, but I thought a change of scenery would be good. What badness could they get up to in the middle of nowhere? They arrived drunk, and at the first sign of provocation from the locals—an offensive remark, idly cast—it all kicked off. Before I knew it, there were scuffles and they chased the estate lads back into one of their houses, and their older brothers suddenly piled out en masse and there was a mad dash for the main road, chest bursting and muscles aching, giddy with adrenaline, until I realized, with the rest of the group running on, the laughter dying down, that we were two boys short; and reluctantly, cursing myself and them, I peeled back to see where they were. My friend Bobby was already unconscious, jaw broken, and Ciaran was being held by both arms as they laid into him. He was taunting them as they did so: "Is that all you've got?" I knew we were out of our depth, so I burst into our house and got my parents. They carried Bobby in, roaring at the locals, and cleaned him up, my mum's hand trembling with rage and nerves, but it was obviously bad, so he was carted off to hospital. We ended up being called to court—a day out of school in suits too big for us. Bobby never hung around with us again.

My father tried to do stuff for the local kids to ease the tensions. He got the council to put in goalposts for them, but they soon pulled the nets down, swinging on them. He carried on, planting saplings and making the area green. I watched him when he worked, digging and planting. Every time a child was born to someone in our family, my father would plant an oak tree. He said it was so the children could see how it grew alongside them, and outgrew them as they got older, and how it would live for centuries, invested with something of them. "There are oaks here that are ancient. With a bit of luck, this will still be growing here in three hundred years' time. Mature for another three hundred. Then die away for three hundred. We'll be gone almost a thousand years." Three hundred years ago, Blackbeard the pirate sailed on the seas, Voltaire and Swift were writing, Jacobites were losing their heads. There was a Holy Roman Empire. Colonel John Mitchelburne flew the crimson flag from St. Columb's Cathedral steeple in Derry, twenty-five years after the Siege, before forming the Apprentice Boys club. Three hundred years before that, the black death still raged. The Prague "heretics" were being burned at the stake. Joan of Arc was a child, and the people of Rouen were eating their pets, besieged by the English. Three hundred years before that was the First Crusade. All in the life of an oak.

My father seemed to be all for returning Derry to the mythic arcadia of oak groves that it was once said to have been. He saw himself in the lineage of the Celts, wearing a silver torque on his arm and his hair long, even though it was said there were no such people as the Celts, or at least not people who identified as such. When there is no refuge in the present, it is tempting to make a refuge of a past that may never have been, or a future that may never come. Everyone does it, to some extent. He'd have been happier if he had lived back then, before Christianity, among the trees. Yet it would have been a brutal place as well as bliss—a place of wolves, bearing the name Doire Calgach, or "the oak grove of he who possesses the blade."

My father did his best, planting as many trees as he could. Births were an excuse. Perhaps the local kids saw it as weakness or just an opportunity, for one day they came down to the front of the house and nailed a crossbar to two of my father's trees and began to play football, shouting abuse at my mother when she tried to reason with them. They then brought their brothers down and performed a Mexican standoff outside the house. Something was said and a hyena laugh followed and a red mist descended on me, and my father saw it in my face as I passed and he said, "Don't." He shouted it again as I broke into a stride and drove my head into the ringleader's chest, sending him skidding onto his back. He got up, disheveled, claiming I was a dead man; but the others had seen him disoriented, however momentarily, and they backed off.

My father was in another room when I came back. I stormed through the house, throwing the wood from their crossbar into our backyard, jittery with adrenaline and feeling simultaneously sped-up and worn-out. I realized, only much later when my heartbeat settled, that it was perhaps the first time I'd ever heard my father raise his voice.

I couldn't understand his pacifism. He was a big guy, after years of bodybuilding. His upbringing was rough, yet he was always extolling peace in a place where even peace felt like war, and failure, by another means. Perhaps his size was deterrent enough. I found his pacifism naive, even an insult at times. When I would get roughed up at school, he'd always counsel calm and understanding until it grated on me and I didn't want to hear it anymore. It seemed to have nothing to do with reality. It felt like a cop-out. His distance added to the feeling. I felt like shouting at him, "What the fuck do you know?" but we didn't even feel close enough—or were too close—to have a row. Every boy thinks his father is a hero, and no boy forgives him when he turns out to be human.

It happened with politics too. When some atrocity in our community occurred, my father was always careful to say that the British people were not to blame (he was culturally something of an Anglophile, loving the Stones, Frank Sidebottom, *Dad's Army*, and so on) and that the loyalist people had believed the lies as much as our side had. He was magnanimous to the point where it stuck in my throat. A typical teenager, I spent as much time as possible outside, coming back for silent, sullen meals and then heading back out again.

It was an odd place, in hindsight; only a few miles from Derry, but it might as well have been in the Appalachians. The local boys kept single-barreled rifles and fierce dogs and listened to shitty metal bands. I couldn't tell if they were stoners or if they kicked the shit out of stoners, or both. They were yahoos. Border villages have that feel to them, a mix of the Wild West and some postapocalyptic Las Vegas; an unreality, or perhaps a deep reality. The nearest settlement was the unfortunately named Muff, just on the other side of the border. The village was full of petrol stations, making use of the currency and tax differences, and slot machines. A dry cleaner's sat snugly next to a funeral parlor. There was a bar ominously called the

Squealin' Pig. A gardai station next to a bookmaker's. It was a quiet liminal space, but other sides would show up semi-regularly. The smuggling had changed since my grandfather's day but it was still rife, mainly with cigarettes and laundered fuel. Occasionally an entrepreneurial spirit would borrow a tractor or digger and pull up to one of the then brand-new but conveniently isolated ATM machines and wrench it out of the wall and carry it off whole. Crossing the border was a respite from the Troubles. People traveled south and exhaled a breath they didn't realize they'd been holding in.

The estate was mixed, and a great deal of the bolshiness and suspicion that I encountered came from years of that tense balance. On the morning of the first July 12 we spent there, I lay dreaming and began to hear Pied Piper music, almost carnival-like, but with a pounding war drum growing in the distance. It followed me from dreaming into a waking state, lying staring at the ceiling. The pounding had become so loud that I felt it in my chest. I rose wearily from my bed, just enough to peer out the window. An entire Orange band, complete with police escort, had marched up to the estate and was now paused in front of our row of houses. The triumphal flute fell away until it was just a thumping Lambeg drum as they marched on the spot, reminding us locals whose territory we were unwelcome guests in. Their banner was emblazoned with psychedelic Victorian writing that reminded me of Sgt. Pepper's, only a bad-trip version. Then, message transmitted, they continued on the Queen's highway until the music was a distant sound and birdsong gradually replaced it.

Between creepy retired UDR men, whose houses I was told not to be enticed into, and redneck country boys, the dynamics of the estate lent themselves to occasional moments of dark surrealism. There was a guy who'd once been a jockey but had fallen and been trampled by the hooves and was now a sorrowful cliché, "never the same again." It left him "touched," as they say. He was Catholic but was pals with the Orangemen, except for one morning per year when they'd march. Then he'd go down, ostensibly walking his dog, and call them all Nazi bastards and so on, while they rolled their eyes before telling him to fuck off home. Later that day he'd be down the local pub, the Magnet, propping up the bar and downing pints of stout with them all.

In the eyes of those who had always been there, the standard of the newcomers was always slipping, always diluting the pure stock. It didn't matter that the estate had been built only in the sixties; it felt like the roots had been there since time immemorial. In some cases, like a stopped clock telling the correct time, they were right about newcomers. Loners would rent bungalows, designed originally for elderly couples, and unsettling events would accompany them. Curses roared in the dead of night, broken windows, cryptic scrawls of graffiti. The knee-jerk reaction among some was to blame nearby Gypsies, but it became clear that the newcomers were exiles from the city, pushed out, having been accused or convicted of sex offenses. The IRA, or a cover group, would pass them a message stating in no uncertain terms that they were to leave the community or be paid a brief and bloody visit. To leave the country was a big ask, so they'd sidle out to the city limits and, for a time, keep their heads down. It added a subliminal air of menace that kids were primed against. We didn't talk to strangers, unless they were female, and even then, we did so in a guarded manner.

The area was called the Woodlands, conjuring up a bucolic Thomas Hardy setting, but the woods were giving way to farms and an expanding golf course. They still existed on marshy land along the banks of streams, as artificial obstacles around the greens, breaking up boundaries, and as a cove down Hart's Lane. The old Irish name was even more revealing and relevant: Ballynagard, the "townland of the garrison." Those soldiers had long been killed or dispersed, but a garrison remained. It was about a mile from the border, which was itself guarded sternly, but idly, by a customs kiosk that would pull in vehicles in an attempt to curb smuggling. A stone's throw from our house, though, was the real divide in the form of the British Army checkpoint. Ostensibly the border followed the county lines between Derry and Donegal, which felt arbitrary, given that the two slipped into each other genealogically, topographically, and so on. This was merely then a rewrite of an earlier fiction.

I'd often wondered what it was like for the soldiers, to be posted from London or Yorkshire or Glasgow to an obscure corner of their kingdom, here to protect ungrateful bastards in the omnipresent rain, dragging their families to uncanny garrison towns that felt both under siege and like a goldfish bowl. Certainly there were benefits—helicopter rides, firing ranges down in the sand dunes on the other side of the Foyle, the feeling of supremacy that came with a gun and uniform and the ability, the blessing, to dominate a population. To me, even as a kid, it looked like such a wretched position that I wondered what the place they'd left must have been like.

The nature of asymmetric warfare was that the enemy was invisible. He drank in the pubs and walked around the shops with his wife, maybe his kids. He or she melted into the crowd. They *were* the crowd. Naturally, it bred paranoia. Once upon a time these threats amid the citizenry were called wood-kerne. Then, strangely, tories. Then rapparees. Queen Elizabeth wrote of the need to civilize the Foyle and "do service upon the rebels." Once upon a time they had vanished into the trees. Now they vanished into the streets. The RUC accompanied the soldiers as a sort of translator with the locals. It was like employing Iago for community relations. Out of shape, semiprofessional, and provincial next to the trained military, they puffed themselves up and were constantly proving themselves, which meant they were insufferable to much of the populace. The people were addressed in the tones of a Calvinist schoolteacher or a perpetually irate manager who, flabby around the gills, fancied himself as still having an edge. The RUC were keen to make examples, to prove themselves.

Our family trips to Donegal, to the beach or the woods, were punctuated with these encounters. Half the time we were waved through and some other sod took the hit. The other half, there were difficulties. We'd be waved into a siding by a cop with a fluorescent baton, the swing of it leaving a momentary arc in the air and in my vision. There we'd be addressed, not always with contempt or a sneer, but consistently with an exaggerated pastiche of authority. It was like a Monty Python re-creation of Oswald Mosley. The aggression, at that point, was passive, but barely. My father's name, being confrontationally Irish, was a problem. The fact that he answered Derry, and not Londonderry, to their second question was a problem. The time he took getting out of the car and the sigh he gave when opening the boot were a problem. His posture was a problem. His wife and children were a problem. I got the gist of what they were doing even as a very small child; the attempt at protracted humiliation and demoralization. When I got to a certain age as a young man, it was my turn. On the way to receive an award at a school event in the evening, already embarrassed and nervous, we were pulled over. The clock ticked until it wasn't worth watching it tick any longer, when it had to be let go. We stood in the rain, my mother, sister, and I, as they frisked my father again and made us wait while his details were corroborated.

I had never seen my father's temper even begin to rise except in these moments. Even then it was through gritted teeth, murmuring under his breath, and by the time we reached home he would be singing again, or telling us about how there once existed a type of penguin that stood more than six feet tall, or how every minute of every day lightning was somewhere hitting the earth, or how in the polar regions at certain times of the year the sun shone at midnight. Yet the feeling of anger and humiliation would not simply have passed but would have fallen and settled into him, as it did me, standing next to my mother and sister in the rain, watching my father insulted and manhandled for saying his own name, and the name of his hometown, to an armed stranger from across the sea.

Sometimes they'd jokingly frisk the children as a friendly gesture and ask us about what they'd find in our coat pockets in a forced amicable way—"Are you good at conkers, mate?"—or flick through football stickers of First Division English football teams and say things like, "Liverpool are shit, mate. You wanna be supporting United." The entire car was searched, from the glove box to the undercarriage to the engine. The headlights of the slow passing cars, full of eyes, shimmered on the tides of rain.

People evolved quickly. They learned to prime themselves in advance. There was self-preservation in avoidance. Keep your head down. "Whatever you say, say nothing." At first this seems out of character for a culture that has prized itself on storytellers and raised bullshitting to a high art. Yet it was part of the subterfuge. If we had a hundred tongues in our heads, the saying went, it would not do justice to the real stories, the ones that counted. These, however, were rarely the ones told. Instead the telling of fictions, anecdotes, jokes, and myths were often a way at keeping certain subjects at bay. It was a way of not speaking.

The local shop and pub lay on the wrong side of the check-point. It was always a long walk. The signs came first: "Stop. Wait until called forward"; "Headlights off. All ID cards to be shown. Await green light to advance." Then the cameras and listening devices were noticeable, up on the trees and the lamp-posts. In a vehicle, we'd invariably be warned, "Watch what you say until we're through." There was, surreally, a house inside the checkpoint, detached from but surrounded by the military. The owner had a fraught relationship with the occu-piers, taking the Ministry of Defence to court for invasion of privacy, given that it was believed they could hear everything he said or did. The base itself was surrounded by high tin walls and lumbering concrete blocks, around which cars would have to slow and wind to prevent sudden accelerating attacks. Up in the watchtower were snipers and lookouts. We'd no idea if we were in the sights at any given moment. I saw barrel tips protrud-ing occasionally. And at nighttime the green glow of night sights turned the landscape into oceanic depths.

The men holding the rifles were not that much older than I was. They'd been kids when I'd been a toddler. Now they were Roman soldiers on Hadrian's Wall and I was one of the savages.

Some soldiers spent their shifts alert, scanning the landscape intensely from their vantage point. Others were glad for an hour or two alone, away from ball-busting, public-school prick supe-riors complaining about dirty kits or ordering them on patrol for dozens of miles across godforsaken moors. Some took a porno mag for company or a sneaky drink. There was usually a grille around the lookout slots to deflect incoming mortars. From our estate we'd watched it go up, factory-made sheets and poured concrete. What it reminded me of changed as time passed—a fort in the early days of the Wild West, a terraforming outpost on a hostile planet. It was a place that set itself up for a siege and therefore was under siege. Even the faces said it. I couldn't see how young the grunts were, for all the marks of camouflage. Sixty shades of tarmac painted on them. A permanent studied grimace.

I tried various techniques to walk through the checkpoint unimpeded—attempting to look distracted, happy; avoiding eye contact, making eye contact; acting natural, acting strange. The result was invariably the same: I was always stopped and questioned, sometimes searched, sometimes hassled. I wasn't all that different from them, hiding my fear and trying a bit too hard to appear like a hard man, unconvincingly arrogant. The difference being that I had no weapon. They kept their rifles very much on show, even when huddled in the doorway of their corrugated tower. Occasionally a disembodied voice would emerge from the slots, high up in the structures. The messages shouted down were always insults, usually some variation of "Fenian," "paddy," or "faggot," but occasionally showing wit ("Oi, mate, lend us your walk"), which made me laugh despite myself. I'd respond to the foulmouthed gargoyles with hand gestures from a safe distance, not knowing if they were still watching.

Now and then, the soldiers on ground level would call me over and produce an English banknote from a jacket pocket and tell me to go buy them smokes, even though I was way underage. I'd seen other kids getting a slap or being lifted off the ground with the swing of a boot, so I didn't flat-out refuse. To avoid what I thought of as collaboration—the walls had more than one set of eyes, after all—I'd tell them I wasn't returning for several hours and they'd wait for the next sap to come along.

Not far from the checkpoint, a large picket-gate estate was being built, and when the work had died down, the local kids would go up and hang out in these huge half-formed shells and

tunnels, smoking and flirting and all the tentative furtive things
that come with that age. Sian was older and cool. She had a
Louise Brooks bob, with the attitude of a punk. "You're doing
it all wrong," she said, exhaling smoke. "You take their money,
ask them all if they need anything. Act real helpful, then you
walk away and you just keep it. Then you come back up via the
fields out at the back road or down by the shore. Then you leave
it a while and make sure you wear something else next time you
walk through. Easy. Think of it as a tax." So I adopted that
strategy and it worked, until one day I absentmindedly came
back the way I'd arrived, having spent the money on ice cream
and comics. It was only on seeing the soldier that I remembered.
I tried turning back quickly but was grabbed by the throat and
earned a punch in the ear for my insolence. It put a shame in
me, a shame that would turn bitter, to wishing terrible violence
upon them. I knew not to tell my parents.

I would never have believed then that people, politicians,
the great and the good, would one day claim there had never
been a border. That none of this existed, including me. They
should have kept some of the checkpoints. Let them fall into
ruin but exist as warnings from history. Moving on was a re-
fined way of covering up.

The motto of County Derry is *Auxilium a domino*, "Help
comes from the Lord." By then it had taken on a jaded, bitterly
ironic tone. The locals had largely forgotten that the army came
initially as heroes to save them, was welcomed as a stabilizing
force at a time when civil disobedience was being crushed, a
bulwark between Catholics and the sectarian police. There had
been a honeymoon period. The tea-and-biscuit period. Mobs
backed up by the police and auxiliaries had been making violent incursions into Catholic areas. The army arrived in Derry
via the river, to the Naval Base. They were officially instructed

to adhere to a "MIDAS" touch: minimum force, impartiality, discipline, alertness, and security. They forgot what happened to King Midas. The problem was that the terrorists weren't seen as terrorists by the population. They *were* the population, in places. And therefore the population could be conceived of as terrorists. It was a gray zone and an excuse for murder.

They were welcomed as protectors. The welcome did not last. The locals forgot they came as heroes because the soldiers forgot.

I hadn't thought of the checkpoint as a target, though it thought of itself as one. That stuff happened nearby but elsewhere, like in the hinterlands of South Armagh, where the IRA had road signs put up that read "Sniper at Work." I never thought I lived in a hinterland, because home doesn't feel that way. It's a center. One day I came back from school to find windows cracked and blown in around the estate. The IRA had hijacked a white van, cut the roof off it, driven it within striking distance of the checkpoint, and fired a mortar from inside. They'd use gas canisters at times, nicknamed "barrack busters" (which then became a term for the large stumpy bottles of cider that alcos drank, as the cheapest way to get drunk). The van launched into the air, veered off into an adjacent field, and exploded, creating a blast wave and no doubt sending the soldiers within into fight-or-flight mode. By the time I arrived back, the drama was over, and they were performing forensics on the scorched vehicle. I had a tendency to narrowly miss such events, later sleeping through an earthquake on a Greek island, not yet aware that I should be very careful of wanting to be part of history. I'd always left early or arrived late. The police standing around behind fluorescent tape. A woman using bowls of water to wash blood off the street and into the gutter. A parent, framed in a window, sweeping glass from their child's cot.

The soldiers at Culmore were lucky. Their colleagues at Coshquin were not. Perhaps they were the same soldiers, rotated. Early one morning a van rolled in. Inside was a building contractor, a Catholic, who'd repeatedly been warned against working for the army but had carried on doing his job, refusing to be frightened. The IRA paid him a visit one night, held his family at gunpoint, strapped him into the driver's seat, and watched him all the way as he drove in and pulled up next to the soldiers. There were shouts and the sound of gunfire and then the entire checkpoint was gone. Commanders were trying to radio to a checkpoint that no longer existed. People were stunned afterward. Eventually a distancing came about, when I began to hear jokes and playground insults. The more callous it was, the more neutralized it seemed. Support for the IRA plummeted in the aftermath, though. It was seen locally as cold-blooded murder. That feeling lasted until the next time loyalists went in and shot up a bar, or the army shot an unarmed person. Peace was continually squandered, but even the brutal, clarity-inducing shock of the violence was squandered and passed over too.

Diary

School was another territory. I kept my head down. The key was to find blind spots. The football pitches. The handball alley. The back gates. Places out of sight, to hang out and smoke dope and talk about Akira or Judge Dredd or Nine Inch Nails or whatever. The school prided itself on having several Nobel laureates, being a factory of the new Catholic middle class. I never felt comfortable there. Each year they focused on getting a select few, the anointed head boys, to Oxbridge. The outlook for the rest was superfluous, regardless of how smart you were. If you were interested in something like architecture and art history, as I was, you were out of your lane and out of your depth, it was strongly implied. So much depended, even there in a beleaguered backwater town, on who your parents were and how much they earned.

Other boys clambered to be prefects, basically snitches. The priests were often ball-busters. Even the secular teachers had a fairly closed outlook. "There will never be peace in this country," a history teacher announced to us one day, not long before the peace process began. Teachers with predatory sexual proclivities were well known and joked about, even by other teachers ("Don't get caught in the showers with Mr. You-Know-Who"), but were allowed to simply drop off into quiet early retirement. We were taught to keep our traps shut. We were also taught to elucidate and enunciate in speech class, which was designed to rid us of our regional accents and any trace of working-class traits, so that we'd be fit to masquerade as civilized people when we invariably moved to London to find work.

I grew more and more inclined to other forms of education, sifting through books on the futurists, the surrealists, Dada, New Objectivity. Art became my education and my faith. I became fascinated by the ephemera of the movements, their pamphlets, handbills, invitations to happenings, photographs of strange characters. It, like the surreal marginalia doodled by medieval monks in the outlines of illuminated texts, was much more interesting and lifelike than the official historical stories.

Some of the masters—a pompous phrase they insisted on, in aspirational mimicry of the English—were plum-mouthed alcoholics with elbow patches, comb-overs, and half bottles of whiskey in their briefcases, who'd grown up in the shires and gradually been washed out to the peripheries. One even came in drunk, stood at the front of a class of fourteen-year-olds, and asked which one of them was man enough to get up and fight him. He was last seen sitting outside the headmaster's office, with a coat draped over him like a defeated boxer, bleary-eyed and staring beyond the floor into outer space, waiting for his wife and the final drive home.

My attempts not to draw attention to myself drew attention. My attempts at invisibility irritated certain priests and teachers.

A dark horse was something to be suspicious of. Hidden depths were impermissible. My hair was always too long or too short, my appearance too scruffy, my subjects too arty. They allowed for certain kinds of freedom, or rather they left cracks and corners beneath the teachers' attention that creativity could flourish in. All my art projects were collages, as I couldn't afford paint, and the textiles I wanted to use for fashion design were even more expensive. I'd cut up free catalogs and stick the pieces together, and the teachers would comment on the influence of Hannah Höch or Joseph Cornell, and I'd silently nod my head.

It was a sanctuary, though. You could bring albums to the art rooms, guitars into the gym when no one was around. Playing real songs that would never be recorded or even named, we formed imaginary bands with imaginary names and drew imaginary logos on our folders. Other kids exchanged rave tapes. We drew elaborate, obscene tableaux on our friends' plaster of paris. Kids went from spraying "IRA" to "NIN" or "NWA." Until Britpop, the jocks seemed to have little interest in music, which suited the rest perfectly. I always carried around an assortment of cassettes inside a secret pocket in the lining of my blazer, which also allowed for some minor shoplifting. There was such a scarcity of access to music that learning of a band or genre was like being party to alchemical secrets. People claimed ownership of favorite bands. I was insatiable, recording scraps of footage on flickering video. Exciting things were happening, but far away, over the seas. Most of the time I hammered through my work in class so that I could spend the day staring out the window, daydreaming. I always sat next to the window. The occasional kind teacher would notice and give me books after class that we weren't studying—Camus (whom I adored) or Salinger (whom I didn't); I hadn't realized they did this for the weirdos every successive year. One of the few young priests would talk to me about the religious collages I was making in art class and my burgeoning fascination with Nietzsche, but he was the exception and quietly vanished shortly thereafter, perhaps caring more than was healthy for his mission.

Being left to your own devices was a brief utopian state, which was not often permitted. To be quiet by choice or temperament was to be a threat, to be judged as plotting, which I was, always searching out escape routes through gaps in the railings or disused parts of the school. The school itself used to be an aristocratic building, intended once as a casino. The old IRA had held out in the building against hostile forces once, while tommy guns blasted all the windows in on them. Middle-class teachers and even priests loved to tell stories like that about the old IRA, while condemning the new one. History was a way of forgetting. There was an old windmill ruin, the site of pitched battles during the Siege, and a library filled with ancient religious texts. If you got past the guards of these areas, they were perfect places to hide, but risky too, given that all it took was being spotted on the way in by a prefect and they'd bring one of the masters directly to you, with a face like thunder.

My shyness and efforts at discretion were undermined continually by the fact that I surrounded myself with lunatics. My friends seemed constantly, perilously keen to get noticed, and I was dragged, often bodily, into their schemes. They flooded the science labs. They would suck the gas taps and blow on Bunsen burners to set fire to each other's aprons. They started a craze for passing out by hyperventilating, which was traced back to them when a kid had a seizure. When I say "they," I mean "we." I was lined up in a hallway and roared at by an apoplectic year-head, still feeling out of body following my own unconsciousness. In art class, when the time came to make sculptures, we would place lumps of clay filled with air holes next to one another's projects so that they'd explode in the kiln. Once, we stole chemicals from a science lesson because we wanted to light invisible fires and get people to sit on them. Fun was always pushed to dangerous levels. Driven in buses to celebrate a cross-community bonding game of rugby, one of my friends opened his blazer to reveal a box full of ball bearings. After the resulting mini riot between the schools, the teachers from the other school came marching down the aisle, picking out the ringleaders one by one. Some were wearing their coats inside out and had ruffled their hair in disguise. I'd have ditched my friends, but for the fact they were hilarious and the only interesting people in sight, deranged as they were.

Once, though, they turned on me. At the bottom of my bag and in my locker I would keep a black book, full of notes, fragments of songs, poems, ideas for stories and films. It was like the inner workings of my head, and I was intensely protective of its privacy. One day my friends were fooling around, turning my school bag inside out as a trick, and they found the book, and before I even discovered it was missing, it had been passed around and ridiculed. They began mocking me as I came walking down to where the smokers stood. I snatched it back, my face flushed, and feeling ill, then took it out later that day to the lane at the back of the school and burned it. The fragments in the book were gone forever. It was only later that I felt angry for betraying myself. No outside enemy could ever win if you had no enemy inside your own head.

Something happened to me after that time. Something changed. It was as if a space that I had secretly formed had been invaded. I still kept to myself, always sketching, dreaming obsessively of imaginary art movements to belong to or of long-lost artists in distant cities, but I developed a quick temper. All it took was an unwanted ruffling of my hair, for instance, and

I'd fly off the handle. I don't know where that rage came from. It didn't matter that I could barely beat snow off a rope. The red mist insisted on action. At the beginning of a new year I got into a punch-up walking home, over a misunderstood aside, with the hardest kid in the school, a glassy-eyed thug who by all accounts ended up in the youth wing of the IRA not long afterward. In the course of the scuffle I was knocked out cold, so my mate jumped in. It was broken up only when a taximan pulled in and intervened. I had a shaved head then, and given that *Alien 3* was in the cinemas, older kids took to calling me "Ripley," which I didn't mind so much, but the attention, their gazes and nudges and laughter in the corridors, felt inescapable. I stuck it out and was left alone from then on. I wore the wounds, came to school, and they moved on to easier targets, but although I appeared impassive, the rage simply grew.

The army intensified this feeling. Every day my friends and I would walk down through the town to get our buses home. To do so, we'd have to walk through the Derry walls at Bishop Street, right next to the courthouse. It was an intersection area, given to attacks, and the army kept turnstiles in the ancient archway that you had to pass through. The medieval walls were retrofitted with the security apparatus of wire and tin and high protective fences. All the windows in the areas were boarded up or had iron grilles over them. The first CCTV cameras watched people pass in hazy spectral form. The noisy, undulating swarm of schoolboys would shrink briefly into a single file as we passed through, and the Brits would occasionally shout abuse from the slit of their lookout post. Two or three times I was spat on and, no longer caring much, began to return the favor. The group would expand again within the walls into a noisy swarm, and the Brits would go back to training their sights on a passing city.

Empty Bottle

Without money to spend, there was nowhere for us to go. We slowly realized how exclusive buildings were. My friends and I were regularly moved on from loitering anywhere, under the threat of arrest. In the prime of youth—the greatest years of our lives, as we were frequently told—we were banished from sight. We gravitated to the edges. Caught out one night, a friend and I tried to sleep in a building site, but there was a huge drop between the planks we were lying across, and all it would have taken for serious injury was to roll over in our sleep. We trudged on into woods overlooking the river, but the rain came down so heavily it felt like hail and we were forced to take refuge by crawling into concrete tubes. I crawled in first and passed out, exhausted, and woke only because of my friend's screams. Flicking a lighter, I found we were covered in insects—in our hair and clothes—and we clattered out, kicking and twitching back into the rain. I thought the morning would never come, sitting drenched on the doorstep of a bricked-up gatehouse. I had a home. I was a tourist in ruin. After that experience, I found myself looking at streets in the city, thinking of where someone homeless might find refuge, and I could find very few places that hadn't been, in some way, sabotaged.

It is the living who haunt places, not the dead. Hanging out around town with my friends, I would cross paths occasionally with my uncle Budgie. He was my cousin but had been brought up alongside my father and his siblings as their brother because Budgie's mother had been young and unmarried when she'd fallen pregnant. She'd been sent off to England to hide the pregnancy, and my grandmother Needles raised the baby on her return. The prying eyes were always looking for scandal. Of all the children and grandchildren, Budgie was the one who looked most like our grandfather, or at least like the army photograph. He had a hint of Elvis, had Elvis chosen boxing rather than rock 'n' roll. Budgie had a mix, not uncommon in the North, of caustic wit and tenderness. He also had a catastrophic drink problem, exhibited publicly. The whole town eventually knew him, after the elder generation of locally famous street drinkers died off. He was a strange anti-celebrity. Reports of his whereabouts would inevitably be one of two possibilities: "Budgie's off the drink" or "Budgie's in a bad way." I remembered him very sweetly coming up to our house with his newborn child and girlfriend, proclaiming a new chance at life, and even as young as I was, I knew it would not last. Budgie ended up in a squalid flat a few streets from our home. It was largely empty, even of furniture, and the drinkers would all lie on the floor at angles that seemed to have followed falls. It scared me visiting him, but I tried not to show it, standing behind my father's legs. Eventually even that shell of the flat went and he ended up on the streets, unprotected.

Two elderly alcoholics, called Sammy and Sheila, were famous in the town; Sheila grew up in Springtown Camp originally. More people knew them than knew who the mayor was. They'd hang around Littlewoods at the bottom of William Street and the pedestrian area of Guildhall Square with their little dog. There used to be subterranean public toilets there, which were then replaced by a fountain before it, too, disappeared. They'd sit there or shuffle around. They were old before their time, and when they died, Budgie and his friends had already replaced them. It was a hard existence that had persisted for a long time (my father remembered men extracting pure alcohol from boot polish to drink), but homeless people had been older before, seasoned itinerant travelers or eccentric old men dressed like ornamental Victorian hermits. Now something had changed, and the homeless street drinkers were suddenly young. Tapping money for drink, lying out in the elements, committing petty crimes, giving—but far more often receiving—violence. Budgie ended up bloated, with a repeatedly broken nose changing his profile. I never thought he'd live that long, but he survived into his thirties, and I began to think, foolishly, that he was perhaps indestructible and would make it, or at least slow down as he aged. I was wrong again. They closed the homeless refuge he'd been sleeping in, cost cutting a few years before full-blown austerity. He was forced to make his home in a disused public toilet next to a car park that had once been called Victoria Market and still bore the archway, without the market. It had no door and an ill wind came in off the river.

Men do not freeze to death in modern times; they do not freeze to death in October; they do not freeze to death in disused toilet cubicles, where people wouldn't even stop to piss, directly opposite supermarkets with bins filled every night with wasted food, and hotels with rows of empty rooms. Men do not die because there are no clouds forecast, just a night that falls into space and a blind moon, the color of ivory. Exposure is a thing of long ago. Drop-in centers do not close. Funding is never cut. There is never nowhere to go. Mothers do not mourn, nor are they sedated. Men do not become alcoholics, as they have no reasons for doing so; they do not alienate friends and family, alienate themselves; they do not sleep on the streets, and they do not fail to wake up. They are not dragged from their coffins by friends in the same mad fog of drink, saying in genuine confusion, "Budgie, stop messing around, get up tae fuck." Shoppers do not walk past tutting—a grown man in a halo of blood outside a supermarket entrance, lying near enough to make the doors open and close. Strangers do not kick his teeth in, or set him on fire for a laugh, or piss on him while he sleeps.

The past is repealed. Men do not break into pensioners' homes for drinking money and trash the place in a blind rage. Men do not place derisory coins in their relative's hands while fobbing them off, embarrassed in front of their pals, then write about it in books. Men do not freeze to death in modern times; they do not freeze in October, not in the West, not here, and definitely not now.

I couldn't entirely blame those who refused to believe that a man could freeze to death in a modern city in autumn. There were times when I was young and schoolmates would nudge me as they passed and say, "Budgie's your uncle, isn't he?" and I would disown him, *three times before the cock crowed*, feeling ashamed and somehow unmasked. Life was not easy for Budgie, and he was not easy with it. People drown on dry land. They are not easy to help. They are not saints. And neither, it turns out, is anyone else.

Pills

The freedom to be left alone was a precious one. Those teenage years were predicated on making ourselves invisible. It was a strange consequence of security areas in Derry, cut off by barbed wire and steel gates, that if trespassers got in, they became imperceptible, fenced off and forgotten about. On what the military and paramilitaries called "dead ground." My friends and I spent our teenage years in such places. We'd long been on the peripheries, lurking on street corners with our hoods up, drinking in alleyways, always on the unsuccessful lookout for a "free house" where we could sink into the sofas and, high as kites, curse the first traitorous blue of morning and the tweeting of robotic birds through slivers in the curtains. We would sit on swings in moonlit playgrounds, playing ghetto blasters and double dropping E tabs, taking great interest in what color and design they were, from cartoon characters to corporate logos. Days later, but under cover of darkness, I would always creep back into the house, and no matter how quiet I was, my mother would wake up at my step on the stair and I'd have to feign nonchalance, with pupils like saucers and the walls melting around me; then a fevered night, unaware if I'd slept or not, with 1920s cartoons playing manically on the backs of my eyelids. I enjoyed the weekends beyond words.

The safest places were the most dangerous, in terms of getting caught with drugs or underage drinking. The RUC were absolute bastards, as were the scallies—"kappa kids," we called them (in Belfast they were "spides")—who'd pounce on anyone with the audacity to grow their hair long or have a same-sex lover or anything different really (yet they always had arbitrary tastes; I saw a pair threaten to stab a busker once because he didn't know any Luther Vandross songs). We fought them frequently, though we rarely instigated it—our appearance was an affront. If you stood out, simply, they tried to knock you down. We gave as good as we got. It was worse the next day, when the aching in the ribs reached a peak, and the split lips and black eyes seemed ripe and wept continually, eyelashes sticky as a Venus flytrap. Once, I found myself having to account in class on a Monday for why my friend and I, sitting next to each other, had four black eyes between us from the weekend. There were no adequate explanations for adults. We never looked for trouble but, singled out as freaks, we never backed down from it, either; to do so would mean living as a shadow. I never liked fighting, even in those long years. One of my legs would always tremble with adrenaline and I'd have to hide it, but I knew there were worse things than a beating, and I counted, foolishly, that there'd always be someone around who would break up the fight when it got out of hand.

We would drink and smoke weed and take pills up on

Derry's medieval walls, which gave us a view of anyone coming and the advantage of higher ground. When too many people started gravitating there, we pushed farther along. It was discovered that you could bypass and breach the security perimeter on the walls, which had supposedly been fortified to stop terrorist attacks, if you dangled over a twenty-foot drop and shimmied around the razor wire. We were taking our lives in our hands, especially under the influence, when everything felt like marshmallows and you couldn't tell how far away your own hands were; but once inside, we couldn't be seen or touched and were free to do whatever we wanted, right under the authorities' noses. The corner of the walls where we hung out was once called Coward's Bastion during the Siege, because it was farthest away from bombardment. Having braved near-death to get in, we raised our cans to our ancestors, the cowards.

If we were near civilization, we had to make sure there was serious peril required to access a place, in order to give pursuers a disincentive to follow us or at least hold them up for a while. Rooftops were best. We got into rooms and attics through skylights and by shimmying across vertigo-inducing windowsills, climbing high barbed-wire fences and scaffolding. The rule was that there must be another way out, no dead ends to get trapped in; preferably concealed, like wired fences unwound in advance, then covered up with leaves, which we'd skid or scramble through on hands and knees. When places were abandoned and in ruins, some creative vandalism was required to create new pathways through holes, or to get beyond rusted locks and doors that hadn't been opened in years. The activities came naturally to us. They were born of necessity. We took up residence as birds do in eaves or rats do in sewers. There was no performance involved. Our activities were expressly designed for invisibility.

Night was our real habitat. In the day we were exposed, but not when the sun set. People merely pass through the night as adults, and engagement is fleeting and purposeful, bolting from car to front door as if between airlocks in space. As teenagers, we fully inhabited the night. We were corner boys, moths in the glare of streetlights. We were of little harm to anyone but ourselves, but we did not realize the shadow we cast for those who passed. We drank in the borrowed light, on waste ground, broken glass shimmering in the moonlight, in the little lanes behind electric generators. All weathers. Taking shelter on the balconies of future offices. Hefting crates over fences. Chasing feral cats from buildings. Drinking when frost covered everything in sight, and the drink turned to swishing ice in the can. Sitting on docked boats. A tape player placed inside stacks of ventilation shafts, amplifying the sound of *Enter the Wu-Tang (36 Chambers)*, *Mellon Collie and the Infinite Sadness*, *Ritual de lo Habitual*, *Angel Dust*. Back when people felt they owned music and guarded it, when it was hard to come by and identity ran through it all like a strangling vine. Cutting paths through shifting undergrowth or gathered in huddles in viaducts. As I was tall for my age, I was sent in to buy all the drink for the underage of the neighborhood, or would walk into venues and then open the fire exits to let the others in. We'd congregate around arcade-game cabinets, perpetually skint, watching the high-score listings and flashing "Insert Coin to Start" signs, then dart around with security guards in pursuit through the aquarium light. Fearless as only the ignorant are.

We often sought out attics in building sites, where you were doubly hidden and could climb out through the skylight onto the roof if anyone did come, or just merge into the shadows. There the challenge was not to move or laugh, riddled with nerves, hearing the watchmen right below us. We learned to stay away from windows, otherwise people would call the cops. Playing three-dimensional stealth games. In truth, unless we were stupid, we rarely were interrupted, but we slipped up now and then. Once, someone was foolish enough to sit a candle near a window in an abandoned caretaker's house, and our shadows were projected onto the wall like malevolent ogres. Someone saw them and phone calls were made. Oblivious, we were all sitting around when the front door burst in and there was wild shouting and heavy boots thundering up the stairs and torches shining frantically in every direction. One of my friends kicked a hole in a plaster wall; another hung from and dropped down onto a lower level through a preexisting hole in the floor. The rest of us fled into a walk-in wardrobe to hide. I knew the game was up, though, and as we were dragged out, I held up my hands. Our eyes were still struggling with the light and the shouting hadn't ceased. Eventually the guns and torches dropped, and we saw that they were cops. "Thank Christ, it's just you," my friend said.

We learned about space while being chased, running for dear life, and often in the painful aftermath. If we made great leaps across gaps, it was best to roll with the landing rather than trying to land statically. Scaling walls and wire fences with the police or army behind us, we'd leap onto them while running full pelt, using momentum to propel ourselves upward, scurrying through vertical space like cats. No hesitation or you'd lose your nerve. If you led the police into the leafy, wealthy part of town, you could shake them up by luring them into dead-end cul-de-sacs and then scrambling through hedges to emerge elsewhere. Other means of escape were to lose yourself in a crowd, to pull your top off, or to jump into a phone box and let on that you had been on a call; or, if your nerve held, to counterintuitively walk back nonchalantly toward your pursuer, if they hadn't gotten a good look at you beforehand. It was all about nerve and the sense that the city should be ours at night. It was only with the arrival and ubiquity of CCTV that the odds stacked up, insurmountably, against us.

The main place we hung out was "down the bay," with the monumental brutalist bridge high above us. There were no cameras there. It was on the rich side of town, where old ladies had squirted us with garden hoses as kids while crying, "Shoo, shoo!" as if we were vermin. Taking a detour—past oil and coal storage depots next to the river, past the derelict docks where we'd climb out onto the cranes over the river and vandalize the vast hangars with their multitude of pigeons in the rafters— we'd come to a point where the road stopped, meaning that the police could pursue us only as far as the bollards. Beyond that there was a Gypsy encampment, full of washing and car batteries; and beyond that again, a vast expanse, formerly the city dump, which still fermented below the grass. In other words, we could see trouble coming and shake off any pursuers. Make it to the Bay Road and we were safe, from anyone but ourselves, that is. We'd lose ourselves among the copses of trees or hiking up the massive concrete staircase to tuck ourselves right in under the bridge, where the walls were covered in a kaleidoscope of graffiti. The sound of the cars zooming overhead sounded like whooshing spaceships in our own version of *Star Wars*. We spent countless nights up there.

Now and then, while tripping, we'd come down onto terra firma and wander around. We were out of sight and out of our minds. I remember seeing multiple moons give birth to one another in the sky while we all laughed in slow motion. Once, I had intense feelings of shrinking and growing, effects straight out of *Alice in Wonderland*, and the headphones in my hands were spooling off to impossible lengths and I was getting all

tangled up in them. The music that was playing in the headphones was insane. I could see it, for starters, despite the fact
that the cassette was not playing. Another time, we were fooling
around on the shoreline and suddenly a dazzling spotlight shone
on us from the river, and I somehow *heard* the light crackling
and fizzing past my ears, like a firework right next to me. "Jesus Christ, we're under attack." Gradually, as some semblance
of coherence momentarily manifested, we realized it was the
search-and-rescue boat, which patrolled the waters looking for
missing persons and dissuading potential suicides.

"Are you fellas okay?" The voice came booming through
a megaphone, rippling like a sidewinder across the water and
then the shore.

My mate was either laughing or crying. I could no longer
discern which.

"Aye, we're grand. We're just tripping."

There was silence. The lapping of gentle waves.

"Okay. Carry on."

And with that, they pulled the boat away and took off.
Lights vanishing, multiplying as we fell to the ground in relief,
and then examined the grass for tiny civilizations.

Drugs weren't easy to get hold of, at that stage at least. At
mushroom season, you'd see grown men walking the fields intently, looking down like large flightless birds. Dealers in syn-
thetics had several barriers: the remoteness of the place ("the
back arse of nowhere," as the saying went), the police, and the
Provos. They might avoid jail but end up learning how to walk
again after the IRA had kneecapped them. Or they'd end up in
the grave. It was a risky business, and so the entrepreneurial
spirits involved in it were either idiots or madmen, whom we'd
meet in remote industrial estates or in their flats as they violently demonstrated nunchucks bare-chested and elaborated on

tinfoil-helmet conspiracy theories. I always let my friends do
the talking, but I had one of those faces—curious and gorm-
less in equal measure, perhaps staring a fraction too long—that
seemed to naturally antagonize dealers. It was a relief to step
outside and exhale and return to a night of your own making.

Box of Fireworks

Our generation was close enough to be witness to and impacted by the Troubles, but far away enough not to be fully immersed. Our involvements had a theatrical quality. I had seen cops busting people's heads with batons, and I'd been swept up in riots. I'd dashed through rains of glass bottles and wrestled myself free from a soldier's grasp once or twice. Even caused a few cheers. Yet I knew that I and my kind were spectators, extras, side characters. When visitors came from out of town, we could regale them with stories, taking them to see the action, walking past burned-out cars. Yet I generally stayed carefully on its periphery.

One morning I woke up abruptly to the sound of my mother weeping. She had a friend nicknamed Tonto, going back to her teenage years. He'd been walking home pissed and had staggered into a riot, when a Saracen tank had accelerated through a barricade and crushed him. His insides had spilled out on the street. People were batoned trying to assist him. I had been at the location earlier that evening, feeling a sense of building tension, palpable in the air. Fool that I was, at fourteen years of age, I found it exhilarating, thinking it was a game or a film. Something, though—something in the air that could be read— made me come home.

We had the space, the luxury, afforded by the suffering of others, to be as critical and complacent and ironic as we wanted about it all. We could rise above it, as many did, acting with a cosmopolitanism that bordered on the pantomime, or wash our hands of it if we wanted. My friends and I would piss ourselves laughing at loyalist websites, in the early days of the net, that played cheesy keyboard versions of "Simply the Best" when you clicked on them. Yet taximen were still being called out to pickups on the edges of estates where they'd be murdered; children making their way to school would still have pipe bombs lobbed in their direction by Orange mobs; pubs were still being shot up; shoppers would still be torn to pieces by shrapnel in malls.

As teenagers, we could live to our heart's content in ramshackle worlds of our own creation. Boredom fueled abandon and invention. One occasion was Halloween, which became huge in Derry, as it was apolitical and afforded a brief opportunity to change our identities and have a break (if not escape) from the fixed ones we'd been born with. There was always a carnival atmosphere, with fireworks exploding above the river and wild hordes partying in the streets. Occasionally fights would break out, and you'd see the wizard's hat of one of your friends suddenly accelerating as they were thrown around within the crowd, and before you knew it, you were grappling with a vampire or the Incredible Hulk or Uncle Sam. Or you'd find them later in a crumpled heap, makeup and blood running down their faces, like a melted Pierrot, moaning, "They smashed me, lads. They smashed me to death." It was bedlam, but—when it went well, and even sometimes when it didn't—it felt like a release from a pressure that resided in the very air around you, as if we were somehow many leagues under the sea and hadn't realized it and had suddenly, briefly resurfaced for a lungful of air.

Even at moments of unwinding, it still paid to be cautious. There was always that voice in the back of your mind. Coming back from a house party late one night, on the other side of town, I was sitting uneasily in the passenger seat of a taxi, trying to think of something—anything—to say that wasn't "Are you busy tonight?" Paralyzed by the prospect of small talk, I shifted awkwardly in the deafening silence. Eventually, from the corner of my eye, I was relieved to see the taxi driver reach for the radio, but then he hesitated. I felt the car slow. "Put your seatbelt on, son," he said sternly. I already had it on and looked at him, but his eyes were fixed straight ahead. There were lights on the otherwise desolate road before us. A checkpoint. One of the mobile ones, manned by the RUC and the army. "Hold on for a second, son," he said and then hit the accelerator. We took off at high speed. I gripped the seat, thinking he'd lost his mind. It was only as we got closer that I could see it wasn't an army checkpoint at all, but rather loyalist terrorists, who'd have pulled us in and no doubt inquired as to my identity and God knows what horrors would've unfolded. The taxi scattered them, but one of them booted the door as we passed, and I could see that they were armed. My heart was pounding. I can't remember if I thanked the taximan, but I remember looking at his license, dangling from the rearview mirror and seeing that he had a Protestant name.

When we used our false IDs to get into pubs, I always took care to sit at the back, always facing the front door and next to

the toilets, in case brutal reality, in the form of a loyalist gunman, came to visit. They had done so on Halloween night, a
year or two earlier, at a pub called the Rising Sun in the little village of Greysteel, just outside Derry, walking in wearing balaclavas, holding an AK-47 and shouting, "Trick or treat," before
opening fire, first on a teenage girl who had replied, "That's
not funny." Another massacre was carried out while punters
watched the Ireland-Italy World Cup match. Yet another had
been interrupted when one of the patrons, in the process of being slaughtered, switched off the lights.

Effigy

In the days leading up to the marches each July 12, teetering Babel-esque structures would be built, one in every
loyalist housing estate. Towers of pallets and tires. From a
distance, they appeared like sea stacks or Indian temples.
On closer inspection, they were festooned with cultural ephemera "from the other side." Mainly tricolors, but more esoteric
fare occasionally. I once saw a Vatican flag, which it must have
taken real searching to find, and stolen Virgin Mary statues.
There was even a wheelchair once, right at the top.

The bonfires would resemble outsider art until they were
doused in petrol and ignited when the sun had set. The night
sky of July 11 glows in multiple directions. Flying in at night,
the city seems to have been recently blitzed. On the ground,
crowds circle the fires, cheering, drinking, singing, staring into
the incandescent soul of the blaze, volcanoes of momentarily
cathartic rage. People look unrecognizable by the fire's glow.

Some look beautiful and some grotesque. I was able to slip in for a number of years, taking advantage of this distortion of light. I had seen the bonfires burn so intensely that the rain turned to steam before it had even landed.

The Catholics responded by inventing their own bonfire night to celebrate the Feast of the Assumption, when the Virgin Mary ascended, body and soul, into heaven. They assisted her with a ladder of acrid soot. What was left afterward were burned offerings, melted mannequins and wreckage, and rain clouds infused with sulfur. Once I had stood as a lunatic threw a gas canister into the conflagration, and a short while later, huge arcs of seemingly liquid flame whipped around and it exploded in a burning mushroom cloud, before blowing the fire into glaring embers in all directions and sending the metal canister rocketing skyward, landing God knows where; and the people cheered, not out of delight but sheer relief to be still alive. The cops immediately showed up and everyone scattered. I scrambled over a fence and, behind relative safety, stopped to catch my breath. The smoke, black as tar, was pumping into the sky, dissolving into the red night as I turned and ran to join my friends, whooping and laughing into streets lit up like an inferno. We must have looked like something out of a Bosch painting.

Occasionally we would go on missions to set other neighborhood's bonfires alight prematurely. We were taking our lives into our hands by doing so, especially if we did it to a loyalist bonfire. I always scouted, without saying so, for escape routes as we entered, in case we were ambushed, and hung back generally from the arson. My cautiousness was partly down to a latent recollection of being burned at a bonfire once, in the time before conscious memory, when my mother had gotten too close to sparks that showered down from the crackling wood and set my mop of blond hair on fire. I didn't fully realize how dangerous it was. Tensions were always heightened at this time of year. Once, a couple of young loyalists had passed out on a sofa in a field while sniffing glue and guarding a bonfire, and both had been brutally beaten by raiders. One never woke up again.

In our own territory we regularly lit fires. We were pyromaniacal guttersnipes, Prometheans of the glass-strewn alleys, and given an empty field, as there used to be at Magee, we would construct a fire, dispatching aerosol cans like offerings into it and then diving theatrically into ditches as the fire ticked and we awaited the miraculous explosive shattering of the quiet Sunday. In the seasons when our playing fields grew wild, we would ignite the gorse and the fire would catch almost quicker than anyone could run, a tiny match setting acres alight, gorse bushes accelerating in flame like herds of wild blind horses being driven into the sea.

Lundy's Day was a big celebration in Derry. Still is. The loyalists would be bused in by the thousands from all over Northern Ireland and Scotland. They'd be steaming drunk before noon, pissing in doorways, chanting, waving Union Jacks, and giving Nazi salutes. Burger stands and cassette tapes of skinhead bands. In such an atmosphere there was a distinct possibility I would have been beaten to a pulp or worse if they'd known who I was or my background, but I was curious. It built into a frenzy when they wheeled out a papier-mâché effigy of Robert Lundy, the loyalists' arch-traitor, who abandoned his people enduring the Siege, climbing down the walls onto a pear tree and escaping with the keys to the gates. I had read enough to know that Lundy had been unfairly misrepresented, as the self-appointed hero, Governor Walker, had insisted that he go; and Lundy had lived on to fight elsewhere, but every faith needs a Judas.

The effigy burst into flames and cheers erupted. Faces

looked crazy in the glow. It was the kind of light in which everyone lost their identities and you couldn't tell who was who. The Presbyterian symbol was a burning bush. Their motto was "Burning yet flourishing." They had won the Siege, but each year they resurrected Lundy to execute him all over again, because in certain minds the Siege had never ended. And certain minds never wanted it to end.

Car Key

I used to walk from the town to our home at the border. The road ran parallel with the river, and before they lined it with streetlights, I would follow the white line, shit-scared, from experience, of dogs (or worse) bounding out from the depths. There were sleeping houses, their facades like skulls. I would pass a small car scrapyard, vehicles stacked on top of one another. A heavy magnet swinging in the breeze, and guard dogs that would test the length and strength of their chains, straining to attack, all teeth and neck veins. In the daytime a constant flow of traffic passed. I remembered bouncing on my father's shoulders when none of the estates were there, when it was all fields. He carried me the whole way. Miles. I never heard my father complain once.

Walking home after a night of drink and debaucheries was always an admission of failure, scouring pockets for shrapnel for a taxi and bemoaning not sharing a bed with another stranger. Some internal radar would take over and guide me home, as my senses were simultaneously dulled and reeled with the drink. I followed the white line, muttering and singing to myself, staggering like a silent-movie drunk. I'd walk through the city first until I ran out of city. In the daytime, reeking wagons filled with pigs for the slaughterhouse would pass in plumes of dust. You could follow their path by the stink. At night, it was different. Occasionally a huge truck would thunder past, lighting up the road like Las Vegas, and then it would be gone and the night would close in again, darker than before, as the red lights disappeared into the distance.

The hardest part of my walk home, the most sobering, was the shrouded bend at the Bishop's Corner, the first place my friends and I had ever gotten drunk, but now almost empty and distinctly sinister. The darkness somehow pooled and deepened there. It seemed like a place where someone, or something, might strike. Destined for ambush. On moonless nights I would curse the dark, quickening my step. However drunk I was, anxiety always cut through the cozy glow, and on moonlit nights I would curse the light, which turned every moving shadow of every branch into overarching limbs. Nature itself seemed to seethe and conspire and close in. Even cities were dark once, before electricity, before gas, before whale oil. Once they were shackled by the dark, and all manner of things, in the mind, owned the night.

Before you came to the convent and the now boarded-up school of Thornhill, there was a field, sometimes filled with horses. They were blue under the stars, momentarily lifting the fear with wonder, the shudder of their warm, swirling breaths. I'd reach over the wire to stroke the blaze on their brows, tentative creatures from some other world.

One night the horses were gone. So, too, was the moon.

Instead there was an unnatural light in the distance. I walked toward it, knowing it was unnatural and did not bode well. In childhood I had read about marsh lights, corpse candles, will-o'-the-wisp, *gunderslislik*, wanting to chance upon them even though they had evil connotations. For a moment I thought the light might be something supernatural, and I was drawn in like a moth to the moon. I passed what I thought were piles of leaves and branches scattered on the road, but their placing seemed odd. As I walked on, I noticed they were mechanical objects, inexplicably scattered. I prodded one or two with my boot. They were heavy, smeared in oil. I had no idea how they had gotten there. As I turned the corner, the light became dazzling, and as my eyes adjusted, I could start to make out the barriers closing off the road to traffic. I realized the objects had all been wreckage. The pieces became more explicable as I walked on: parts of an engine, an obliterated wing mirror, a scalped hubcap, so far from the scene ahead that I could barely imagine the forces that could cast them there. It was the aftermath of giants.

The fire brigade had erected floodlights, arc lights that shone like a Nativity scene, a medieval passion play, Candlemas, an alien landing, or a messianic birth. The glass glistened almost innocently. I walked through the still-stunned air, an intruder unnoticed on a busy film set, and they didn't seem to see me—not the firefighters with their cutting gear still glowing, or the ambulance crew logging the time, or the police drawing rings around the shrapnel, a scene at once sacred and profane and mesmeric as a morning dream.

Usually the joyriders, always older than I expected, ditched their cars long before this point, after the requisitely satisfying hand-break turns and wheel spins around estates and the mad bolts down expressways. Usually they drove them into the ground in circles, in thrall to Archimedes, or just rammed them into school gates and ignited the evidence. I worked with a caretaker in a local school, and we'd have to clean up such aftermaths nearly every Monday morning. This joyrider was unlucky: unlucky to find the police on his tail, unlucky to take that route in a bolt for the border. Yet it was the same physics as a game of pool. He got the angle and speed wrong on that deceptive bend. I had seen three crashes unfold at that same corner, each almost warranting the "Accident Black Spot" sign that was then used to memorialize deaths at such places. This was by far the worst crash. The car was no longer a car anymore, wrapped around the tree. The dimensions were all wrong. It was a painting by an insane cubist: a shape, all angles, previously unseen by nature. Imagine the laws of motion, the stampeding gale of horsepower, the massive deceleration, the forces that engulf those inside the vehicle like tons of water through a breached hull, and the space to constrict, to embrace and conjoin muscle, metal, and bone. He was in the afterlife or oblivion, quicker than he could possibly realize.

Every day afterward I walked past the scene and the marks were still there on the road. The petrified squeal of the tire tracks in chalk. You could read the patterns of crash lines, the gaudy amber arrows sprayed toward the pavement, then parallel lines churned in the grass directly into the tree, still standing, almost imperceptibly shifted off its axis, like it was rooted in the iron core of the earth. Every day the marks on the road were there, unnoticed by everyone at the nearby bus stop. The path by which a young man exited this world. Then one day they were gone, and this was another nowhere again.

Videotape

The wasteland, a former hockey pitch, would turn from a taiga of frost to a concrete pasture of wildflowers in the summer and then back to frost. We'd drink there in all weathers. We'd get pissed and have dummy fights, as the batteries and the songs on the beatbox slowed down and warped. When our presence had been noted, indicated by a coating of burglar-resistant paint on the walls we hopped over, we began drinking round the back of a Chinese takeaway. A few of my mates then were loco. They were funny, charming, but they always pushed the limits. It started innocently enough, daring one another to shoplift the stupidest thing we could from the minimarket, but a sense of harm continued to enter.

Once, they found a manhole in a field and spent hours prying it open, and then covered it with leaves and got a friend's older brother to come, under the ruse of showing him a bird's nest full of bright-blue eggs (the lie-telling always had an art to it), and he walked over, pontificating on his avian knowledge, and fell in mid-sentence, groaning from the bottom of the shaft as the uproarious laughter turned distinctly nervous in character. Another time, a kid broke his collarbone on one of our "death swings," and we tried chasing him to silence him as he ran home squealing. We'd set fire to gorse, as we always did, and that would soon spread out of control, but it was no longer funny and instead was stressful as the fire engines arrived. It was like handling dangerous chemicals. They were the kind of guys who see Begbie and Tony Montana as characters to aspire to. Squaddies in a parallel universe.

Paul always had this lumbering recklessness. He'd do anything for a dare, always proving himself, always shadowboxing. He'd punch hornets' nests if dared. He would invent films that no one else had seen. Claim he'd been to places he couldn't possibly have been near. Always talking about zombies and ninja films. Always articulating affection through rough-and-tumble that would very quickly escalate. He had brute strength too—a big kid who hoarded food under his bed, overweight but built like an ox; one punch and your arm was dead for a whole day. He was a mixed-up kid but didn't seem to dwell much on anything either. It was a dangerous mix. He was a few years younger than the rest of us, and gradually, as the age gap became more significant, he began to hang around with the younger lads of the area. There seemed to be even more of a streak of malice to their activities. We all did similar things: we lacked their malevolent intent, but what did intent mean when the end results were the same? What difference did it make that you thought you were good inside your head?

Soon Paul was getting into fights with random passersby. A mutual friend, a lunatic himself who used to try to derail trains for the craic, told me that Paul was an accident waiting to happen. I started to hear *stories* and I began to give Paul a wide berth. It was obvious it would all end badly. He couldn't be told and was bolstered by his new role, going from the youngest to the oldest in his groups. He no longer had limits. When I said to watch himself, as he had been told a hundred times previously, Paul acted threatened and threatening.

The local kids were soon conjuring up schemes like poaching, robbing taximen, or deliberately getting locked overnight in a supermarket, but they started becoming more reckless. The last time I saw Paul, they had a stuntman scam. They'd run out in front of a car, leap up onto the hood, and then skid dramatically onto the ground; then, as the person exited their car with their hand over their mouth, they'd flail around and ask the person for hush money. They called it "the perfect crime."

One night they were hanging outside around the takeaways, and Paul, egged on, randomly picked a fight with two guys who were leaving, and words were exchanged and he clocked one of them. The guy was knocked out and cracked his head on the pavement. They switched off his life support later that night in hospital. He was a former "blanket man"—a particularly venerated part of the republican movement for what they'd gone through in prison. Before the hunger strikes, these prisoners had grown their hair long and refused to wear prison clothes, and smeared their excrement on the cell walls as a protest, to be recognized as political prisoners in a war and not as criminals. The man was also a father of four. Old enough to be Paul's dad. He'd survived the Troubles, and Paul killed him. After he'd served time in a juvenile lockup, Paul had to leave Derry under threat of death. The last I heard, he was living with a relative who was a priest in Belfast. Maybe he had a new name, a new identity. We never saw him again.

Mix Tape

My teenage years really began with the opening notes of Pulp's "Babies." Or so it seems now. Absurdly intense, I was uncomfortable in my own skin as a young man. I felt too tall, too skinny, too pale, too angular. In a western, I would not have been the hero, the outlaw, or the sheriff, but instead an apprentice coffin maker. The temptation, with being an introvert in a world run by extroverts, is to construct a mask. I began to see it, as Britpop eventually reached us through *NME* and VHS tapes. The middle-class boys adopting the Manchester swagger, the middle-class girls punching the air to "Common People" on the dance floor. I thought of creating masks, identities to hide behind—until, that is, I met her.

She was a friend of a friend—a book obsessive, music obsessive, film obsessive. She looked like Amélie and had plans for greatness, which she declared without embarrassment or arrogance, but as if stating a fact. She had a boundless love for discovering culture, which unguarded me.

"Everything's been fucking said and done already," I'd say, prematurely cynical.

"But not by us. Silly man."

She smiled and kissed me, and she tasted ecstatically of cigarettes and vanilla. I was smitten.

She was, for me, the discovery of worlds. She was kind, which I was not accustomed to in strangers, making me compilation tapes with Chopin's nocturnes, Satie's *Gymnopédies*, Holst's "Neptune, the Mystic," and Mozart's Requiem—music that I'd never imagined existed. She played the piano and the violin and spoke French, and lived in an attic room plastered in pages from *The Face*, and adored books, most of all *Le grand meaulnes*. She seemed nostalgic not just for all the lost ages but for the time we were currently living, as if aware it would not last.

For me, the universe deepened on meeting her. It became more fascinating and cinematic than I'd thought possible and made me believe that we could be more than mere bystanders. She lent me poetry books, and told me about the Beats, and brought me to see art-house films in a cinema where the lone projectionist looked three hundred years old and was probably a ghost and the dust in the projection light waltzed and swirled; and we fed our coins all day into jukeboxes and pitchers, and we shared our nights with each other like some immense and precious secret. The sun and moon felt new in the sky. She was the first to show me that you had to risk being laughed at to do anything worthwhile, that more people were undone by fear of derision, of vertigo masquerading as coolness, than by disaster. She was a moment of color in a monochrome film, movement in a series of stills.

The dawn, however, always returns. Her parents disapproved

of our relationship. I used to hope, every time calling at her house, that they would not answer (they probably wished the same). They didn't like my background and judged my prospects to be insufficient for their beloved, but they largely held their tongues, given that she was due to go overseas to university, and the long-distance relationship we'd planned was laughably unrealistic to them, and reality. Traveling to Barcelona with my family at seventeen, my first time out of Britain, I asked her to come, but she said she couldn't. I explored the city, becoming enraptured by it. Even by the small differences, like the fact that shops didn't need to pull down shutters at night for fear of riots. One day I trekked for many miles along the Catalan coast. I'd never heard of land art, or Li Bai carving poems onto cliff faces, or Wordsworth writing poems on the walls on an island at Grasmere, but I thought if I created something in a remote cove, carved some kind of message, then something of the present would survive, even when I knew deep down it could not.

We drank in life, deeply and joyously, but despite our efforts, we could not stop time. Nor was love enough. It was a simple story: we wanted the world, we got it, and so we lost each other. It was the first bittersweet taste of innumerable such experiences to follow.

She left for university and the life that her books had promised her, and which she had promised her parents. I was quietly bereft. I did not speak of the storm in my head, but it seemed somehow to radiate out into the weather around me. We still wrote letters to each other, but words never seemed to survive the translation the distance, in time and space, brought. There were worlds of accumulating unsaid things. Letters were lost, phones with threads of messages broke down and were thrown into drawers, e-mails went unanswered. The late-night calls had growing silences. Her accent began to change. She would appear in my dreams, and my next day would then be haunted. She visited me one last time. I listened to her stories, insecurely countering them with my own, and she left the next morning. I stayed awake that entire night, knowing it would be our last, gazing out the window at stars that shone down on us and had burned out long before we'd even been born.

ID Card

The choice of moving to Belfast as a safe option was foolhardy. It was near enough to feel like I was in geostationary orbit around Derry, but it was still unstable. I knew the first day I'd made a mistake. I knew in the very first class of a law degree, which I'd been enthusiastically encouraged to take by my school and my family, that it was doomed. The weight of expectations—the first Anderson in my lineage to get to university—bore down like a leaden sky. Before she'd left, my girlfriend had warned me, saying I had to do what I really wanted to do, but I was dumb enough to know better. Before long, I was skipping classes on jurisprudence and torts and contracts just to sit in the courtyard of the university, reading secondhand books in a dangerously drifting daydream.

I would phone home every day or two. My father would answer and instantly pass me on to my mother, as tradition demanded. The mention of the Maze prison on the news interested me. They were closing it. Sending the inmates elsewhere. There were calls to turn it into a culture center or a football stadium, or to bulldoze it entirely so it didn't become a shrine to the "men of violence" (a sanctimonious phrase used by the politicians and religious leaders who profited from division so profoundly that they could rise above it, and absolve themselves from it). The name Maze fascinated me, with its images of labyrinths and Minotaurs.

"You know your da was there?"

"Where?" I asked.

"The Maze. When he was *inside*."

I froze. I had heard murmurings—such talk was hidden in clear sight—but always had a sense not to pry, not to look through the keyhole into Bluebeard's chamber.

My mother wouldn't talk in detail over the phone, but from resulting conversations I pieced together enough to know that my father had served time as a young man. He had been sentenced to eight years, for possession of explosives and conspiracy to murder. My father, the former terrorist. It sat uneasily in my mind.

I thought of it a lot on night walks through the city, trying to understand this new information, given that it ran so counter to the man I knew, or thought I'd known, my whole life. At night the city center of Belfast still became a ghost town. Pub bombs and shootings had shut down certain areas, but even the main thoroughfares were haunted by the memory of death squads like the Shankill Butchers, roaming for Catholics and misidentified others, to drag in and carve up with butcher's knives in the back of black taxis. The Butchers were such maniacs, the story went, that the leader, Lenny Murphy, was set up by his own loyalist allies, as he was making them all look psychotic.

Another story went that he'd inadvertently killed a Protestant woman. Either way, his whereabouts were handed over to the IRA, which promptly ambushed him alongside a friend and riddled them with bullets. With a truly malignant degree of cynicism, those who'd set him up then avenged his death, in the typical tit-for-tat fashion, by killing more innocent Catholics.

The peace process had begun by then. I was as relieved as anyone, especially after the atrocity at Omagh, but I could not share the feeling that things were suddenly much better. It seemed a delusion at best, perhaps necessary, temporarily at least, but one that could turn into a lie if we were not careful. Psychologically, it was a liberation to have the army taken off the streets. To have some semblance of normality. The sight of shop windows unshuttered at night was startling. For some time, though, I could not get to sleep, even when tired, and it only gradually dawned on me that it was because the nocturnal soundtrack of helicopters was no longer there. The silence of peace was deafening.

Belfast still had a certain postapocalyptic quality then. People stuck to their own areas on the outskirts rather than be identified walking back from a communal place. It was tragic because you sensed that very few citizens of Belfast wanted it like that. It was a self-segregation. And it was dangerous moving through it. There were places, intersections, where it was possible to identify a person's background, political allegiances, and religion from which direction and side of the street they were walking along.

At first I had a sense of romance and would walk around the streets, listening to *Astral Weeks* on a Discman, with the CD rotating in my pocket. I soon realized the danger of attempting to visit areas because of the attractiveness of their names—Cyprus Avenue, Tiger's Bay, Sandy Row. Belfast put the *psycho* in *psychogeography*: I'd quickly learned that it was ill suited to the flaneur. You took your life into your own hands, or rather you placed it in the hands of others. Northern Irish language was debased during the Troubles, with dreaded things like the "Nutting Squad" being veiled in innocuous, abnormally normal language. I'd read about "romper rooms," named after the American kids' television show—loyalist marching-band pubs where they'd have a man or woman, a Catholic or again a mistaken identity, tied up and tortured on stage as the revelers drank, before finally being dispatched in an alleyway out the back. I'd learned of how they taunted one of the victims, after finding out she was a singer, to "Give us a wee song," before she was murdered and her body stuffed in a garbage bin. In such places, with such histories, you did not go off course.

On the surface was the appearance of calm, and some eagerness to make the fledgling peace process work, but a silencing came with it too. Underlying issues were unaddressed. "The face will grow to fit the mask," went the reasoning, and so we all donned our masks.

Nursing a hangover one day, and seeking the hair of the dog, I called in to see a barman friend for a pint. I'd propped up the bar for an hour, talking and joking around, when suddenly the barman nodded over to an old sod sitting with a pint of stout at a table. "See that guy?" I turned my head. "He was one of the Shankill Butchers. Got out early, with the Good Friday Agreement."

I stared over at him again. He was just some old prick. Nothing demonic about him. I stared back at the barman. He was cleaning glasses.

"He's all right actually," he said, half to himself.

"He'd have carved you and me up," I replied.

"That was then, this is now."

I drank up and left.

At night I would go down to a pub around the corner from the Sean Graham bookies where a massacre had taken place. It was on the edge of an intersection, and the locals would be hemmed into their homes every year, violently if necessary, to let Orange bands march through the area. I'd rap on the metal latch and a face would appear, always rude, and I'd hand over money for a carryout before being informed, "Now fuck off." The city was famous for its hospitality. Then I'd go sit by the river. These were the quiet nights, and I relished nothing more than the dance of the streetlights on the water.

The peace was not to last, for me at least. For a while it seemed I was a magnet for trouble. Bad encounters in pubs and nightclubs, namely. I had an unfailing knack for being dragged into unwanted conflict. I initiated none of it, but couldn't extricate myself. I was thrown down staircases and had bouncers open doors with my head. One had the audacity to bob and weave, before punching a tooth clean out of my jaw because of a "misunderstanding."

On one occasion I told a guy to stop touching a girl, and the gentleman in question tried to stick a glass in my throat, bruising my windpipe. As I caught my breath, the assailant vanished in the crowd, but I looked up to see his friend laughing and something in me snapped, and I struck him as hard as I could and he fell onto a table of drinks. In the resulting melee, I had several fingers broken by the bouncers, who took me out the back to rough me up. I talked my way out of it, but not before they'd found my student card and announced, "Ha-ha, you're fucked."

I had a meeting with the university the next week. I went in nervous, wearing a borrowed suit and with my fingers in splints, only to find—to my surprise—that they'd decided to drop the case because my assailant was training to become a doctor and so it would be unfair to put his career at risk. I lost all hope in the place at that point, and with the added fact I was skint and on the wrong path, I walked apologetically out of class mid-tutorial shortly afterward, never to return. Maybe it was self-sabotage, but it was made all too easy.

I didn't tell my parents for as long as I could, and then only my mother, as she'd be more sympathetic. My father, when he found out, went quietly ballistic, though I saw none of it. I'd blown all the dreams they'd had riding on me. The great white hope had crashed to earth. My pretentious claims that I'd become an artist or a writer—that I always should have been that, because that's who I was, whether I liked it or not—just threw petrol on the flames. I was hankering for an argument with them so that I could feel less guilty. To give a form to the formless. To give the chaos and fear a name. I knew, though, how it would play out. My father would seem deflated and would talk sense, and I would lose my temper and regard him as a hypocrite, given what I thought I'd learned about him, and he would quietly leave and go out to fix something in the backyard that didn't need fixing, and I would feel lousy about it and want to apologize, but the words wouldn't come out. So I resolved just to stay away more, and slowly phase out contact and rely on solitude.

My father's hostility to writing wasn't just that he didn't believe me or thought I was headed for the gutter. It went deeper. He loved books, as his father had, and as I did, but it gradually began to dawn on me that he was only partly literate. He could certainly read and did so continually, but he could barely write. He had been thrown out of school too early. And, as my sister was diagnosed as dyslexic, I realized that my father was too. Though they had worked hard in their careers, the diagnoses came too late for them both. Both had been hounded by teachers for being stupid at school; both had sought escape routes through misbehavior and absence; both had been failed. All that time, as I indulged myself with dreams of some absurd kind of sainthood of writing, I hadn't noticed my father quietly handing my mother all the forms he ever needed to fill in, merely adding his signature at the end.

By this stage I had already set off to become a writer, a laughably ridiculous venture even then. Money was always a problem. I'd kept hold of my now defunct and out-of-date student card, to flash my way into the library, where I'd spend my hours enveloped in imaginary projects. I could buy coffee and hot chocolate there with pennies in the vending machine, and huddle next to the radiators on the top floor with a view of all Belfast in 360 degrees. I'd pick floors with subjects that people rarely visited, and on occasion would catch some sleep there.

My mind was filled with a million ideas and directions, bouncing off one another and continually inverting. I struggled to focus, and my writing showed it. I wrote Jacobean revenge plays set during the fall of the Spanish Republic. A cabaret on the Maginot Line. Novels about time travel, tour guides of imaginary planets, indestructible angels with dementia who'd lived through millennia of history. Poetry collections printed on tarot cards and slipped into random books, or placed as messages in bottles and thrown into rivers. Nonfiction studies of night and madness and the apocalypse. I gradually built a library of abandoned or unpublished books. I thought of writing as the eye of the storm, but in truth it helped to fuel the storm. I was prone to intrusive thoughts and sleepless nights, drinking by candlelight, living the life of the poet in the garret, a century after it was fashionable and to no discernible audience or readership. I lost track of the stacks of notes that filled every drawer.

I ended up living in a flat with friends who were never there, were off staying with their partners, because the place was cold and in a dodgy area. The first couple of years it had been one for all and all for one, and everyone partook in the madness, but now it was dinner parties and easy listening, early-onset middle age. They were the kind who'd never been in a scrap—not out of virtue, but because they'd never needed to. They wouldn't even break one up if it endangered their haircuts. Yet, in the long run, they were right and I was wrong. Rising above it all was an enviable position. Still, it left a bad taste. I'd seen people walk past domestic-abuse incidents or step around unconscious young fellas who'd been kicked up and down the street. Once, it had happened to me; having had my hoodie pulled over my head while being beaten by three assailants, I'd thrown one over my shoulder and inadvertently knocked myself out by head-butting the ground. I'd woken to find my attackers being dragged away; only the bravery of their girlfriends saving me from being stomped.

My flatmates were decent but their holiday in the chaos was over. I had no way, perhaps no desire, of escaping it. I concentrated on escapism, writing copiously, fueled by speed and drink when I could afford it. My room was no longer a base but something between a hermitage and a scrapyard. I'd covered the walls and ceiling in collages. The images were mostly cut out of magazines and secondhand books. Strange figures from Bosch. Paintings by the Blue Rider group. Book covers for Hamsun, Kafka, Akutagawa, Lispector. Maps of islands and deserts. Rimbaud's "The Drunken Boat," Dürer's *Knight, Death and the Devil*, and Picasso's *Family of Saltimbanques*. I dreamt of being part of imaginary movements, writing manifestos and creating events that would cause riots and revolutions. In reality, I lived in a monastic cell. I would go out into the world and be as debauched as possible, and always return to what seemed a bubble of somewhere else in the city, a nutshell of boundless space, surrounded by prompts and pathways and iconography. A tiny place where there was space to dream. I told myself it was a way of escaping, but I was really delving further and further into drama.

There was as little rest as there was clarity. I fell in with fellow reprobates, a different side of the city from the redneck discos and crate-digging dilettantes. We would go to illegal underground clubs in derelict buildings with dodgy bouncers, boarded-up windows, padlocked fire escapes, lit with candles; every room, every floor with different kinds of music, pulsing, losing ourselves for hours, dancing until sweat ran down the walls, then back to orgiastic displays where no one could tell who was who and where one person ended and another began, laughing the delirious laughter of the damned. "Where's Jim?" I heard my friend ask. "You're Jim," came the reply.

We'd burst through the nights, drinking and fucking and breathlessly dancing our souls away. For a long time I found myself propelled by the momentum of abject hedonism, taking every drug under the sun—amphetamines, opiates, downers, dissociatives, hallucinogens—and drink, always drink, as an anchor. For a long time it was all thrills, however manufactured. You could dance yourself out of your own body, or accidently burn a skinhead on the forehead with a cigarette on the dance floor, and you'd just end up hugging and declaring mutual love because everyone's serotonin was stratospheric. Having grown up in an environment where people couldn't put their arms round each other and family couldn't say the words "I love you," but had to gesture it through an improvised sign language, it was like a dam bursting. It would catch up with you, though, and soon you'd endure walks of shame home the next morning, or the next next morning, hypervigilant and paranoid, skittish as a ghost as real people passed on their way to work; or you'd come round mid-sentence to find you were delivering some conspiratorial speed-freak lecture, the contents of which you were not consciously party to—self-induced glossolalia—in front of a group of appalled strangers, high up in a tower block. Or forgetting you were in a tower block and trying to leave, and staggering out onto the balcony and almost over the railings, and the ground fifteen stories below rearing up with vertigo, as if suddenly transported into the sky. Or forgetting you were on a ship and, intending to stagger home, going out onto the deck to find the land, some indistinguishable land, gliding past. Or waking up from sleeping on a sofa in the window of a furniture store.

Without adequate sleep or routine, I had begun to lose my grip. I started getting nervous tics, like scratching frantically at times, which I tried to conceal. When I did pass out, I had recurring nightmares of being attacked and defending myself with obscene levels of violence—slicing eyes, throats—that left me profoundly disturbed upon waking. I kept having invasive morbid thoughts, when on trains or in cars, that tires would blow up and there'd be high-speed crashes if I jinxed the journeys with certain minor, unrelated actions. I had a worrying propensity for self-damage when I was under the influence. I had slices along my arms, inflicted for reasons not entirely known to me, and which I'd done in a daze, perhaps in order to focus myself. At times it felt like I was watching someone else. I'd had to start wearing long-sleeved shirts after the scars began showing up, to my mortification, under the ultraviolet lights of a nightclub. Yet I carried on the business of forgetting, casting all moderation aside, paying little attention to the meaning of our lives, because it didn't feel like there was any. Where the self-destructive impulses came from, in the blood or in free will, was unclear. A lover said to me, "You sabotage everything good for yourself at the last minute."

I didn't argue but just asked why.

"Because you are afraid."

"Of what?"

"Of succeeding. Of ever permanently getting what you want."

We had seemed invincible then, friends and lovers and I, or were dumb enough to believe so. Come morning, the devil took what was his. There was always a brutal payback. Come morning, we'd burn up on reentry. "I'm all right" was a sign that nothing was all right. We clung to each other as co-conspirators. There was always a moment, though, in the cold merciless dawn, when even the birdsong sounds cursed, that you'd have to face reality alone. Partying for days and coming round, propping yourself up in some pub with a pool cue as a crutch. The brutality of the pitiless Monday morning, closing in. With my skull splitting and no whites in my eyes, stepping over bodies on the living room floor, trying to find a cup or plate in the kitchen that wasn't overflowing with cigarettes. Tempted to stand on a few bodies on the way out to work in my crumpled uniform. One such session was so prolonged and hedonistic that a friend became a born-again Christian at the end of it and I never saw him again.

I worked in warehouses, call centers, a factory line. Mostly I worked in a supermarket on the edge of a loyalist area. Before and after football games, fans would come in, literally marching up and down the aisles of biscuits and nappies, singing songs about being "up to their necks in Fenian blood." The security guard, too scared to apprehend them, would stand around, shuffling his shoes or chatting to them on first-name terms. The workers had a message that would come over the intercom, "Could Mr. Smith please come to the basement?" There was no basement. It meant a bomb threat had been called in, and it instructed them to start covertly ushering shoppers out, without starting a panic. Stubborn older folk, who'd "seen it all before," would often continue shopping, even when they'd turned the lights out, carrying on by the glow of the fridges as the bomb squad arrived. At the end of every day, as part of cashing up, I'd be sent with the guard's colleagues to look under the shelves of the store for incendiary devices.

"What is it exactly we're looking for?"

"I dunno. Wires and shit, I guess."

People got on well enough working together, but things turned frosty around the marching season and the Old Firm games between Celtic and Rangers. I'd feel a change in the air pressure, the temperature. Grunts on the stairs, messages pinned to the pinboard, hostile latrinalia written on toilet doors by workmates. Sometimes I'd be asked where my accent was from, as if it were separate from the rest of me. I would tell them different imaginary villages in the northwest. The name would change each time. The sectarian issues flared up and certain areas were still no-go. It paid to keep your wits about you, but I found myself settling into complacency, which was a dangerous luxury. Once or twice, people would show their true colors. When migrants were starting to get burned out of loyalist areas, there were glimpses ("They're over here stealing our jobs and scrounging our benefits"). While many were congratulating themselves on how hatred and division were being overcome, they failed to recognize that it was simply shifting elsewhere. It was still needed by some. It was, perhaps, all they had.

Stereo

Whatever I went through, my sister went through far more crazed situations and was far more streetwise because of it, from seeing the aftermath of the assassination of a policeman on Shipquay Street to years of partying on the rave scene. She reminded me of the phrase about Ginger Rogers when anyone overly praised Fred Astaire and left her out: "Try doing it backwards and in heels."

As a child, my sister and her friends had navigated and reinvented the neighborhood space in their own ways, playing games that culminated in the creation of a death-defying place they called "the bars": a rudimentary length of iron railing, which they'd turned into a gymnastics spectacle. They would spin around it upside down and at high speed, performing tricks, with their ponytails whipping across the concrete. Her later stories, many of them very recent, were hilarious and grim

in equal measure, usually ending with, say, a friend losing a
finger on the way to a rave but trying to carry on with the sesh
regardless. My sister told me once of a party in Derry that had
gotten out of hand, and the Provos pulled up in a car and burst
in and smashed up the speakers and started wrecking the place,
scaring the shit and the noise out of everyone. You could hear a
pin drop afterward. Everyone started streaming out in all directions. The paramilitaries went back to their car with balaclavas
still on, got in, and turned on the ignition. Suddenly there was a
voice from the back seat. They turned and stared at two guys,
off their faces on the seat, thinking it was a taxi. "Take us to the
nearest off-license, mate. It's all kicking off in there."

In places where the law had lost any legitimacy through internment or raids or harassment or straight-up killings, there
was a vacuum. Where there is an absence of justice, it will be
filled, and there will be little control over who fills it. Who will
protect people from their protectors?

At any hour, the rattling on the door was unwelcome. There
was always hostility between the locals and fly-by-night students
in the terraces of Belfast. One evening we were sitting having a
drink and a smoke in a friend's room when we noticed showers
of sparks and smoke at the window and, rushing down to the
front door, found that someone had built up piles of leaves and
rubbish at the entrance and set it on fire. On another occasion
a friend was, somewhat ironically, playing "Born in the USA"
one lunchtime in her bedroom when a brick, from a passing
critic, came through the window. Another friend, testing the
tectonic range of his speakers, had opened his door to two
IRA men, who bundled their way in. He ended up scuffling
with them, almost getting the better of one and ripping the
invader's shirt open in the process. "Jesus, you maniac. You
could've been killed," I said to him.

He paused for a minute. "You know . . . the thing that went through my mind at the time—the thing I couldn't get out of my head—was the fact the guy had pierced nipples. It's strange, the things you notice. Maybe they weren't Provos. Impostors. The unreal IRA."

My friend had been playing with fire. Across town, another incident had occurred. An old lady had a heart condition, and the girl who had just moved in next door wouldn't keep the noise down. Lots of people had complained. She had these parties. Bass thumping through the walls. So the lady's husband made a complaint to the right people and the matter was dealt with. There wouldn't be any more parties. That night the sound through the walls changed. Ten loyalist paramilitaries burst in. Beat four of the party badly, with pickaxe handles and baseball bats. All were hospitalized. The girl, a thirty-year-old mother, didn't survive. The police charged only the old boy who'd made the call. The walls were silent after that.

Skylight

A room came up in another house in Belfast with old friends, and I thought I'd move in and take some time to get my head together. We could sit around playing *Mario Kart* and smoking and telling stories, and I'd get back a sense of balance. Get back to zero. It was bedlam, however. They were hilarious but deranged. On my first night we had a celebration that ended with my friend falling through one of the windows, slicing the tendons in his wrists. I visited him at the hospital, bringing him spare clothes that were deliberately too small for him, which I'd picked up at a charity shop. We sat out on a balcony, smoking with patients who were wheeling around drips. And the fun took a further, darker turn. There were the same laughs with friends so fucked they'd try leaving rooms at the hinge side of the door or by stepping onto the wall, thinking the room had tilted. And another who'd passed out while taking a piss and fallen headfirst through the frosted-glass bathroom window, coming round staring down into the backyard.

Our actions began to have dire consequences. Lost jobs, failed relationships, mental-health problems. What began as *seize the day* became *obliterate it*. One of my friends ended up in a coma after falling from a garage roof while drunk, even receiving the last rites before recovering. I couldn't bring myself to see him when he was at death's door, and never forgave myself for failing to do so. Other friends began to lose their minds. Some turned violent. Some suffered psychotic episodes and developed paranoia, reading conspiracies in subtitles and adverts. The illness mirrored the emerging era. Where once they'd have ranted about the KGB and aliens tapping into their thoughts, now it was the CIA and al-Qaeda. Others disappeared. You'd see them years later, changed through illness and medication, and they were not the same people you'd once loved, and perhaps you weren't either.

The house started falling apart. I'd wake to find holes punched in the walls, or threats about the noise, or the banisters kicked off, and no one would have any recollection who'd done it or why. My record collection gradually vanished and then my books. Eventually one of my friends was sitting on a radiator, having a smoke, and he knocked it onto the ground. He was so stoned he didn't notice the water pumping out of it onto the floor and down into the floor below. He explained later that he thought the water, pumping from a reservoir high in the hills, would just "run out." It wasn't long before the floor/roof caved in, and we were filling a garbage bin with water every few minutes as we tried to find the stopcock and shut off the water supply. It seeped through everything. The place was fucked. There was now literally a room that no one could enter. We had to flee the house, knowing the landlord was involved in shady circles in Belfast and had a reputation for beating up tenants for merely missing a month's rent. Once we'd fled, I remembered that I'd left some prize possessions in the attic, so I, my friend, and his girlfriend sneaked back to the wreck of the house. I kept busting their balls by saying, "There's the landlord!" as we tiptoed around the place, gathering everything salvageable. We were still packing up when we heard the landlord's key in the lock; they hesitated for a second until they saw the terror on my face, then we barreled out the back door. We ended up being chased down alleyways by the enraged landlord in his car, at one stage splitting up and then colliding into one another and bursting out laughing until our stomachs hurt, as the landlord circled around the streets at high speed.

I moved on to sleeping on a friend's couch. My aim was to dry out, find my bearings again, reconnect with the place. Fresh air and good thoughts. Long walks again. Time for thinking. One evening in the usually safe university area, on the corner of Malone Road and Chlorine Gardens, I was strolling along, recalling how I'd read that plague victims were buried around there, some pretentious flight of fancy, when I noticed a car slowing down to match my step. Three young men were inside, windows rolled down. The passenger in the front barked, "Hey! Boy!" I walked on, initially thinking mistaken identity and hoping they'd realize it. He kept shouting, more agitated this time. I was avoiding eye contact and already feeling as if the street beneath me was a lift descending. My stomach dropped. From the corner of my eye, I caught a glimpse of a sawed-off shotgun pointing right at my face from the back seat. I just kept walking, but instinctively cocked my head to one side, and they all burst out laughing and revved the engine and sped off. And I just stood there, my heart in my throat as the world continued

on, oblivious, around me. I felt like the dumbest motherfucker
who ever lived.

By the time I made it to my mates' house, I felt sick and was in
need of a drink. I asked them if I should go to the police, having
failed in the panic even to notice, let alone memorize, the model
of car or its license plate, or enough detail to make a facial com-
posite of its occupants. I felt humiliated, like an awkward child
again. All I could remember was the sheen on the stunted barrels
of the gun, like copper pipes. That stayed in my head involun-
tarily. And all I could see, regardless of what my friends said,
was a look of disbelief behind their eyes. They didn't believe me.
These things didn't happen anymore. They didn't happen to the
likes of us. That's what hurt most bitterly. "We live," Conrad put
it, "as we dream—alone."

I went back to the river, never feeling more solitary or in
greater despair. A deep depression grew in me. There were signs in
the river warning of electrical wires beneath the surface. I gave
myself many reasons not to jump in—what it would do to those
left behind, to those who'd find me—but if truth be told, at that
moment cowardice was all that stood in the way. And I ended up
sitting there, the glowing sky hiding the stars, laughing to myself.

Winter came and I found myself living in the attic of a freezing Georgian house. The students who populated the area had
slouched home for the holidays. Street after unearthly street lay
empty. Every rooftop and pavement was covered in snow two
feet deep. I trudged a path through it, like the first steps on a
new planet.

The library was empty, bar a skeleton staff. I took the stairs
and my familiar window seat on the top floor. The streets below were almost obliterated with snow, and I struggled to orient
myself, eventually picking out landmarks around the cardinal

points: the Botanic Gardens, the Holylands, and beyond them the winding River Lagan.

As I made notes, the sky darkened and a snowstorm began to lash down biblically upon the city. I was high enough to feel the windows buffeted by wind and sleet, and I swore the lights momentarily flickered. The city was almost completely obscured through the glass.

I gathered my notes and made my way home through the storm, barricading myself in against the elements for several days. When the weather cleared, emptying itself out or moving on to other lands, I returned to the library to continue my writing and research, only to be stopped at the front desk by the receptionist and a security guard. Only members of the university could use the facilities. I tried explaining, but I knew from her body language that it was a lost cause and she was delighted in catching an interloper, so there was no point. The halls were empty behind them. I left half-agitated, half-embarrassed.

For the next week I couldn't look at any writing. It started to occur to me that the continual commentary in my head, the intrusive thoughts as I lay awake at night, was also the voice that kept me writing, making plans for projects, dreaming up imaginary movements. It was not an innate or entirely positive thing. By the time my housemates arrived back, I had turned bearded and semiferal and was greeted with surprise. It had been a week since I had said a word to any living creature. We caught up, and they reminded me that a friend's birthday was being celebrated that very night, so I cleaned myself up, downed some Dutch courage, and headed out to the club. The renewed vigor I felt didn't survive the queue, and by the time we were in and jostling for drinks amid the deafening soundtrack, I was starting to wish catastrophe on the very earth. Having toasted my friend and shown the minimum social propriety, I found a corner to make a last stand and set about drinking myself into oblivion with what money I had left.

"Yu. X. Es. Er."

"What?" I leaned forward, covering one ear.

"Your ex is here." My mate pointed over to a country girl I'd been seeing. "She knew you were coming. She's brought a guy along. Don't look over."

For the next two hours I sank the huddle of drinks I'd bought, then pulled on my coat and told my mates I was off to the gents.

The cold air hit me as I stepped out of the fire exit into the alleyway. I wasn't as drunk as I should have been and felt it bitterly. It wasn't that far back home. I didn't want to return and at the same time I couldn't bear to remain. In the hope that a better idea would fall out of the sky, I walked vaguely in that direction, feeling more sober and shortchanged with every step.

I had just started to cross the road at the intersection of Donegall Pass and the Lower Ormeau, in the shadow of the old gasworks, when I heard footsteps running behind me. Suddenly a figure jumped up on my back, almost affectionately. Before turning, I assumed one of my friends had followed me out of the club and was making sure I got home okay and was fooling around. My main concern was to get off the road in case we were knocked down, given that the area had its fair share of boy racers and joyriders, but then I turned and saw the leering face of a stranger. I backed off, but I was turned at an awkward angle and the stranger had momentum as he came toward me, trying to push me, almost playfully, off my feet. I staggered back onto the pavement at the other side of the road, realizing what was going to happen, and thought, in an instant, to hit him as hard as I could and then take to my heels toward the nearest pub. I swung a punch into his ribs and another into the side of his face as he lunged forward, but he already had me grappled and I felt a boot coming in hard against my side from a second person, whom I hadn't even seen. I knew I was done for, wrestling with the first one, who was trying to drag my shirt over my head, but boots kept flying in and I could feel my strength starting to ebb. Somehow I got my leg around the first assailant and threw him onto the ground, but the momentum carried us both down and we went face-first onto the tarmac.

I'd been in many scraps before, but this felt different. It felt like it would not stop. There had been no reason for it to begin and none for it to end. I struggled to get up, as if I was caught under waves that would not cease, struggling for air and dazed from the fall. There was blood in my eyes, and I found myself trying to talk to the assailants, although I had no idea what I was saying. They paused just long enough for me to turn and run—run until my chest felt like it would burst, hearing them right behind me, one of them laughing, trying to clip my heels at least once, like it was just a game, before they peeled off and I continued running, along the white line and down the alleyways, heaving myself over the wall and dropping into our backyard. I locked the back door and collapsed onto the sofa.

When the party landed back, I split upstairs, in danger of feeling like a freak-show exhibit. The walls felt like they were closing in. Every tooth in my head was throbbing. My jaw felt like it was on wrong. I opened the skylight and hauled myself out onto the slanted roof, three or four floors up. I clambered up to the chimney and sat next to the aerial, the chill of the air soothing on my face.

"Hope you're not thinking of topping yourself." A head poked through the skylight. "'Cause you'll only break your back." My friend Liam crawled up the tiles toward me. "Jumping off that is a safer bet." He pointed at the tall building in the near distance. The library.

"They won't let me in there anymore."

"Probably for the best," he said and laughed. "Here." He handed me a beer bottle, using his lighter to open it.

"Thanks, man."

"I used to come up here when the landlord came looking for the rent. I used to peer in and see him pacing around, pulling his hair out at the state of the place. Must've had twenty smokes waiting for him to leave."

He paused.

"I'm glad you're still alive."

"Thanks."

"Listen, man. You need to get the fuck out of here. I mean, all of this."

I smiled and we clinked bottles. A line from Oscar Wilde's *De Profundis* came into my mind: "Men have gone to heaven for smaller things than that."

I felt inordinately, inexplicably lucky. "I'll write about this one day."

"Write about what?"

"Nothing."

I was smiling like a gleeful idiot through a mouth of bloodied teeth. Staring out at a city that lay like a sea of slate beneath a moon that knew all secrets, above the jeers and the songs and the howls and the laughter of the not-yet-damned.

Doorbell

Something changed then. I wasn't quite sure what. Perhaps it was simply that I did not want to destroy myself anymore. That there was something to life that I could not defile. You could hate everyone and still see there was something miraculously precious about this miserable, beautiful life.

One evening, while we were drinking in a spit-and-sawdust bar, a would-be thug harassing some female friends of ours was invited outside by my mate. In the space of time that it took for me to grab my coat, the thug had been beaten unconscious and was lying prone in the car park, his face covered in blood. "Let him sleep it off," my friends joked and went back into the bar, but I couldn't leave him, scumbag or not, so I lifted him up and took him to the emergency room. It wasn't about him. It was about being able to meet your own gaze in the mirror without looking away.

I knew none of this would go away, though. And I had

no intention of beating myself to pieces against the sea, like some saint or hippie. I had to get out of town, go elsewhere—anywhere—where there might be space to breathe, but excuses were easy to find and the absence of money was one unavoidable issue. There was, however, an intervention from on high.

The knock came in the early hours. Then a furious ringing of the doorbell. I was not yet asleep but about to go to bed, and it threw me. I thought about letting on there was no one in, but I already had music playing, giving away my presence. I was also passing right beside the door when the knock came, meaning that I could barely breathe without making a noise on the floorboards. The door had no latch or peephole. It thudded harder the second time, echoing through the rooms, and an authoritative voice boomed, "Open up." I looked around for something to grasp, but there was nothing. Eventually, when it was clear the visitors were going nowhere, I relented and, bracing myself, opened the door tentatively. Two police officers, male and female, were standing there. One had his walkie-talkie in his hand, and the smaller had her hand by her pistol. "Can we come in? There's been a report of a disturbance."

"Sorry, there must've been a mistake. I didn't report—"

"Can we come in, sir?" The last word said through gritted teeth.

They pushed past me and told me to take a seat. There had been an armed robbery at the top of the street, and CCTV had captured the assailant heading for the door of my tenement. I was on the ground floor. "You also match the description," they added.

I laughed, but they didn't smile.

"Look, I haven't been out in days." I pointed to the mattress on the living room floor, the only room with heating, and to bottles and papers everywhere.

"We'll just have a look round, if that's all right?" They didn't wait for an answer.

I assumed the gun-toting mugger lived in one of the flats above and perhaps was aware of the cops being here. Maybe he was listening in, ear pressed to the floorboards. It was not even enough just to stay inside and keep your head down. Even then you were not left to your own devices. I resolved at that moment to depart the city—for the siren call of other cities—and never return. I left the next week, without leaving a message, with thirty quid in my pocket.

PART FIVE

A Death in the Family

Bus Ticket

Nel mezzo del cammin di nostra vita." Flying home from Italy, fifteen years later, I'd bought a secondhand copy of Dante, carelessly assuming it would be in English. I flicked through it while waiting for the bus from the airport, in the vain hope it had translated itself.

Belfast was changing, booming. You heard it everywhere. The way people insist, a bit too much, that they are clean or better now. Belfast was European. You could tell because people air-kissed over Frappuccinos. A sign in the airport read: "Welcome to Westeros." Taxi drivers did "Troubles tours." Pints cost seven pounds. Hard drugs had seeped in, but the kneecappings now happened by appointment. This was progress. The shipyards—once the bastions of unionist employment, to the exclusion of foreign and papal elements—were dead, but the giant cranes Samson and Goliath were kept as symbols. Of what wasn't certain. They'd named a quarter of the city after the *Titanic*: a ship they proudly built that took 1,500 souls to the bottom of the ocean. As I walked through the arcade full of empty shopping lots, the stalls were selling *Game of Thrones* calendars and flashing phone covers. I felt terribly tired.

The intercom sounded with a once-familiar litany: "Augher, Clogher, Fivemiletown." I went to the vending booth. "A single to Derry, please."

She didn't look up. "Single to Londonderry it is," then slid the ticket under the glass before an abrupt, "Next."

I muttered, "Fuck sake," under my breath.

I found a seat near the back of the bus, walking past rows of people avoiding eye contact, with their bags placed territorially on the seats next to them. I sat my bag next to me in turn and immediately feigned sleep, resting my head against the window. The bus hissed, shuddered, then took off, winding through the city. I still had my eyes closed, knowing every tree and every minute of the journey from Belfast to Derry, though it had been years, and wanting simply to evaporate the time between places. I heard the bus pull up at traffic lights as I nestled in for a nap. Suddenly there was a huge thud and what felt like a firm punch to the side of my face. I looked out to see a group of teenagers making obscene gestures and realized they had thrown a brick at the coach. As the bus drove on, I held my aching jaw. Everyone on the bus was now looking at me as if I were somehow the source of the noise, given that it was my window they'd struck. I kept my head down until they turned away and ran my tongue along my teeth. I couldn't taste any blood, but one of my fillings was loose.

"Motherfuckers!" I cursed, more audibly than intended.

The bus turned onto the West Link motorway, the escape out of Belfast. I glanced out the window, still nursing my jaw, and saw one last line of graffiti, painted with a brush in large white letters. "Fuck Off Back to Ireland," it read.

Soon the motorway took us around the mountain and into the countryside. Seventy shades of green. I could no longer see the beauty of the place, even though I'd been away, and far and wide, for fifteen years. It was like being face-blind. I'd known it too well. Besides, I'd never stood—and never would set foot—in any of the fields I could see rolling by next to the traffic. Those lost spaces next to motorways were not an explorable landscape but rather a no-man's-land. The view was like a film that played over and over again on the cinema screen of the window. The only thing that might change it, make it seem real, was if the hellish tumbrel that was the bus crashed. "Christ," I thought, "I could do with a drink."

The bus ascended onto Glenshane Pass, up into a mist-strewn landscape. I turned to gaze out the window. It was the only part of the journey that ever interested me. A wilderness. Down at sea level, in the cities, the fog surrealized familiar things. Here it suggested the edge of things, or even everything. The pine forests and the waterfalls fell away into nothing, the moorland dropped not into valleys, corries, eskers carved in the Ice Age, but into a gray-white abyss. There were trees all across this land once, turned into charcoal and barrels and ships. Unprotected, the land was left wind-scoured or sodden. Forests of evergreens were patchworked on the hills, in rectangular blocks, but it seemed an artificial substitute. In the foreground passed the gates of the stone quarry, the landscape of which had been torn out and reconfigured into the city that we grew up in. Waterfalls cascaded down the mountains as the bus sped past, coming back to life only after the rain. Entire rivers are ephemeral. They disappear in certain seasons, but the land remembers them.

At its peak was a truck-stop pub, the Ponderosa, named after the pines that grew at height in warmer climes. The building had tall aerials and a generator outside. I'd passed it many
times, never stopping but always wondering who would drink
there—haulers, no doubt, perhaps a curious tourist. It was a
landscape so remote it seemed to have had only cursory deal-
ings with the twentieth century, let alone with the Troubles.
The hills were unforgiving in bad weather, and a person or a
light might be spotted from miles away. So, too, however, would
patrols, and there were hiding places for those who knew the
lie of the land. It was a landscape of appearances and disappearances. A few months after the Bloody Sunday massacre, a
Parachute Regiment Land Rover was driving along here when
it was blown apart by a roadside bomb of explosives packed
into milk churns, detonated by a hidden watchman. The army
learned from the incident and placed their own snipers to guard
the pass, which was the only convenient way by road into the
northwest. It must have been intensely solitary in those wilderness hours, not an enviable posting, though perhaps some
soldiers liked the quiet. Two figures were hiking, several years
later, when a soldier emerged from the undergrowth and ordered them to halt. All three drew their weapons, and the soldier was not quick enough. I wondered, gazing at the landscape
rising and falling as we sped through it, where he had lain, in
the frozen dew with the sky and rain filling his unblinking eyes.

Men died in remote places like these. Alone and in groups.
Places like South Armagh, where there were so many traps that
the British Army took to traveling around in helicopters rather
than by land. Blown up at television transmitters. Informers
shot, ditched like rubbish by bins in alleyways, nudged by foxes.
Pools of frozen blood. A booby trap tripped in a derelict building. Two brothers lying dead on a lane, having set off to meet

their girlfriends. A body by the city's waterworks. Bleeding to death in a bedsit. Quarry. Half Moon Lake. Forest. Lonely places to die and to be found, and for those frozen oceanic hours in between. Bye spots. Silent but for the creaking of branches in the wind.

The lights of the cars ahead were ships in a fog-bound port, monks walking in procession with red lanterns. They slowed down to a safe crawl. An indecipherable flag in the outlands, blown to a rag. When the weather got truly bad, Derry was cut off, even more so than usual. We passed through Dungiven, or *Dunlivin*, as it was tempting to call it, with its murals of dead hunger strikers, and then Drumahoe, the last village before the city, which proudly flew flags of loyalist terrorist organizations and the Parachute Regiment that had committed the Bloody Sunday atrocity. It wasn't just the victims who never forgot. We passed Altnagelvin Hospital, where the bodies of those boys and men shot at that march had been autopsied, and where virtually everyone in Derry, after a certain date, was born. A giant illuminated star, now turned off, adorned the roof.

You live beyond the third act. Or you die at the end of the first. Life is inconvenient like that. In stories, the protagonist always leaves for good. They are not supposed to come back. I returned after a message from my mother: "Your cousin Robert is dying." It was unexpected, for me at least. Robert had always been that handsome ladies' man, quick-witted, a glint in his eye and a swagger, but he had suddenly gone off the rails. Falling dangerously in love with martyrdom, however justified, was a self-sustaining destructive reaction. It didn't do well to nurse a grievance, to feed off it. His liver and kidneys were destroyed so quickly it seemed intentional. He'd ended up bloated and discolored in intensive care, unrecognizable. By the time I was able to arrange to come back, he had already died. I made it in time for the funeral. They had already gone through the wake with all its ceremony, making sure the body was not left alone, keeping a candle burning in the open window, covering all the mirrors so that the dead would not realize they were dead.

We all shuffled along, shaking hands with relatives we hadn't seen in years, commenting on how we'd all weathered the passage of time. After a buffet in an ex-workingmen's club, we ended up back at the house. Robert's sisters were quietly distraught but seemed preoccupied, with friends around them, always nipping in and out of rooms. When I heard bursts of crying, it was through the walls. A cluster of people started drinking, shot through with adrenaline and a nervous energy that prevented drunkenness.

I was called over. "You know Robert's son, Andrew?"

I shook his hand. "Aye, we've met before."

Andrew looked improbably young, younger than his late-teenage years, dressed up in a suit as if he were going to his first job interview. When I'd met him before, he'd had his father's edgy wit, at once charming and prickly. Now he seemed understandably lost. We ended up talking. Andrew was deep in despair and appeared unreachable. In the background, people were haggling over the CD player, what to play. To fill the silence closer to them, I leaned in and talked to Andrew. It seemed he was already elsewhere. Nothing he said appeared to connect, and I gradually began to feel words fail me; everything sounded contrived, a platitude. How easily people fall into cliché, whatever their intentions. Words were insufficient. Not only that, but they seemed an insult, part of the problem—a way of covering up, insinuating that the person should move on. We ended up just clinking glasses and saying, "Fuck it." Andrew's eyes were simultaneously glazed and intense. He'd no job, no future, no money, no hope, no father. I could offer him nothing in the end but silence.

The mantra these days is "talk about your feelings." It sounds like good advice and perhaps it is. It is said, though, by those who can already speak freely. For others, there are consequences to talking, to admitting to colleagues, friends, family—many of whom are struggling too—that you are struggling. There are difficulties in even finding the words, and then in facing the distinct possibility of someone mumbling something awkward or dismissive in response, breaking eye contact. Words have a weight. Sometimes they are lead.

I spent most of my time back home frequenting what pubs remained from my youth. Coming back for Robert's funeral made me realize I'd hit an impasse. The first pangs of middle age. Battered by too many years of too many nights, too many airports and projects and breakups and moves, and bereft of momentum in any other direction, I ended up home, through sheer gravity alone. If you're lucky, that's where you land, temporarily, on the way down. Home, of course, was not the same. It had virtually the same dimensions, bar a handful of changes. Certain gaps in terraces; estates where there had been fields. Buildings that had lain abandoned, empty save for their occasional clandestine intrusions, had been renovated behind darkened glass and keypad entries. Derelict buildings had signs of life decorated onto them. I felt homesick in the midst of home.

The strangest thing wasn't the places that were gone, altered, or disguised, but rather the buildings that remained, which hadn't changed yet still felt somehow unreal to me. As if they'd been replaced by exact replicas in an unaired episode of *The Twilight Zone*. It had not been very long, but I had walked, it seemed, into a facsimile of the past. The bowling alley had the same gigantic ten-pin on its roof. The Guildhall still had its glowing clock face, verdigris-copper cone, and golden weather-vane. It was all there in front of me, but I could never again see it as I once had. I knew few people in the pubs in which I holed up in dimly lit corners, and those I did recognize glanced at me with silent, furtive acknowledgment, as if we had committed some terrible crimes together once in the past—crimes I could not recall and of which neither of us wished to speak. It was not the buildings or the place that had changed, but me, through age and absence. The pub filled and the drink kicked in, but apart from ordering the perpetual "same again" and nodding to the barmaid as she lit the candle, lodged in the empty wine bottle on the table, I said nothing to anyone. Weary of both love and promiscuity, I kept my own company. Where to begin was difficult. Where to begin again nearly impossible.

I spent my days walking, searching for things in space that had most likely been irretrievably lost in time. I found, to para-phrase an old Camus book that I'd unearthed from my teenage stash, that in the depths of summer, there was in me an uncon-querable winter.

Once or twice I would chance upon old school friends and would read in their faces their surprise at how I'd aged. They'd talk about the good old days, and I'd quietly nod along with a half-smile. Nostalgia seemed a fiction you tell yourself, and I was never a good enough storyteller to believe my own fic-tions. Someone had some old photographs on their phone. I didn't keep any myself. It was interesting; we all appeared to be getting increasingly young in the photographs. I stayed long enough to return the round politely and then make my excuses and move on to the next pub, hoping they didn't follow. When the bell rang for last orders, and the bouncers did their rounds, and the bars slowly emptied, I'd watch the last drunken strag-glers melt away in the rain and would find myself always at the quayside. I gazed down from the bridge, dropping bottles into the water to see how they navigated the currents off into the darkness. There was something hypnotic about the river. Looked at from afar, it was a huge mass of water, dark and glacial, complete and permanent. Yet the closer you looked, the more transient it appeared: every bit of it—all the swirls and currents that shimmied on the surface and glitched the reflections of the lights. Rivers exist in deep geological time and yet they are forever restarting.

The morning after the wake, I woke hungover. I slunk downstairs and sensed there was something wrong with the silence. I asked.

"Robert's boy is missing. Andrew. They found his belongings on the bridge."

Wallet, Keys, Mobile Phone

Disappearing completely is not an easy task. You can try to step out of your life, but life holds on. Everywhere we go, we leave traces. We are shades on CCTV, time stamps on bank withdrawals, coordinates on phone signals to satellites. To disappear completely now takes effort, skill, a technological Indian rope trick. It is far easier to die than to disappear. No one saw Andrew vanish. The things he left behind—his wallet, keys, and mobile phone—were ominous, given how crucial they were to modern existence. I paused at the bridge on which they were found, thinking of those missed calls and unread texts transmitting through the atmosphere.

I stopped to tighten the laces on my boots. My father was already across the road, up ahead by the ruined gatehouse. He began walking on when I'd almost reached him.

I followed, purposeful as a stray dog, and thought of things to talk about, to pass the time and distract us: music, the woods, the birds, the jet trails of a long-vanished plane high above us, the pale ghost of the moon in the sky. In the end, I said nothing. We climbed over the cold clasp of the metal cattle-fence and onto the path, wet as sculptor's clay, then through the brambles, parallel to the field and down, down into the thicket that descended to the river. The path was frozen at its shadows and set at a treacherous angle, the sidings thick with thorns. I pulled my sleeves down over my hands and walked, attempting to test the firmness of the ground without dropping pace, once or twice almost losing my footing, heart momentarily stopping in a brief jolt of adrenaline. My father seemed unaffected, striding ahead until I had lost sight of him completely through the briars, which swallowed up the way forward after he'd passed. I could still hear him singing. It suited him, the wildness. He belonged, it seemed, to an earlier time. There was something innately pagan about him, more suited to the days when every corner of the landscape had its own small god.

When he reached the clearing and sea level, my father was already staring into the mid-distance, scanning the river's silver skin. Da didn't notice my watching him. When I was young and could glance unseen, I would study the map of his face. It was full of character, weather-beaten from working outside in countless seasons as a gardener-groundsman for the council. He'd become even more Lincolnesque with age. His long straggles of hair were grayer and thinner, but still a statement. His tattoos a little more faded with his sleeves rolled up, but still prominent, inescapable. He still dressed with admirable disdain for convention: a prospector's waistcoat, Gypsy scarves, Chelsea boots. There was a traveling fair somewhere missing a member. Always quiet and self-contained, he had a certain fatalism that had recently become pronounced in him. He seemed suddenly vulnerable, after years—decades—of appearing elementally solid. He had not taken to age well, which was surprising, even unsettling. You spent your youth wanting to escape your home and living away, and then in middle age you get the sudden, terrifying realization that your parents won't be around forever, or even for that much longer. Something had put the fear into my father—maybe it was mortality or the past—and it shook me too, though I said nothing of it. What could he be thinking, now that he was returning, once again, to retrieve the dead from the river?

And yet in moments like this, bounding over the slick rocks and rivulets, he looked like his old self again. I thought of the times when, as a child, I used to try, through sheer willpower, by concentrating intently, to make time slow down, come to a halt and finally reverse, but the clocks kept ticking and time flowed on regardless, and us with it.

We emerged from the trees to a part of the river called the Narrows. As we stepped down off the bank, the riparian edge of the woodland gave way to shingle, which whispered under our boots. The gravity of the moon had dragged the river down, and the things it contained were left behind, scattered as detritus. It looked like the scene of a catastrophe, one that had happened impossibly long ago. I kicked through the wreckage. Rusted cans. Collapsed lobster cages. The jawbone of an animal, bleached white.

The Armada had washed up not far from here. Splintered galleons, the pride of imperial Spain, turned into flotsam and jetsam on a merciless shore, their names lost now in time, their bodies (those that were found, at least) looted for keepsakes. And now they had returned, the descendants of the plunderers, to beachcomb again for the drowned. "Where are you, Andrew?" I thought. "Just give me a sign and we'll take you home."

We scanned the slipstreams of the river, together but separate. It was odd to be searching for something—someone—I didn't want to find. The mind played tricks. Here and there I'd see a darker patch on the surface or breakers hitting rocks, signs of riptides and eddies, and swear there was something there, something that resembled a silhouette, but the kid remained hidden. What would we find? It was not worth thinking about, yet you inevitably did. What were the boy's immediate family going through? For all the well-worn formalities of the newspaper appeals and police reports, it was the stuff of nightmares and yet, as little as I knew him, Andrew did not belong to nightmares.

The wind began to pick up. Somewhere in a slow, silent dance of water and half-light, I was drifting and we could not find him. The river was mute. Across the expanse, factories were silently pumping artificial clouds into a sky mirrored on the water.

My father was farther down the beach, surveying the horizon through binoculars. I began to kick through the dreck left in the wake of successive tides, looking for clues—anything really. Streamers of knotted wrack seaweed cloaked the rocks, from mustard fronds to onyx barbs and bladders. I recited their names in my head, learned in childhood yet still curiosities: wing kelp and sea whistle, oyster thief and dead man's bootlaces, peacock's tail, sea oak, landlady's wig, dillisk and black carrageen. They looked like the fossilized tendrils of an alien race, because they had come from an alien world. What did that world make of the strange periodic visitors from the surface, floating and then falling down into this other universe?

It was a fearful realm to contemplate. The depths of the Foyle had long unsettled me, even when, as children, we toyed at its edges, knowing we shouldn't. A world of monsters was concealed from us by the water's chrome surface and by the rationing of light in its depths, but you'd get occasional glimpses. The slick devils of eels that we hooked by accident, all teeth and black oil. Eating blind fish around the sewage pipes. The rats we hissed and threw stones at, darting along at right angles beneath the dock pilings. The eyeless things powered wholly by instinct.

Yet the water in the shallows was crystalline. I reached down and let it run through my fingers. Though it was the depths of winter, it was still colder than expected. I tried to imagine the shock to the system, upon going suddenly under; how long it would take for the body temperature to drop, for the muscles to seize up, for energy to ebb away, hoping it was mercifully quick. I remembered foolishly diving into the sea while camping once, too early in the year, and how my lungs shrank to the size of a walnut in a fraction of a thought, and, winded, I barely struggled to the shore. It was the cold that got you, they said. That and the undercurrents.

Two friends of mine were sitting, smoking on a pier once. A car drove up and the driver just sat there, gazing at the sea. Thousand-yard stare. They watched him as he watched it. Then suddenly he hit the accelerator and launched the car off the edge. It belly flopped onto the waves and, much quicker than expected, tilted and slid down into the depths, its taillights disappearing into the murk. My friends sat there, dumbfounded. Seconds later the driver burst to the surface gasping, "Jesus, lads, it's fucking freezing." Maybe it's an urban myth or a memory or a memory of a myth, but it has the ring of truth.

The river was deceptive at this point in its meanderings. Three steps in and you'd suddenly plummet downward. They'd kept Allied submarines down there, hidden in the unseen fathoms. There were still traces of its past military life along the shore. For a better view, I clambered up onto a man-made parapet of concrete sandbags, grazing my palms against the rough surface. At the end of the last world war, the Nazi U-boat fleet, having surfaced and surrendered as far north as Norway and as far south as Spain, had been gathered here. The crews, stunned that their thousand-year Reich had lasted only twelve years before obliteration, stunned that they were somehow still alive, were taken off into custody, while their vessels—116 submarines—were towed out into open waters northwest of Ireland and scuttled. Operation Deadlight it was called. Along the ocean floor are iron rooms rusting and transforming into coral, in an unseen sea change.

In the cold war that followed, Derry was reputedly designated a nuclear target by the Soviet Union and would have received a payload fifty times the power of the Fat Man and Little Boy atom bombs that obliterated Hiroshima and Nagasaki. The aim would be to knock out the naval yards and the submarine trenches, incinerating or irradiating the city in the process. Standing at the docks, looking north along the river toward the sea, I wondered how long would pass—seconds, milliseconds—before the heat and the blast wave hit. I wondered what would be left. Silhouettes flashbulbed onto whatever stone remained standing. This local tragedy would, of course, go virtually unnoticed in the wider world, given that Moscow, Berlin, Washington, and hundreds of other cities would be sequentially seared from the face of the earth. I thought of figures out at sea or up on the hills, by the ancient stone sun fort of Grianán of Aileach, gazing down, shielding their eyes as a second sun appeared in the sky and a boiling tower, built from what was once a city, rose into the sky. I thought of the eerie silence when telegraph and radio operators couldn't contact the entire city of Hiroshima.

The BBC planned for such eventualities, with prerecorded

messages to be relayed to those lucky or unlucky enough to have survived, in the reassuring Received Pronunciation of the continuity announcer, whether he was still alive or dead: "Stay tuned to this wavelength, stay calm and stay in your own house. Remember there is nothing to be gained by trying to get away. By leaving your homes, you could be exposing yourself to greater danger." It was a message for those homes that, by blind luck or topography, still remained. Clouds of radiated smoke and debris of what was once Derry would join what was once Belfast and begin to drift northeast over the sea, to the Scottish islanders struggling to get a signal on their radios, wondering what the ominous glows on the horizon were.

Among my earliest memories was being carried on my father's shoulders at the front of Campaign for Nuclear Disarmament marches, walking beside my mother and aunts, all of them in hippie kaftans. There was a black-and-white photograph on the cover of the local paper of one such parade in which we were discernible, crossing the river on the top deck of the Craigavon Bridge. Banners bearing messages like "Protest and Survive," "Refuse Cruise," "Ban the Bomb." Years later, as a cocky youth, I'd casually jibe my folks and ask if Northern Ireland had become an irradiated wasteland, how would they tell the difference? My mother answered seriously, with an unexpected reproachful wistfulness, that many nights she lay awake, thinking the apocalypse could come at any second, and would gather up my infant sister and me in her arms through the night to have us with her, just in case the four-minute warning had already been given and the nukes were on their way. As it happened, the end of the world failed to occur, for them at least, but the mushroom cloud cast a long shadow over many lives. It was only later that I became aware that her fear of the bomb, however looming and all-encompassing, was just the surface—a totem. Something else was shadowing her; not the colossal destruction of nuclear annihilation, which wipes out entire cities in seconds, but the creeping death that seeps into families on days when everything is normal for everyone else. The death of her mother had given her a sense of doom and gloom. Trying to shield her children ran the risk of un-armoring us in the process.

The earth was charred on top of the lookout from a long-extinguished bonfire; springs like metal orbits unwound from incinerated tires. The ruins of a building, the roof fallen in, stood farther upriver. Another was completely shrouded in ivy and other plants, a cube of abundant forest, with only a window in the green revealing that it was man-made. A foul-tempered goat had once made its home there and had chased me out onto the rocks, but it had long since vanished, leaving silver fleece tangled on the wire.

My grandfather Anthony would have known how to read the river, how to find the boy. The shallow turbulence of the riffle, the signs of pockets of depth, how the river speeds at certain points.

The sun had begun to sink in the sky, and the light was changing. A chill had entered the air, and I turned up my collar against the wind. My father suggested coming back in the morning, given that our chances of seeing anything now were slim. I agreed, but said I'd stay on, clear my head, take the air. My father nodded and turned and walked away, singing as he went. Da was always singing. I remembered a scene from Kurosawa's film *Rashomon*. The rain forever falling as the desperate huddled under the refuge of a crumbling gate in a country falling to pieces. "We all want to forget something," one of them said, "so we tell stories. It's easier that way." Songs were Da's stories.

I propped myself up next to the green lighthouse and took my hip flask from my coat pocket and watched as my father disappeared up through the trees. I took a swig and leaned my head against the stone. Sunlight splintered through the canopy in the near distance. I closed my eyes for the briefest of moments and felt the warmth on my face, a lizard saving up the heat from a distant star before the night comes. It would get cold soon, and dark, but the least I could do, having failed Andrew when we last met, was to sit with him awhile.

Dusk exploded in slow motion, the stars already appearing through a sky on fire. Should I feel guilty to see beauty at such a time? It appeared to me like a painting by Turner or Titian, the palette changing by the minute. Ruby of arsenic, copper patina, Egyptian blue, Schloss green, chrome yellow, spirit of Saturn, orpiment, vermilion, cinnabar, and cadmium—all the poisonous pigments that drove artists into madness and the early grave. But what sunsets they painted! I wondered if anyone else was watching this as it carried on around the curve of the planet.

There was a story of a lady leaving Derry for America. Inconsolable, she had turned around for one last look at her birthplace and saw the silhouette of a man hanging from the gallows, framed against an exquisite sky. I struggled to remember who had told it (Steinbeck perhaps?), passed down as it was from generation to generation, but memory is a slippery fickle thing. It would have been this direction, on this river. I sat there drinking, and the light slowly seeped through the dusk and then ebbed away, until all that was left were stars and questions, endless constellations of questions.

Ballast

I walked all night, walked myself sober, looking for anything in the river—any sign. The morning was the color of cobalt. Frozen tire marks traced over and over one another like a charcoal sketch of cathedral arches on the ice. Winter asphalt Gothic patterns that the sun would soon erase. Across the fields of frost, that same pale sun finally emerged. This far north, this deep into winter, day comes fleetingly, like an afterthought, an accident of light and geometry.

Birds perched on the telegraph wires. In a silent cacophony, they took off into the sky. High on the hills were white towers, farming the wind. I walked through the still-standing forecourt of a bulldozed petrol station. Farther on, I reached the area referred to as "out the line." Here you followed the ghost track of a vanished train line right next to the river. The ballast stones were loose underfoot. The rusted rails and decaying sleepers were overgrown with weeds. Even knowing it had been closed for decades, I still had the urge to look over my shoulder, for safety, as I walked along it. In March 1957, as part of their border campaign Operation Harvest, the IRA hijacked a Great Northern Railway cargo train in Donegal. Ordering the crew off at gunpoint, they fired up the engine, picked up as much steam as they could, and then leapt off it. The train carried on at full speed into the Foyle Road station, bursting through the barriers with such force that it ended up twenty feet deep in the concrete. People posed next to the wreckage afterward. A crumpled poster on a pulverized board still invited "Fly BEA to the Sea." The trains were now long gone. So, too, was the station. Even British European Airlines was gone. Maybe even the bandits.

I passed an abandoned halting site, full of rubble, named Daisyfield. An electrical generator marked "Danger of Death: Keep Out." A white heart sprayed on a low wall. A fraying wooden sign demanding "Justice for the Craigavon 2." A fenced-off crane. A poster half-peeled off with a faded face: "Rewards available for information." Satellite dishes on the walls of houses, tinged with rust, still speaking to satellites in a silver halo of debris around the planet. A plaque boasting "Best-Kept Neighbourhood 1980." The year I was born. Year of the Monkey. It looked like a place devoid of meaning or history, but this innocuous stretch was once a perilous one, being a small patch of waste ground in a valley overlooked by higher ground. A soldier keeled over here, shot from a rooftop up on Bishop Street. Another was shot at the filling station by a sniper in the cemetery. Another at a street junction, from the grounds of the college. A middle-aged bus driver, a reservist in the UDR, was dragged off his bus to the frantic protests of his passengers, bundled into a car, and found bound, gagged, and lifeless here. Two men were seen limping across the fields at the border, one with a rifle, and the army opened fire, leaving a body near the customs post. A man went on an errand for his pregnant wife and did not return home. He ended up here. Once, I had thought of this as a place devoid of any history, but nowhere really is.

The tide was out and just about to turn. Even this far inland, the river was tidal. At points it looked so metallic, you could imagine walking across, but at other points there were mudflats and very slowly stirring patches of slack water. Half-buried bicycles and shopping trolleys appeared like postapocalyptic wreckage. Scavenging birds left their tracks in arcs across what was, for any heavier creature, a dangerous mix of mud and silt. Descendants of the dinosaurs teetering around out on the surface. I thought of the tale of a girl, apocryphal perhaps, who slipped in and became stuck in what locals called the "glar" and slowly drowned in effluent, panicking to extricate herself but succeeding only in forcing herself farther down before they reached her. The incident, and the fear of slow drowning, was talked of with the same fascinated childhood dread as quicksand, or the tales of mammoths and dire wolves getting stuck in tar pits.

Then there were the suicides. Perhaps it had always been an issue, the river always there, beckoning the lost to escape to somewhere else. In recent years, post-Troubles, it had become an epidemic, especially among young men. There was simply no future for them, or rather the sense of no future prevailed. Their reasons were as complex and nuanced and individual as each case, but there were certain universals. A sense of despair. An absence of any opportunity for a better life. The vertigo that might come at considering leaving the city, and the anger that came with having to. Drink and drugs offered the appearance of an escape in the same manner that digging further into a hole might. They were the left-behind in a city left behind. In the days of the

Troubles there was a conspiracy of silence: don't say anything, lest you say too much. It was the age of hard men and squealers. In the supposedly halcyon days that followed the conflict, the mantra became, Don't speak, in case you spook the horses. Everything is fine. Indeed, you are privileged, or the perpetrators of everything wrong in society—a view expounded from both left and right. Suicide became, and remains, by far the biggest killer of male Derry youths. It is a voiceless epidemic.

Hundreds of attempts, too many of them successful, occurred each year. Almost one a night, it worked out. Rather than offer everyone the possibility of a future, plans were touted by the council and local architects to cut off access to the river, with decorative walls and fences. Hem them into this life. Well-meaning messages were put up along the river in desperation, with instructions, "You are not alone. There is hope." Perhaps they even worked once or twice. Yet the deluge kept coming.

On the columns of the flood wall I passed faded letters, each four feet high, marked "A," then "R," and finally "I." The river was still calm, but slowly it was turning, as if its gyres and currents were wheels and gears winding up. The slightest trace of turbulence behind the jetties revealed a glimpse of force under the stillness.

The winter sun was low, struggling over the horizon, but it was enough to begin to crack and melt the sleeping ice on the trees. They began to drip, and initially I mistook it for rain. Soon the trees crackled. We forget how strange they are, rising out of the planet toward space. All of them have turned subtly south over the years toward the sun's arc. One side was speckled with moss; the other burned with shadow. I ran my hand along the fissures and grooves of the freezing bark. It felt like the braille of some untranslatable language.

There was no sign of the boy.

I wondered what the first people to live here called the river. How many names it'd had down the years. Archaeologists knew from the remains of raths they found, when digging up fields for housing estates, that Bronze Age people had ventured out of their forts on higher ground into the woods to forage, to hunt birds and hogs with flint, but above all they relied on the river for trout and shellfish, sailing on currachs of canvas over wood and pitch, taking them back to salt for the hard months. This source of sustenance must have had names. On Ptolemy's study of the world in the second century A.D., the river was marked Widwa. The Foyle came later. It commemorates Feabhal, the drowned son of the ancient chieftain Lodan. Death is written into its very name. Every river is a threat as well as a gift.

I arrived at the old railway station. It was long defunct, and even the museum that had replaced it was now long closed. This was the end of the line, the terminus, of one of the extinct railway lines that cover this island. An old County Donegal Railways timetable was framed on the wall. The times for stations that no longer existed. "Meet your friend in Letterkenny." "High Mass in cathedral at 12 noon." Monday, June 29, 1931. The Socialists have just won in Spain. The German government informs the British that their banking system is in danger of collapse. Prohibition in America. The HMS *Poseidon* sinks in the Yellow Sea. Salvador Dalí unveils *The Persistence of Memory*. Up ahead was a surviving steam engine, albeit hollowed-out. Its red and black paint flaking into rust, sidelined and fenced off to prevent vandals or drinkers from going near it, dying a slow death in the rain. I sat on the cold stone of what was once the platform and surveyed the rising water.

The river was like quicksilver. As I leaned against the railings, a bird came flying down, foraging amid the wildflowers and weeds on the tracks. Looking at its dark wings, I struggled to differentiate in my memory, though I had seen them all count-less times, the difference between ravens, crows, and rooks. It turned and leapt up onto the wall, and I could see it was a jack-daw, with its unmistakable doll's eyes, which look as if they are painted on. It flew off, splicing the sky into a montage with its wings.

Waves were striking and swirling over loose bricks and slabs, like masonry from fallen towers. The little islands of rocks—"skerries," as they were known—were vanishing. A lone bird swept along the surface of the water, its fragmenting twin keep-ing pace below it.

Before the water rose too high, I stepped over the railings and, holding on to them, reached down and hauled up a gnarled piece of driftwood. I held it up to the light. It was covered in tiny holes. "Gribbles," they called them. Shipworms. This had been part of something. It had a story within it, probably a cen-tury or more old. I swung my arm and launched it, spinning, onto the river and watched as it floated speedily away.

There is the slightest trace of oil on the river, its color like abalone shell. The light falls into the depths, processing all the things it has reflected, like photography.

As the tide came in, it reclaimed the territory it had lost be-low the wall. The seaweed waved and vanished. The last things left were at the tideline. Blue mussel shells. Dog whelks. Peri-winkles. Among the dreck being swallowed up were "nurdles," hooked onto the plant life. "Fish eggs," they were called, or, if you were romantically inclined, "mermaid's tears." Man-made plastic pellets that take millennia to wear down and choke the insides of marine life. A lasting, purposeless remnant of mankind.

Over the pathway, a bird, with its hollow bones, is buffeted by the wind. One second fighting against it furiously, the next allowing itself to be swept up in it. For the briefest of moments, it achieves an equilibrium, levitating in clear sight.

Downriver some planks had been washed up. The timber looked relatively fresh. Dunnage, perhaps: material they used to stabilize cargo in the containers that kept every city functioning. I had watched the long, thin ships move slowly in so many places around the world, from the Baltic to the South Pacific. Always there, always unnoticed.

A slow cataclysm of time was evident at the shore. I gazed back out the line and could see the land that the city was built on. Layers of rock had been riven and peeled away. It was cracked and hewn and sculpted, as if by some mad god. Even the concrete behind it would not hold out forever. Everything they built was in defiance of atrophy.

It was not unusual to see creatures at the river. On the more easeful stretches, especially of the lough, you spotted herons, even storks with their spindly legs that moved oddly, almost mechanically or surreally, like Dalí's elephants. Several times I saw a drove of sheep led astray, ambling along, some sprayed with color. Once I came upon horses that had somehow made it to an isolated part of the river. I couldn't quite work out how they'd gotten there, between a large banking and the river on either side. They were scuttling on the rocks. Four, five of them. I assumed the tide had come in and stranded them. Their reflections mirrored on the water as they stooped to drink. They were skittish as I approached, so I held back. I hiked up onto the fields to see if anyone was looking for them or if there were stables nearby. When I returned, they were gone. Nowhere to be seen.

My grandfather used a phrase to describe waves out in rough conditions: white horses. The equine sea. Many myths linked the two, almost always with some menacing result. In northern Europe, the *bäckahäst* was said to drown anyone who climbed on it by plunging into the water. The Celt-eating kelpies could be escaped only if you fled across running water. Mythology was not just the graveyard of religions. It served purposes. Old ditch-haunting drunks explained away blackouts and disappearances with tales of falling into the crazed dance of a fairy ring for a few days (hence the still-used phrase "away with the fairies"). Myths explained dinosaur bones and ruins dug up on farmland. Superstitions. Fictions. Alibis. Yet I took no chances and stepped across the little streams leading to the river.

There was snow on the Donegal mountains, hulks of sleeping granite, in the distance. The treacherous scree we once scrambled up, as boys on adventures beyond the border, was welded fast and sleek as glass now. It would be spring before it would thaw properly and the ravines would reactivate into waterfalls and streams. Down here, ice had coated the roads, turning the dew on the grass into ripples of quartz as if the wind had frozen mid-motion. Spiders' webs had turned crystalline. Even now, though, before sunrise, the frost had begun to retreat to the shadows. The salt on the roads was already staining the leather on my boots.

Driftwood sailed by, gnarled and mutated, from a forest somewhere in the past.

I walked along the shore and stopped to pick up a flat stone. The sun was glistening on the river, shining on sinners and saved alike. I skimmed the stone across the surface, once, twice. At the third instance it sank beneath the waves and settled there, likely for centuries.

For a split second, I swore I saw some glint of movement below the surface of the river, life in the universe beneath. It moved faster than time, faster than thought, and vanished again until I was left doubting I'd seen anything at all.

A boat suddenly appeared, carving a "V" in the water. It slowed, almost cutting the engine, to pass under the bridge, between the supports, then fired up again and took off, bouncing on the surface, curving between the buoys. As the wake came in, the reflection of my face fragmented.

The low golden winter sun cast long, languid shadows. The wind slowly grew in power over the undulating grass. Birds rose off the fields like smoke. I trekked back up the rocks, almost losing my balance once or twice on the precarious slipways and outcrops, before making it onto the relative safety of the path.

The other road took me into a fine imitation of wilderness. Behind ten-foot wooden panels were black dunes of coal. Opposite were gas yards and oil terminals, behind cameras and razor wire. At the river's edge, you could push through the trees to a little cove and walk right out onto a secret view of the city, from discarded concrete slabs, riprap, or accropodes, shot rocks either dumped there or deliberately placed to minimize erosion from the rising water. Future echoes for the buffer zones and breakwaters that will be needed when global warming really begins to come calling. The river had been cleaned up a great deal even since my youth. If pipes were still pumping night soil into the river, they were now discreet. I noticed the wind wisping off the surface and dark clouds gathering. The weather was turning. The sky was more turbulent than the water. A low front was coming in. The barometer in my grandfather's attic was stirring in the dark.

There were little messages on the wires. I thought they were advertisements. Instead they were inducements to live. It seemed futile, desperate, but who was I to judge?

I trekked through the trees for fifteen, twenty minutes, seeing if I could find anything. By the time I emerged out the other side, the weather had already gotten worse. I put my collar up, buttoned my coat, and fastened my scarf. Clouds like rusting metal hulks were hanging there as the sky raced past them, flowing over the earth, bringing air from far-off places. I'd been caught out by weather before, mistiming a mountain climb, high above sheer cliffs, and getting hit with a storm, barreling down the slope as fast as I could. Another time, high up on a plateau, lightning began to strike, and I realized that I was an hour's hike from anywhere resembling safety and that I was the tallest object in sight.

I remembered the trees marching right down to the river. There were roots and a stump where one once stood. Others had ribbons tied around them, as a sign of which one was to be felled. The wind had almost blown one away, offering the possibility of a stay of execution. The shadows of clouds raced across the harrowed fields. Swifts whipped through the fields in impossible pirouettes.

The urge for pilgrimage preceded, and will no doubt outlast, the faith. I ran my hand along the stone in some mute forgery of prayer. The path along the docks was a popular jogging run with a bicycle path. Both were empty now, save for a figure in the distance walking a dog. The path was there for the scenic views of the river and St. Columb's Park opposite, via the curving Peace Bridge, and for its calorie-burning distance. Promenades are for walking and resting, not exploring or uncovering, but traces still remain. A section of train tracks embedded in concrete. Rusted rings for tying mooring lines to, staining the stone beneath. The iron bollards, heavy as anvils, where the ships tied up, had a fresh lick of black paint. Needles and Joseph—two decades apart—went into the river somewhere along what is now a pleasant stroll. Where the bustling docks were, there is a marina for pleasure boats. Memories that I forgot I retained returned to me as I leaned over the brink. As children, tempting fate, we'd clamber down the stone wall onto a pipe platform just above the river, precariously close to the currents. There we were hidden from view and therefore somewhere precious, as well as dangerous.

The clouds were barreling across the sky. The sun had long been swallowed. I gazed at the river and thought I saw something, then ruled out anything human; a seal perhaps, maybe just an exposed rock in the oil-black river. If it was watching me back, it was awfully still. I walked on. The wind was whistling through the metal fences. A flock of birds formed into shapes then chaos, then shapes again.

I climbed up the steep hill to the road. A mobile-phone mast stood like a blind sentinel. A broken umbrella lay blown inside out. During a lull, I dashed across the dual carriageway and hopped over the metal crash barrier, sliding down the banking. Above me, up at the beginning of the bridge, a windsock whipped around violently. It looked like an unfurled flag of an unformed country. The land along this stretch of the river used to be called Ballynashallog, "the townland of the hunt." A land of ecotones—transitioning from field to road to woods to river. With the wind coming off the water, I turned toward the trees, hoping to find somewhere to sit it out. A trail, a bridleway, formed by journey after journey of horses and farm machinery, took me round to disused stables, several hundred years old by the looks of them, and then the ruins of the mansion Boom Hall. Its doors bricked up. Its roof fallen in. Its upper windows unreachable, framing the sky. A cat scurried out of the bushes and darted off in another direction.

Boom Hall had been the site of Charles Fort, which guarded

the boom, bloodily and ultimately unsuccessfully, during the Siege. Both sides of the boom were defended, and there were so many hostilities there that it was fearfully referred to as "Gunsland." The mansion had been the home of earls, bishops, businessmen—its ownership charting the changing fortunes and character of the establishment. During the war it was occupied by the women's corps of the Royal Naval Service. It was gutted by accidental fire in 1970 and left to ruin. I walked right around it, but all the entries were blocked up. As boys, we used to get in under the steps of the main entrance, down in a small moat where the servants would presumably have arrived. We'd scurry about on the rubble inside, trying to climb up on fallen broken masonry like loose scree, to where the second and third floors had been. What were once luxurious rooms were just empty cubits of air above us. We couldn't be seen from outside, but it was risky too, as there was only one way out if someone followed us in. I had never entirely felt at ease there.

Shortly before the mansion burned down, it had been abandoned. A group of Travellers, it is said, relieved the building of its remaining valuables, including furniture and food. Before they carted them away, they laid out a long table with an impromptu banquet and ate and drank merrily—the last of a long line of the great and good to do so.

The storm was gathering force and I knew I'd have to find shelter soon. It was coming in on the leeward tide. Waves snarling at the sky. An uneasy truce broken. I moved deeper into the trees. On the edge there were already bluebells, wood sorrel, bracken, bog asphodel. Signs of partially swamped land, I knew that much. What once grew here was recorded in old almanacs. I found something resembling a hollow that still had a bed of golden-brown leaves. It seemed to offer some semblance of shelter, but as I walked in, there was a chorus from above, like an aviary alarm system, and suddenly dozens of crows took noisy flight, stripping the branches bare, save for their empty nests. Birds burst from trees like piles of leaves kicked in autumn. The birdsong of spring—trill, warble, peep, chirrup, whistle— reduced to a harsh caw, breaking the promise of silence. The sky was a delta of light framed by the trees. The canopy sway- ing. I remembered hearing somewhere that the willow bends in a storm while the strong oak breaks. The rain broke through the trees. Another word came into my mind as I leaned against the bark—*petrichor*, the scent of the rain after a dry period.

What intrigued humans about the woods was that which once repelled us. They were uneasy places on the periphery of settle- ments, full of potential dangers. You once went there by necessity, not choice. They were fearful places of transformation. Where the branches would suddenly turn into creatures, and where un- seen things could be heard in the undergrowth. Fit only for those seeking refuge or foraging. Bandits, hermits, and would-be saints. They were places you could almost imagine being sentient, the way a single step would set off a shudder through the entire envi- ronment, a chorus of disapproval having detected your trespass, the animal that scares the other animals away. It *knew* you were there. In stories, from those of Baba Yaga to the Brothers Grimm, people tried to personify this, but it was beyond human. Its think- ing was not ours.

The weather suddenly worsened into a black squall. Deep churning clouds, black with the weight of water directly over- head. Before he went into exile for starting a bloody war with another local saint over a plagiarized book (the land of saints and scholars was by no means an innately positive thing), Columba had once said a prayer—a spell really—that no one be "shattered" by lightning in Derry, and I hoped if there was a god, he'd been listening. The downpour came through the trees like the sea's roar. I could just about hear the thudding of a gate somewhere, wrenched almost off its hinges. I knew I'd have to make a break for it, the trees offering scant shelter. The muddy path, strewn with slugs, was an oil spill.

I was soaked right through by the time I made it under the bridge. On both sides were walls of water, the feeling of being behind a waterfall. This was once our base. The brutalist viaduct was still covered in a kaleidoscope of graffiti, but innumerable layers had been added since I'd last been there. I pulled myself up onto the ledge and leaned into the corner, trying to keep the wind off. Next to me was a door to the passageway that ran the entire length of the interior of the bridge; pipes ran along the underside of the bridge. I felt a vague sense of vertigo, only now appreciating how high up I was, and how high we'd been up here larking around as teenagers. It struck me as insane that we used to get wasted up here, with the steep staircase below, but the danger simply hadn't occurred to us then. I tried warming my hands by cupping my breath in them. They had a purple tinge, like an old boxer's. The bridge curved in mid-air and turned, sweeping down to land on the other side. It was held aloft by vast pillars, some on dry land and others on small man-made and uninhabited islands filled with trees. Archways for boats passing underneath them. The kid had vanished from the bridge I was now huddled under.

The downpour was coming in waves now. The scent of nettles in the rain. Given that the rain was coming sideways, I decided to make a dash for the edge of the woods, where there might be more shelter. I almost slipped once or twice on the fresh mud, but made it.

We were always finding little copses as children to hide within, to exercise the subversion of invisibility, having access to a world adults could not enter. One was in the grounds of a psychiatric institution on our way home from school. We'd crawl through a tunnel someone had made and emerge in a perfect hollow. There were markings on the trees, unidentifiable names and dates carved and the ruins of a tree house, left by others who had since grown up. Relics of the childhood of others. All the trees were laid waste by winter. A gaunt, starved landscape, tied to seasons that the cities tried to ignore. Spring would come and summer; the empty arc of branches would turn into cathedrals of green. The entire planet had to shift first. In earlier minds, there must have lurked the fear this winter would not end, nor even this night.

The trees creaked in the wind. I thought of the sounds of the sea. The groans of the *Endurance* being slowly crushed by pack ice. Tapping in Morse code on the hull of the *Kursk*. Sounds of pressure.

I pushed deeper into the woods, toward the river, going over the litany of trees like it was an incantation, taking my mind off the cold—wych elm, silver birch, ash.

Deep within the *Inferno*, Dante finds a wood. It has no clear path and seems in perpetual winter. The leaves are not green, the branches are not smooth but tortured and twisted, the fruits are thorny and poisonous. Tormenting harpies nest there. He hears wailing but cannot place it. He breaks off a stick from a thorn bush, which begins to bleed and then replies, startling him, "Why did you break me?" The very trees are the souls of the damned, the suicides, the "self-murderers."

Whatever pity there was in Dante the traveler's account, Dante the theologian placed suicides in the Seventh Circle, the circle of violence. The Church was marginally more merciful. It merely sent the victims/perpetrators of suicide to limbo, alongside those who had lived before Christ and the souls of unbaptized children. It was one of the ways the priests kept the congregation in line. Hell was too extravagant to be real, but limbo seemed believable. A place of no torment, but no pleasure and no hope. It was even said that the entrance to limbo lay not far from us, in a tunnel once visited by St. Patrick, on Lough Derg.

In the past the authorities, civil and religious, exacted a heavy price for acts of suicide on the loved ones who remained. It was illegal, being seen as a way of escaping debt or defying God's omnipotence; and therefore, it was reasoned, anyone surviving an attempt, or even the bereaved family, should be punished. The Church tried to portray suicide as an English import and innately un-Irish, while simultaneously operating the death cult of Christ and the saints. But the taboo was not just a Catholic one; the Protestant Book of Common Prayer contained the Order for the Burial of the Dead, "not to be used for any that die unbaptized, or excommunicate, or have laid violent hands upon themselves."

The people I knew who had taken their own lives did not belong in limbo. And the religious authorities had no right to condemn those who had suffered to purgatory. In recent times the Church's view had changed. Nowadays it was assumed that the person had taken temporary leave of their senses and so was not in a position to exert free will. They were no longer buried at night in disgrace, or in unconsecrated ground, or at crossroads, like criminals destined to wander between the winds or publicly shamed or sent off to be dissected. The papers spoke of accidents or unfortunate cases. Eventually the Church abolished limbo entirely, emptying its chambers, setting them all free. After centuries of condemning the dead and tormenting the grieving, they ruled that it had never existed and that all the misery endured by their loved ones was for nothing, except control.

The rain and wind were abating, though the storm clouds

still hung low in the sky. I decided to make a break for it. Fortune favored the brave. I made a dash for the pebbled shore of
the river. I should have noticed that there were no worn paths,
no desire lines, ahead. The landscape was slick with rain, and
momentum took me a great distance before I realized it was
much more sodden than I'd initially thought. What looked like a
straight of green from a distance was actually far more treacherous. The mounds of grass that appeared stable and dry had clefts,
or were just fragile skins of moss that would collapse, forcing me
to step on them only briefly, forcing me on. Some were hidden
and others almost Zen-like, reflecting the sky with bone-white
fallen branches extending over them. I struggled forward, too
far in now to retreat, and for every three footings I managed to
reach, there was one where I plunged down into freezing water,
lucky to retain my boots, which were covered in thick, clinging
mud that slowed my step. I aimed for the shingle, which looked
far more clear and far less treacherous in comparison. And exhaling as I reached it, finally touching down, I realized it was not
solid at all, but an apparition of landscape that began sinking as
soon as my weight came into contact with it, and I was forced to
sprint across it. I could not turn back, and there was thicket on
every other side of me, bar the river.

Around the bend of the impossible shore, nothing but more
shore. I cursed the place, really cursing my own stupidity. All
the nature writers I'd read knew the semiology of the land. I
knew the names, the sounds—cygnet, ironwood, willow—but
I barely knew what they meant, and even less what they told
me about the landscape. The flora might show me paths to dry
land or access to wind and light, plants that might indicate
copses, shade bearers, a thin shelter belt and thus a way out. I
could not read the signs. I had stood in the Gaeltacht parts of
western Ireland and wondered at Irish signs, separated from

the language. Even beyond words, the land seemed lost to me, or at least untranslatable.

The storm was battering now. The sluice of each wave was overtaking the last. Finding wreckage of bonfires, a rusted barrel with holes eaten through it, I took some solace that there must have been a way out, but each time I seemed cut off by the river. I would double back on myself, try another route, a third one. I attempted to hike up the banking, but could not get a decent grip on the veins of tree roots, Lovecraftian under the forest's skin, and slid down in the iron-red clay. My hands were swollen from stings and cuts. I turned to the sky to catch the rain in my face.

There was no reception on my phone. It was perhaps a blessing. I had no choice but to hack up through a sloping wall of barbed undergrowth. At points it was worryingly steep and I had to cling to overhanging branches, taking deep breaths to summon up another push. Little streams running down the banking made it even more precarious. Finally I reached an accidental staircase of roots and made my way upward through ferns and the omnipresent nettles. I came to the bottom of a large field and tried to duck under the barbed wire, getting my coat snagged in several places. As I struggled to dislodge myself, my top stuck to my back with sweat. The field was a quagmire, with shotgun shells scattered around.

Through the trees was the boarded-up school, and next to it a Convent of Mercy. A statue of Jesus and Mary and a crucifix, white in the rain. It looked like the punch line to a bad joke. I lay down on the wet grass, catching my breath, listening to the distant sound of a dog barking, and let myself get soaked through to the skin. Staring through the dripping leaves into a sky that fell into infinity.

Twine

Certain boys from our estate never got older. Their tale was used to keep the other kids, even years later in my youth, away from the tantalizing path down to the river. There were two separate groups of drowned young men, but time had merged them into one. The first were boys who'd taken a raft of plastic barrels and tires, tied together with twine, out onto the water and were never seen alive again, the call going up when their raft was recovered drifting.

"They were ten, maybe eleven. Two brothers and another boy. He was an only child. They were a quiet family. They became much quieter after that."

This day, with the weather cleared, Tony had joined me walking along the shore, searching for the latest lost boy. Tony had lived with us for two years in Cedar Street when I was a teenager, landing back from America with all manner of outlandish tales and piles of records and underground comics. He would take me and my less unhinged friends out to remote places to fire his shotgun. He'd become like an older brother.

We talked to pass the time while scanning the river.

My mother had mentioned the drowned lads to me, claiming the river was cursed, given how many had gone into it down the years. I disagreed. It just offered access to a way out. It paid no attention to the cargo it carried.

"There was a rundown Gaelic football pitch where the school is now. Your uncle and I were up playing with a few others—I was a bit of a tomboy—and the boys came up and hung around, played a bit. They went off then and they never came back."

The other boys were older. The other group who drowned. They'd been drinking in the pub and, full of Dutch courage, decided to take a boat out and row over to Strathfoyle to try to chat up the girls.

My mother knew them too. "Geoffrey was seventeen. They stay that age, unlike the rest of us. He got drunk with a couple of others. I can't remember their names. And they made a mistake. He used to tease me. He'd never admit he was friends with what his friends called a Fenian—never really acknowledge my presence in company. But he would joke around when no one else was there. He was quite sweet actually. I liked him, despite myself. Your uncle knew him better."

I mentioned the conversation to Tony as we walked, then asked him if he came down to the shore much in those days.

"All the time. Culmore Point was like an untouchable area back then. It was rich. Properly rich. Money went further then. Staunchly unionist. A separate village really. The city hadn't come out this far yet. And it felt like it. There was an orchard with a high wall. We'd climb trees, get into trouble, get chased.

Tried climbing Culmore Fort many times. Got up high, but never to the top. You don't have fear at that age."

The fort down there wasn't the original one. There used to be a small castle with triangular battlements pointing to the river. The story went that the skeleton on the city's coat of arms, sitting looking bored on a moss-covered rock, was a rebellious Gaelic knight starved to death there by his treacherous cousin. No one quite knew the full story. It had been passed down for so many generations that it had changed, like Chinese whispers, and the facts were lost, even though the iconography remained. People in Derry joked that it was someone waiting for their dole check. Now the fort was just a stone tower used to store boats. Pylons soared above it, bridging the river with high-voltage wires straight from the power station. You could hear the electricity from time to time.

"We got into the lighthouse once, though. It's bricked up and painted over now. You see that little lough there? It's pretty shallow, then suddenly it drops down deep. We'd row out the dinghies to the larger boats and just sit in them, fishing or fucking around. Drove the owners mad. They'd shout, 'You wee bastards,' and wait, fuming, for us to row back in. Didn't give us any incentive to hurry to shore, to be honest.

"Anthony wasn't happy with us being there, unsurprisingly. If he saw you heading down the lane, he'd wait and give you a welting that evening when you returned. I don't know how he held on to the anger all day. Fuming, he was. 'I'll teach you to do that again.' I suppose he was just worried we'd drown, but Christ, he had a funny way of showing it." Tony laughed. "I used to walk along the river. They had the dump at Gleneagles. That's why they've never built on the Bay Road. They say it's to keep it as a nature reserve, but most likely they can't decontaminate the place. Reclaimed land. It was rubbish piled up, literally, into the river. Have it floating off somewhere else for someone else to worry about. They didn't give a shit about the environment back then. Probably still don't, but they were brutally honest then. Now there's a layer of soil and grass on top. They have methane pipes hidden around, releasing the gas, to stop the place from exploding. Who wants their house built on . . . all that garbage? People don't even know it was there anymore. We'd go down, play in the dump, looking for prams to take the wheels for go-karts, or wire and elastic to make catapults from."

All the days that were lived were shadowed by waste. Built up in piles to be compressed, then finally covered over. Bubbling and fermenting away underneath the clay. The pressure mounting.

"It was sad, though," Tony continued. "Some people were so poor they'd wait for the dump truck to pull up and start sifting through the fresh garbage. That was one good thing about the shops getting blown up; they had to dump their food as smoke-damaged, even when it wasn't. We'd get good stuff every time Superfare went up. Boxes of Cadbury's—that sort of thing. We'd physically fight over them. They'd barely finished rebuilding it and it'd be hit again. You ever hear what happened to the two young fellas there?"

"I don't think so," I replied.

"To cut a long story short, they blew themselves up," Tony said. "I heard they were due to plant a bomb in there and warn the staff—there was a war on property and businesses at the time—but it detonated as they were leaving the car. The story that went round Derry was that the boys went in, planted it, shouted to the staff, and the manager locked them inside, intentionally or otherwise. I'm not certain what is true, but that story became the one people believed. Two teenagers from Shantallow, they were. One of them was Protestant."

"Damn," I replied. "You wouldn't bat an eyelid driving past that place. Just another shitty supermarket." I stared out at the river. "You always hear of ghosts in old Victorian houses. You never think of them walking around the aisles of supermarkets. Did you know those young kids who drowned? The ones from the woodlands years ago?"

"Aye. One of them survived."

"Serious? I didn't know that."

"Aye. Dan died. Sad, as he was a decent fella, but his brother survived. The wrong one lived, in my opinion. The others had gone in and floundered, but he swam to one of those floating buoys and clung to it all night, screaming his head off. You imagine what that was like?"

"Jesus."

"He was fucking crazy, though, even before that. A bad bastard, to be honest. Wired to the moon. Complete space cadet. He was in the UDA. You remember them?"

"Vaguely."

"They were a paramilitary outfit. Did terrible things. Thing is, they were legal—right up until the early nineties, I think. He was mad as a fuckin' hatter. Even by their standards.

"We had a bonfire down at the lighthouse one night. We were just kids. I don't even think we were drinking yet. We used to go down and shout over insults to boys in Strathfoyle doing the same thing. The water carried the voices. We couldn't get at each other—not that we'd have done anything. He came down with a friend of his. Probably saw the smoke from the top of the hill. You could feel a change in the air when he arrived. He came up with this smirk on his face, hands in his pockets: 'All right, lads.' He hung around like he was waiting for something. I knew he was a head case, so I tried to pay him no heed, let on I wasn't bothered, but he made me nervous. He hung around with this sense of . . . intense menace. And he knew it. He was smiling to himself. It was like something sinister came along with him. My mates were trying to keep their cool too. I could see them, trying to act all normal, like mini-adults. People like him look for weakness. They sense it. Feed off it.

"Then, as if it was nothing, he took out his gun and held it up so we could all see. I swear my heart stopped and I was rooted to the floor, but I tried not to show it. Then he unclipped it, emptied the cartridge into his hand, and threw the bullets, one by one, right into the fire. We just froze, until one of us suddenly bolted and then we were all off, all confused, like we were running in different directions at once, tumbling over ourselves. I made a dash for that concrete structure that covers the pipes down there and squeezed myself in, and my mates followed behind me, trying to push their way in too, but there was hardly any room. We were there two or three seconds literally, and suddenly you could hear the crack of the bullets whizzing around and hitting things. I just pressed myself as far as I could behind the concrete. And that crazy bastard was walking around the whole time, laughing, circling round the fire.

"There were rumors he was involved in an assassination of a local politician who went down on this side of the river, out in the sticks. The killers knew the bridges would go into shutdown, so he got them back across the river by boat. Who knows? You hear these things like Chinese whispers."

"What became of him? He still around?"

"He used that gun on himself, in his shed, of all places. Sorry end, but I can't say it didn't suit him."

I tried to imagine that night he'd clung to the buoy. The depths of that. Sweet Jesus!

"I guess it was boredom that brought us down here. We'd copy my da, I s'pose. Catch flatfish and eels with a rod and line. We'd make swings out over the river. The Brits would race powerboats down the Foyle. We'd shout to them, get chases. They had a launchpad at Ebrington. They went unbelievably fast, the bottom bouncing over the waves, soldiers clinging on, being thrown around like ragdolls but trying to look cool, like they were in 'Nam. They'd often have three soldiers on board, but it could be anything up to ten. All armed to the teeth. We'd light fires to draw them in and then brick the boats. We were warned by Anthony repeatedly to stay away from the narrows. The most dangerous part of the river, he'd say. I was fishing with a friend once, and he cast out and I felt this horrible tug on my cheek and realized he'd put the hook right into my face. We couldn't pull it out; we had to push it through the wound—or, rather, the nurses did, after I'd walked home with the rod attached to my face. I got a double whamming for that." Tony laughed, shaking his head.

We walked along. I pointed to a blue frayed rope dangling from a branch out over the Foyle.

"That one of yours?"

"Could well be. That may have been our hanging tree." He laughed again.

Across the water the factory lights were blazing, even though it was daytime.

"That's Coolkeeragh power station. British Oxygen used to be there. It was a military airfield before then. You know Anthony worked over there for years? After he gave up the full-time fishing. DuPont, it was. Pushing vats of chemicals around. The factory made bulletproof vests. You believe that? With all the shit going on in town.

"He'd still fish on the side: moonlight fixing nets, weaving knots, with his waders up to his waist. That was '78 or '79. He took me out on the boats. He had a knowledge of the Foyle that was like a computer. Like a satellite. If someone went in, Anthony would get the fleet up from Greencastle to look for them. There was an exception, though."

"What was that?"

"Suicides. If they thought the person went in deliberately, they backed off. I don't know if it was not to meddle with the person's intentions or whether it was forbidden by the priests. They were all staunch Catholics. Suicide was really frowned upon then. It was a mortal sin. Might still be."

"Strange, when you think of all the saints they worship. How they died. And Jesus."

"Aw, they love their martyrs, under certain conditions. It's the rest of us that are the problem."

We walked on.

"What about the younger boys? The ones who drowned?"

"Well, your ma's right. They did come up to us on the day they died. It was weird, come to think of it. We kept playing and they left at teatime. We didn't get no tea that day. They went in, ate with their families, and then came back out, telling lies to their folks no doubt, and dodging us for some reason—maybe they wanted the game all to themselves. They went down to the river when the sun was setting. We found out the next day they were gone."

"What a thing . . . Christ! What stopped him? Anthony, I mean. Working on the river? He came off a motorbike, didn't he?"

"He smashed up his leg bad. Compound fracture. Bone shattered and came through his skin. Real bad. I know because I took my turn looking after him, and it wasn't pretty. That was the late seventies, but Anthony was phasing out the working world already. That was his excuse to wind it up really, or maybe it forced him to face reality. Kitty ran upstairs, unable to handle it, when he was brought back injured, so we were left with the handling. Not a model patient by any means. He recovered, though, pretty much fully. Years later Anthony had veins that needed seeing to on his legs. I'm not sure if it was related, but it was a minor operation, to ease the pains that he felt, or claimed to, when the weather changed. He got it into his head the operation was a big deal. That it had gone wrong, when it hadn't. Some leftover taboo about being a cripple. Took to the bed. Never left it again.

"He was doing night shifts in DuPont when he came off the bike. He was like a bear with a sore head, working shifts. Clock time, not tide time. Couldn't get used to it. He'd made himself a real pain in the ass, trying to keep the fishing thing going, tagging along on other guys' boats. Forcing himself on people by helping them, accumulating debts, hauling up lobster pots and all that. He'd no idea of leaving people alone."

Something like footage came into my mind of Greencastle, the port where the fishing boats were mainly based on the Foyle, just past Moville. Boys with silver trays of fish. Someone washing away the overspill. The heady reek of marine life. Tires and pots hanging, jangling from the sides of boats. Bobbing awkwardly against the quay, trying to lasso a rope onto the bollards there. And a word that I'd read that stayed in my mind— *Abraham-men*. Originally these were beggars who were either formerly bedlamites or were imitating bedlamites for money. They eventually migrated to the docks, out-of-work mariners or those masquerading as sailors begging for money. It had once been a dangerous business to hang around the docks, as press gangs stole men into the Royal Navy—and rum, sodomy, and the lash—from that very quay. Maybe Anthony was the last of the Abraham-men.

"He could be friendly when there was something in it for

him. And even then, only ever to those above him. I went out with him once or twice toward the end. He liked that, holding court with stories. Didn't matter who it was or whether they wanted to listen. He'd talk about every kind of fish, how fishing in the Atlantic in winter was so cold his shirt would stick to his back with frozen sweat, or nets that got caught on downed planes and rusting ships.

"One thing I noticed: he had the most amazing eyesight. He'd be talking and then swing around to something in his peripheral view—a shoal or a salmon leaping really, really far away. It all looked the same to me, but he could spot it. He'd point to the horizon and say, 'You see that ship out yonder?' And I swear I'd scan the horizon for a good ten, twenty minutes before it appeared, microscopic in the distance."

Tony paused, thinking of something. "You know he spoke Gaelic?"

"Fluently?"

"Yup."

I could hear Anthony's booming Paisley-esque foghorn voice. "It's the quiet ones you watch, I guess."

Tony laughed.

I thought of Anthony and his crew praying in Gaelic in case the Holy Spirit spoke the mother tongue.

There's an imaginary destination called Fiddler's Green. The afterlife for sailors. A place of uninhibited joys. You got a key to it when you died, if you'd served fifty years on the sea. Anthony made sure to quit before the prospect of bliss neared.

"There used to be houses down there. That old overgrown ruin. The roof's fallen in now, but the local Orange families owned them. They were used as sheds by that stage, but they'd lived in them once. They were born on the river, those kids, and then it took them."

I remembered the houses. Some were still there. Completely enveloped in plant life. Windows gaping black rectangles in a riot of green. The rooms decorated with generations of graffiti. The words "No Future" faded by seasons.

"What did they keep in them? Smuggling stuff?"

"I think it was fishing gear, but you could never be sure. They guarded it ferociously. Their auld boy—tough nut, he was—if he saw you anywhere near the path, he would be onto you. Thought nothing of giving you a fist to the ear. They kept a vegetable patch down there, and he'd be down two or three times a day. He was a real bitter old Orangeman. He'd wave his stick and set his dog on you. Took to wearing his sash around the estate when he found out they were housing Catholics there. He didn't believe we should live anywhere near them. Bothered him to see us going where we pleased. There was a lot of paranoia around. You know the big house down there at the end of the lane?"

"I've seen it through the trees."

"We found out it had secret staircases, passageways, a tunnel to the river. Christ knows what trouble they were expecting or how inflated that story was, but I had it on good authority. That's the thing, though: we were always treated as if we were the ones who suddenly arrived here, as if we had somehow invaded. As if they were the ones needing protection. Preemptively. I suppose they knew about revenge."

"I guess that was the intention. Make you a stranger in your own land."

"My patience with the auld boy gave out one day. He said something he shouldn't have when I was out shooting rabbits. You remember the shotgun I had? Got rid of it when I had the kids. Can't have a thing like that lying around. God forbid. I was out shooting when I saw that bitter old bastard Orangeman. I'd emptied the gun, hung it over my shoulder. He hadn't expected me there but he froze. He'd called me a 'Fenian bastard,' called me 'boy,' expecting me to know my place when we were on his turf. I walked right up to him and said—really slowly, so he'd get it into his thick skull—'You . . . don't treat us . . . like that . . . anymore.' And that was that. My hands were trembling afterwards, but sometimes you have to do what you have to do.

"The sons were all right. It was generational too, to an extent. They were around nets all their lives. What they think happened is they pushed the raft out, with a net to catch fish. They anchored it down somehow, threw the net in, and waited awhile. When they were pulling it in, it got snagged on something. They all tried pulling individually, but it stuck fast, so they tried collectively. First rule of small boats: never stand up, especially with more than one person. The net gave and the boat tipped, flipped upside down with them. And that was that. We were due to play them at football the next day, the new estate versus the old estate, but they never showed up.

"You can't imagine how dangerous the narrows are. All that water being squeezed through the channel. You can barely see a trace of it on the surface."

It was hard to believe, given how calm the water's surface was, that it moved with the force of an iron juggernaut, a constant landslide, a quiet tsunami moving through the city every day, barely even noticed by anyone who lived on its banks.

"Anthony knew the river so well that he had names for every single bit of it, from Derry to Inishowen Head. He knew the lie of the land below the waves. Experience, stories. Who the fuck knows?" Tony began clicking his fingers. "What's that thing they do with lead and line?"

"Depth sounding," I added, regretting it as soon as I spoke. "Bathymetry, I think it's called."

Tony nodded. "Aye, some shit like that. He even knew where

and when the dead would resurface. He used to say it takes ten days, and the stomach bloats with gas and it floats. They'd work shifts, all day and night. He could read invisible currents as if a map was on the water. He knew the river well because he was afraid of it. He used to say that a ship passing would disturb the silt, churning it up, and bring bodies to the surface. He knew what places to dredge and what places to ignore. I remember seeing two or three trawlers at work. They had these huge grappling hooks, dragging wood and wire along the riverbed. Pulled-up cables and things best left alone, no doubt.

"You'd get the loved ones down at the river, though it was no place for them. I was there when they found one missing boy. He'd snagged out on the nets, opposite the gas pipes. A fisherman out pulling up pots got into a right state discovering the body unexpectedly, the face staring up at him from the depths.

"Anthony knew the river inside out. I remember when he found a body, a kid I knew called Geoffrey. I remember my auld boy crying afterwards, when he'd come home. That creeped me out, 'cause I'd never seen him like that. Geoffrey's father was on the boat when they found him. They had to hold him back. They kept his boy in the water until they'd got to the docks and ushered the father off and away."

The sea change that happened to a body in the water for many days was not the magical metamorphosis of Shakespeare. It required a closed casket at the funeral. The bodies ended up discolored all over and inflated. The skin would peel off. Their sex, race, let alone identity, became hard to tell. Anthony said they were like pregnant women floating. Sometimes fish would get into the soft parts and pour out of them when pulled onto the shore. Crabs crawling out of eyes and mouths.

We stared out at the water.

"Once, some family members hired a boat and found a

body, and the fishermen had to go out and relieve them, drag them away basically, because they hadn't been prepared for what they'd found and were in hysterics. They learned to keep relatives away when the body was found."

Out of sight. Such things could never be forgotten. Such things could replace what memories they had of the living. Such things were a cancer to memory itself.

Tony continued, "Anthony was a professional. A real determined bastard. He went at it day and night when he knew the bodies would be rising. And he hauled in a lot of bodies down the years. Truth be told, he played on the savior aspect: 'I brought your son back to you.' Like he'd saved a life."

The grave is, at least, tangible. Though there was a romance to those willingly buried at sea; for the unwilling it was a means of erasure. There would be no tomb, no marker on land, no burial in consecrated ground, and hence no rising on the Day of Judgment. It was a resting place of eternal restlessness, reserved for heathens and the disgraced. The bones of Wycliffe, damned as a heretic, were exhumed, crushed, and burned and his ashes thrown in the River Swift. The Nazis hanged after the Nuremberg trials were cremated and had their ashes dumped in the River Elbe. It was said that Hitler, his wife, and the Goebbels family followed them. Bin Laden was buried somewhere in the Arabian Sea. No body, no shrine. Yet the innocent, too, were lost in the sea.

Vikings, who had scoured this land and built on it, believed the uncared-for unburied dead became revenants, and the restless would visit and profoundly disturb the living family members, which usually foretold more death. To bury them in peace was to end a cycle.

Recording Device

My father was in the living room, his feet up, having a drink, watching old footage of 1970s bands on a German television show. For some time he had been wobbling, struggling with his health—I don't know. The fact that Da kept it all silent, stoical, except the times he no longer could, only made it more quietly terrifying. As he got older and he got aches and his tendons became frayed, he no longer had the distraction of jogging the bridges at night or hitting the gym. It seemed more than physical. He had enough time on his hands to realize there was more spent than left. I worried if there was something else at play, something early-onset. Or perhaps something late-onset. I remembered a quote from one of the art books I used to cut up, by the artist Otto Dix, referring to experiences in the war—one of the wars—about how trauma got harder with the years; how time didn't heal old wounds, as people said, and things got worse or returned as the adrenaline rush and distractions of youth died away: "As a young man you don't notice at all that you were, after all, badly affected. For years afterwards, at least ten years, I kept getting these dreams, in which I had to crawl through ruined houses, along passages I could hardly get through." As life settled, narrowing into routines and certainties, it just kept narrowing for some people, to the point of claustrophobia. The walls kept getting closer. And the sky with it.

Not long ago, talking about what happened in the Troubles might get you killed. And so people were silent or, when they spoke—consummate story- and joke-tellers that they are in the North—it was a way of *not* addressing subjects. It was a diversion. Silence, nevertheless, prevailed. Now people do not talk for fear of rocking the boat. Now they are silenced by the mantra that tourism and investment will cure all ills. There is no truth-and-reconciliation process. Collective amnesia is official policy. Journalists overhearing confessions from the "bad old days" are subject to having their homes raided by the police. We are told that this silence is different. This is a better form of silence. The schools remain segregated. The cities remain internally divided. The trauma is, against the lessons of psychiatry, buried. The peace process is disrupted and undermined, but it has always had a problem, for all the relief that the respite of violence has given. The North remains a patient in a medically induced coma.

My father had started drinking late in life. Previously he'd suffered from what I thought were cautionary hangovers, as if his body knew the inclinations in his genes and had an internal alarm system, given that he'd two alcoholic parents, and punished him as a deterrent. Then suddenly he started drinking heavily, regardless, in middle age. It didn't seem to suit him, and I doubted what good it did, especially given the quantities he was downing. I recognized my own hypocrisy, given that I drank too much. I justified it by telling myself I had grown into drinking, while my father had plunged into it. I would sit up with him and we'd watch vintage music programs—*The Old Grey Whistle Test*, the German show *Beat-Club*, prog rock and blues revival bands, Tim Buckley and "Van the Man"— and we'd talk about old bands and all those records in boxes in the attic. It was one of the rare times we'd be animated together.

"Would you change it at all?" I asked him.

"What?"

"The past. If you could go back."

He laughed. "You can't, though, can you?"

We kept watching the music videos. There was no need to talk after a while. The passing of a bottle said more than language could. Eventually Da went out to the kitchen to get a drink, but then I heard him shuffling off upstairs to his bed. I sat there thinking, drinking. It was a while before I even realized the footage had stopped on the screen.

One night I decided to talk to him finally, properly.

And Da told me. He told me about growing up in the camp. About his da dying. About surviving, playing at the edge of a whirlpool. About shootouts and arrests and internment. His brother, a bricklayer, on the run. He remembered a stolen car with bullet holes in it screeching up to their house in the early hours of the morning, and how spectacularly blue the sky looked. He carried a scar on his leg that he'd told me long before was from climbing a fence, but which resembled a flesh wound from a bullet. How he was set up by an informer, chased into the Phoenix Bar, and captured. He was charged with explosives and membership. He was sixteen. He told me about interrogations. He told me of fear so deep and immediate it was like a person, a presence, a shadow in the room. He told me about helicopter journeys across the country. He told me of blindfolds and being thrown out at an indeterminate height. He told me about the dreaded Crum—Crumlin Road Gaol—where they went to town on suspects, and guilt or innocence was incidental. He told me of white noise and beatings, and stress positions and sleep deprivation. He told me of torture and the doctors they brought in to monitor it, and how they worked on you in shifts and went home to their homes to play happy families at the weekends, and came back and started over again; and the whole time they were away, you hadn't slept for more than a second that you could grab standing up. He remembered their faces. He told me about Long Kesh, a former Allied aircraft base, and "the Cages." He told me about prisoners sent from the prison hulk HMS *Maidstone*, moored in Belfast Lough. He told me about returning to live in the Nissen huts after only a few years in a brick house, from one kind of jail to another.

He told me of camaraderie between prisoners because of, and despite, having forty to eighty of them in each hut. He told me of how they personalized the partitions, how they read everything from Frantz Fanon to Brendan Behan, and gave classes and played football and hung their clothes on the wire. He told me of knowing the main players—"heads," they were called, which meant a good guy, someone who knew the craic, in terms of music and culture—including Bobby Sands, who was just one of them; not a martyr or a saint or a villain, but a young fella whom he remembered played guitar and made-up songs. He told me of escape plans and of the guards digging water-filled ditches around them to prevent tunneling. He told me of carving woodwork to pass the time and of records being smuggled in (Brian Eno's *Here Come the Warm Jets* came to mind—it wasn't much to his taste). He told me of almost-admiring rumors that the loyalists once smuggled in a goldfish. He told me of messages being smuggled out. He told me how the huts had burned in '74.

They moved them to the Maze, the brutalist concrete of the H-blocks. Their political status as POWs was removed and they were to be treated as criminals. They were placed in individual cells, and the screws were hostile from the beginning. He told me of the surveillance. He told me of burning away the hours of the one youth you'd ever have. He told me of tapping messages along the pipes to other cells. Shouts and messages passed via the doors. Continual noise. He told me of how the prison officers searched the prisoners, taking them to the circle, making them squat naked over a mirror and probing their behinds, then their mouths with the same glove. He told me that pain was not enough; shame was also required. He told me of how he and a cellmate had pushed their mattress up against their cell door as they listened to riot police come down the aisle, cell by cell, beating the occupants unconscious. Waiting their turn. Not much more than kids, they were. He told me about stress and how it is buried. He told me of the five years of protests and how, right as he was being released, it was all escalating toward the latter-day Catholic martyrdom of the hunger strikes; Bobby Sands writing on the first day of his dying, "I am standing on the threshold of another trembling world." Bobby was not the only one.

Except none of this conversation happened. We just kept watching music. All the information I possessed came from unverified snippets from other people or was overheard in unguarded moments. They were likely true, and there were many more truths never expressed, but we could not begin to talk about any of it directly, because how or where do you begin?

Bird Feed

How did he become involved? Was it Bloody
Sunday?"

"You know your da—he's the quiet man and
just fobs the subject off. He was there and it had
a big impact on him. Your aunt told me that. He had been lucky
to get back alive. All the young fellas were. He said he knew,
from the sounds, something different was happening."

My ma paused for a second or two before continuing.

"That wasn't entirely it, though. His older brother had been
interned. They were constantly getting grief from the army and
police. The thing that did it, though, if you piece together the
snippets, was this story about a wee boy who kept pigeons—"

"Pigeons?"

"Aye, some kid on his street kept them out the front of their
house. He was a harmless critter apparently and was tending
them one day, and an army patrol just came along, in one of the

tanks they called a Pig. You remember those? They had Sara-
cens, Saxons, and Pigs. And they just started shooting at that
wee lad. They knew they could get away with it. One of them
was laughing. Your dad watched it happen; he was distraught,
said it wasn't fair and resolved to do something. Everything
changed at that moment."

"Jesus. I thought *Kes* was grim."

"They joined the young republicans, the Fianna, thinking it
was like the Scouts. They didn't know what they were getting
themselves into. Pandora's box had already opened."

We tell ourselves stories about war. Of good guys and bad
guys. Redemption and sacrifice. Yet the nature of conflict is
such that when it is unleashed, it is almost impossible to remain
good. Man, at such times, becomes wolf to man. Everything
still was, and remains, a choice. It came down to moments, de-
cisions. None inevitable. Either choosing to act, react, or choosing to walk away, to create rather than despoil. Easy things to
write when the boot is not on your throat or the barrel pointed
at you or your child.

Several days passed and I was called back overseas, back to
my life. As I packed my things, my mother was hanging around,
silently lamenting.

"I'm not leaving forever."

"I know. It's just not the same without you and your sister."

"Ah, you'll be grand. You don't need my sorry arse around."

I left a pile of books and asked her if she could drop them
into a secondhand shop. I sifted through them for something
worth taking on the plane.

"That thing I mentioned the other day . . ."

"What's that?"

"The story about the boy with the pigeons."

"What about it?"

"It was him. The kid was your dad. His sister told me. It wasn't someone else. They shot at him and he was terrified. Barely made it inside the house. No way to live," she concluded to herself.

I froze, books still in hand.

"She said they used to go down the docks into the old warehouses, grain stores, and climb up into the rafters or find pigeons colonizing cupboards and grab them, stick them inside their jumpers. They'd keep them in the shed for a week or so, and feed them and domesticate them. Then they'd fly them. He was looking after them. That was his obsession, and then the army pulled up one day."

I shook my head. "That's . . . quite a thing."

Silence. I stared out my old bedroom window. Birds were sitting on the telegraph wire.

"I don't think your da knew what was happening. How could he at that age? His da had been in the army, his uncles, his grandfather. Not long before that, he'd been a paperboy, delivering *Belfast Telegraph*s. He used to drop copies round to the soldiers in Brooke Park. They'd send him on errands, to pick up things from the corner shop. Maybe he even looked up to them. Wanted to be one of the lads. All those strange accents. He remembered one of them showing him a Polaroid of his girlfriend. And then they turned . . ."

Ideology is overrated. Few people are really that romantic or deranged. It's emphasized because it distances as much as it gives the appearance of explanation. This is not to say there are not ideologues. Ideologues exist, but it's best to pay attention to what they do rather than what they say, or what they say they do. Often there's a dishonesty there, even to themselves. The ultra-righteous frequently have less-than-righteous motives, but it goes further than that, into the realms where you can see in the fanatic a profound disbelief in what they claim to espouse, an intense doubt and failing at the core of their supposed faith, and thus all the more need to shout and attack and convert.

You can only be absolutist with little or no experience. This is one reason the young are radical and the rich can be casually cruel. As you live and experience, you learn that people are complex, contradictory, nuanced. People do not fit where ideologues place them.

There are other much more compelling and truthful reasons for conflict, some noble, some cynical; not least, fear, revulsion, and a sense of injustice. Countless signed up after harassment. The Bloody Sunday and Ballymurphy massacres, when the British Parachute Regiment went on a killing spree of Catholic civilians, were huge recruitment drives for the IRA, showing the protest route of the Social Democratic and Labour Party to be woefully insufficient, earning them an unfair sobriquet in graffiti: the "Stoop Down Low Party." It worked both ways. Many prominent loyalists became involved after seeing blood-soaked bundles, containing what had moments earlier been little children, being brought out of what had been the Balmoral Furniture Company and elsewhere.

Violence begets violence. Those immersed in it know it; those who profit from it at a distance know it even more. Not much is truly holy in this world, but precious is the person who does not pass on the pain and the desire for retribution, that self-sustaining spiral; who says, "No more," not out of resignation or defeat, but out of something that might be called love, if it even needs a name.

It became clear to me now what my father had given me. He had broken the cycle.

"You remember Cedar Street?" my mother asked unexpectedly.

"Of course."

"You remember your dad got his tattoo changed?"

"No."

"You know he has my name on his arm. It didn't always say that. It used to be something else. Three letters."

Beginning with "I" and ending with "A."

She continued, "That was a different world then. It might look the same, but it was different. He didn't want you and your sister exposed to any of that. That was the most important thing for him. Family. Protection. It always was."

Just then I had a sudden memory of my cousin Robert nudging my father as he demanded to see his new inking. "And they say romance is dead, eh?"

Flotsam and Jetsam

The city lights twinkled in the distance. Usually the glow of the city extinguished the stars above too, but I could see the constellations, like campfires or microscopic phosphorescence or distant burning civilizations. The lighthouse at Culmore no longer shone. Its light had lasted from the discovery of gold in California until the discovery of the Higgs boson particle below Switzerland. It did not shine, but I knew it was still there. Under the bridge I could see the white light of Ballynagard Lighthouse, pulsing every three seconds. There were no ships in sight but it kept on, the river mirroring its light.

I sat on the rocks, gazing but no longer searching. He had been found earlier that day. Close to the town. I'd been told by text. They had brought Andrew back home to his mother. I'd been too late, much too late. I found myself apologizing out loud at the riverside.

The frost was already creeping over the rocks, turning them to glass. I wondered what it would take to freeze the river again. These were the rocks where Needles had washed up. I gazed out at the other city, upside down in a mirror world, shimmering and reflecting on the water. It would be easy, too easy, to be elegiac. Suicide was too raw for that. It felt like both a tragedy and a wounding. My grandmother Phyllis had not chosen her fate, but the others had, in different ways. Needles had feared a slow, painful death and so she had chosen a quick one. She met it head-on, and as sad and as wasteful as it was, I was forced to trust her. Her life was hers to take, but she shouldn't have felt the need to. Nobody should.

I was leaving in the morning. I stooped and picked up a small piece of wood from the shore, sculpted by the water. I couldn't tell what it had come from. Maybe it was nothing but dreck. Maybe flotsam. Maybe ballast. Times will change and people will come and say that certain things did not happen. The entire existence of some will be washed away. Yet there are stories within this junk, and souls within these stories. There was no ending to it. In a day or two, another young fella would be reported missing or seen going into the river. There is nothing to do but offer each other—those who are left, those still trapped within this miracle—the possibility of a life worth living, in defiance of "No Future."

The darkness is coming. Let it wait.

Acknowledgments

Thanks are due to my family, friends, and loved ones for their remarkable support. Thanks to everyone I spoke with, concerning the subjects in this book and the vast quantities of material that did not or could not make it into these pages, for their bravery in opening up.

I am indebted to a number of texts, and writers, for guidance while writing *Inventory* and its lost predecessor, *Tidewrack*.

Chief among these is *Lost Lives: The Stories of the Men, Women and Children Who Died as a Result of the Northern Ireland Troubles* (Mainstream Publishing, 2001), by David McKittrick, Seamus Kelters, Brian Feeney, Chris Thornton, and David McVea. Documenting the killings of the conflict in which we grew up, it is dark and essential reading for anyone delving into this part of the world.

"The Spoil of Mariners" (*Lapham's Quarterly*, September 25, 2013) is a beautifully written account, by the gifted writer Colin Dickey, on the theme of maritime scurvy, which I am indebted to as an introduction to the topic.

My deep gratitude to Kevin Barry and Olivia Smith for their kindness and support, particularly as a portion of the text herein appeared in their exquisite *Winter Papers*, albeit in a different form. Along with the likes of the mighty Susan Tomaselli, Lucy Caldwell, and Damian Smyth, they are a force for good for Irish writers, at home and in the diaspora, and for literature in general.

Thanks to everyone I've collaborated with at Chatto & Windus and FSG for their hard work, talent, and trust, and to my exceptional agent, Eve White.

Thanks to all the local historians who work tirelessly to record places like Springtown Camp and who help to rescue memories of the past from erosion and oblivion.

And, finally, my debt to the dead, may they rest easy, and to those who have survived, may each day be better than the last.

A Note About the Author

Darran Anderson is the author of *Imaginary Cities*, chosen as a best book of 2015 by the *Financial Times*, *The Guardian*, and *The A.V. Club*. His writing has appeared in *The Atlantic*, *The Times Literary Supplement*, *frieze*, *WIRED*, and *The Architectural Review*. He was born in Derry, Northern Ireland, and lives in London.